FUN TOMORROW

˙FUN˙
TOMORROW

LEARNING TO BE A PUBLISHER
AND MUCH ELSE

John Morgan Gray

MACMILLAN OF CANADA
Toronto

Canadian Cataloguing in Publication Data

Gray, John Morgan, 1907-
Fun tomorrow

ISBN 0-7705-1710-2

1. Gray, John Morgan, 1907-   2. Publishers
and publishing — Canada — Biography.
3. Macmillan Company of Canada — History.
1. Title.

Z483.G74A3   070.5′092′4   C78-001319-0

Printed in Canada for
THE MACMILLAN COMPANY OF CANADA LIMITED
70 Bond Street, Toronto
M5B 1X3

For John and Liz
and for
Colin, Rachel, and Joshua
with love

❧PREFACE❧

I N MY LATER YEARS IN PUBLISHING I pressed many people to write their memoirs. Those who had not taken part in great events seemed to think that an ample excuse, but I was inclined to think that everyone had a story to tell if he or she could tell it; that all such stories were the new material of our social history. So, in due course, I was bound to try my hand.

As my title implies, I have enjoyed my life in publishing and outside it. In the course of the manuscript I explain the origins of the chant "Fun tomorrow" in the early days of our marriage, when there seemed no contradiction or special recklessness in closing our days on that happy note. Life was not to be so simple, but each day had its happiness and fun, and there is probably not much we would change in it if we could.

In two or three cases I have used fictitious names for people in the book. As disguises they are very thin and easily penetrated by any critic. But I hope the critics will feel, as I did, that the pseudonyms may spare families embarrassment, and that the correct names will add nothing to the truth of the narrative.

I am indebted to many people for help and encouragement, and especially to Frank Upjohn and to my personal editor and encourager, Rache Lovat Dickson. And I salute with gratitude the talent and care of Diane Bennett and Mabel Molloy in translating my script into copy that editors and printers could work from. As always, Tony has stood by offering the support that only patience and love can provide.   J. M. G.

TORONTO
May 1978

FUN TOMORROW

⚡ 1 ⚡

WHEN THE BRITISH SAILING SHIP *Thames* foundered in the Bosporus in 1837, the captain and all hands went down with the ship. The captain was my great-grandfather, John Gray, and he had intended taking his wife and young son Robert on the voyage. It had been a long-promised holiday for Rachel Gray, this journey to the eastern Mediterranean, but at the last minute one of the babies at home was sick and the doctor forbade the trip. Captain John, with a full cargo and crew, could wait no longer. He sailed out of Shields into the North Sea and beat down for Gibraltar without them; and since young Robert was to be my grandfather, I'm just as glad he did.

The sad news came at last to his widow in Durham, and close behind the shock and grief stood the hard question of the future. Many of the family's assets had been swallowed by the stormy Bosporus, and in a world that knew nothing of welfare states a widow with small children was often in a desperate situation. In Dundas, Upper Canada, Rachel Gray had a brother, Robert Holt, after whom young Robert had been named, and to Dundas a few years later she came. It was a small but flourishing village that obviously, at the head of Lake Ontario, had a great future. Only Toronto (which had recently changed its name from York), Kingston, and perhaps Niagara might grow greater — certainly not the village of Hamilton close by. She knew a little about Canada, for Captain John had sailed to Quebec more than once, but she could hardly have been prepared for the harsh crudities of what was still a frontier community.

The brave move for the young widow was to prove wise. In the result Robert seems to have grown and prospered relatively more than Dundas. He grew up stern, hard-working, and rather successful. About the precise nature of his occupation and about the man himself there are few records and only fragmentary memories. At an early age he moved to Toronto, whence his import business took him often to what was then called affectionately Little Old New York, and there he found his wife. She was a member of an old New York Quaker family, Isobel Cowperthwaite, little more than a schoolgirl at the time. "Oh, don't marry an Englishman, Belle," her school friends warned her, "he'll beat you."

They settled down in Toronto to raise a family of five boys and two girls. Robert was getting on. He owned a substantial office and warehouse on Wellington Street and in what his friends regarded as a wild speculation bought property on the north side of Queen Street, west of Yonge and half a mile from the lake shore. "What are you going 'way up there for?" his friends asked, and he is said to have answered, "I'm building for the future." Until Timothy Eaton bought the property as part of the site of a fine new store, it wasn't clear just how wisely he had built.

By that time Robert Holt Gray was dead. He had received late one day in 1896 a large shipment of spices, tea, coffee, and silks from the far east, and had considered seeing to insurance at once; but by the time they were unpacked and stowed, he decided to leave it until the morning. He shook hands with his work people as he always did, locked up the building, and went home. During the night the building and its contents were destroyed by fire and his affairs were brought to the edge of ruin. For several months he struggled to rebuild the business, and though he won the battle, he lost the war. He died within the year, but all creditors had been repaid one hundred cents on the dollar.

Robert Gray had been at least consistent. What he required

of himself he expected of others. When his fourth son, Bert, was of secondary-school age, Robert Gray could consider Upper Canada College — "the Eton of Canada" as it had been called — perhaps appropriate for his son. So to Upper Canada Bert was sent. The honeymoon with these exalted circles was short-lived. After a few days Bert was discovered slipping off to school in the rain without his rubbers. "Put on your rubbers," ordered his father. After a good deal of shuffling it appeared they had been lost — lost, how could they be lost — well, they had disap-peared from his locker at school — do you mean stolen? — well, borrowed perhaps. "We'll see about that," said my grand-father.

Long afterwards, a remote and elderly cousin in Durham re-membered a visit by Robert Gray as a young man and de-scribed him as "a ginger chap". This may have referred to red-dish fair hair and fair complexion bequeathed to many de-scendants, or to quick temper. On the morning of poor Bert's disclosure, the temper was in the ascendant. The reluctant and unhappy Bert was towed along in the wake of the striding pil-lar of Victorian society. The Headmaster was confronted and the problem quickly stated. Instantly, the suavity that all head-masters keep in store for angry parents came into play, the shrug, the spread hands, the weary smile — boys, you know, boys do pinch things, that is borrow things, from each other — and do you condone theft at this school? — oh come, surely that is a little strong — "Let me be sure I understand you," said my grandfather with great solemnity, "are these the attitudes one is to expect in a school for gentlemen's sons?" — well, one must make allowance for boys, you know. Stiffly my grandfa-ther made it clear that these were not the kind of allowances he was prepared to make. He was withdrawing his son from the school at once, and he would bid the Headmaster good morn-ing. Thereupon he did both.

There are other little echoes of "the ginger chap" in the role of stern Victorian father, echoes returning often in my father's time, sometimes in mine, and, just occasionally, in my son's. When he presided at table flanked by six children and one or

3

two sisters or sisters-in-law, who seem to have been permanent guests, children were to be seen and not heard. Childish complaints about the food were answered briefly, "Eat that or leave the house." And a serious misdemeanour brought a quick command, "Go to your room and wait there till I come." But I never heard of thrashings as an aftermath. Cooled off, he could reprimand gently, if firmly.

This was the solid prop now knocked from the centre of the house. It was less of a disaster than his father's death had been in the previous generation, but the family's comfortable certainties were gone. The eldest son, Frank, had already graduated from Osgoode Hall and was in the law office of Mortimer Clark (soon to be Lieutenant-Governor of Ontario). And young Frank was showing initiative, for shortly after, he ventured to introduce a typewriter into the office while Sir Mortimer was away on a long trip. This reckless modernization was at first frowned on, then reluctantly approved. Frank was on his way to a partnership. The next two oldest boys, Fred and Charlie, were already in business and in a position to help, but for Bert and my father it was the end of schooling; the end of glorious summer holidays on Long Island and at Niagara-on-the-Lake.

My father had been born late to my grandparents, fifteen years after Frank, and in her glad surprise at an unexpected boy my grandmother, who knew her Bible, had christened him Samuel — a gift from God. For good measure he was also christened Morgan after her favourite brother, Morgan Cowperthwaite; he chose to be called Morgan. At fifteen he left the Model School, which then stood behind the Normal School where the Ryerson Polytechnical Institute now is. He went to work as an office boy at Eby-Blaine, who were in a similar line of business to that of his father.

With so many bread-winners there does not seem to have been hardship following my grandfather's death — except perhaps the hardship recognized too late of lost education. Within a few years the boys were part of a lively circle. My father and his friends were all in the Queen's Own Rifles, sailed at the

4

Yacht Club, and on New Year's Day bundled into sleighs and went calling on their friends and paid their respects to the Lieutenant-Governor. Once, many years later I was with him in the Oak Room of the King Edward Hotel and he said, "The last time I was in this room we had all come in from the King's Plate, and we stood with one foot on the bar and one on a table and drank the King's health." It sounded like a gymnastic feat worthy of the occasion.

That must have been about 1902 or '3, for in 1905 he married my mother, Helen Harris Putnam, and there were no more grey toppers, no more champagne. It was partly that as a young married couple they had very little money, and partly, no doubt, that my mother strongly disapproved. In later years she liked to remember that the first time my father took her out they went to the RCYC (Royal Canadian Yacht Club) and my father offered her a claret lemonade. She refused with embarrassing abruptness, wondering what kind of a girl he thought she was.

Her background had been very different from his, and she never escaped it. Her great-grandfather, Seth Putnam, had come to western Ontario in 1796 as part of the Ingersoll settlement. In the next four years he built the first road in the district, running from Burford, south of Brantford, almost to Chatham, along the south bank of the Thames. It had been a crude enough road, merely an old Indian trail widened, with trees cut off to ground level and the trunks rolled into the gullies to make a rough bridge. And when it was finished in 1804 or '5, settlers along the road who had all promised to pay toward the building found that they had no money. The Executive Council of the Province when appealed to reported solemnly that as a principle it was wrong for government to make good the default of the settlers. So Seth Putnam had four years' work for nothing, though the primitive road — long known as Putnam's Road — for all its roughness was a great benefit. Simcoe's Dundas Road was just begun and Colonel Talbot's Road was still some years in the future.

My grandfather Alanson Putnam told me once that for

5

building the road Seth was later offered a large grant of land in the middle of what is now the flourishing city of London, Ontario, but Seth knew better. He chose his land around the present village of Putnam, south of the river and west of Ingersoll, and in due course his sons William, Thomas (my great-grandfather), and Joshua drew land near by. There they had at one time a sawmill, grist-mill, distillery, and tavern. Now there is little of Putnam but a cemetery, while London real estate is better than gold.

The Putnams were part of the wave of American immigration invited by Governor Simcoe. Before that the family had been in Massachusetts for 150 years and Seth had served as a revolutionary soldier under Washington. But in the War of 1812 the oldest son, William, fought as a Canadian in Merritt's Dragoons and later was a captain in the Middlesex Militia. Like many Upper Canada people of American background, including many Loyalists, when unrest developed in the 1830s, the Putnams, who were not active rebels but outspoken critics, were for Reform — and that was the wrong side to be on, especially in the London district.

Having never known my grandfather Gray, I wish I had listened more to my grandfather Putnam. Through him one could touch hands with the pioneers. His grandfather had fought in the American war of the Revolution and his father, Thomas, as a small boy had witnessed a meeting between Tecumseh and Proctor in 1813, hidden behind a couch in his father's house, and had been taken in for questioning in the Rebellion of 1837. As an old man "Squire" Putnam had moved to Brantford where he died and was buried in 1880. Thomas's older brother, William, had been less fortunate. Arrested, released, and forced into exile, he had died leading a "Patriot" invasion of Windsor in 1838.

Many of the Putnams went to the United States after the rebellion, settling in Iowa, which was just opening up. Thomas stayed in Canada and prospered, but his four sons, having all learned farming and a trade, as required by him, went to the United States and did well.

My great-uncle Warren Putnam, for example, had quite a presence, the effect a little spoiled by a growing paunch. He had somehow become surgeon-general, or some such title, of Vermont, and from time to time dressed in a rather splendid uniform. He was fond of saying "My ancestors were courtiers in the court of King Charlemagne." No one knew where he found this astonishing information but neither was anyone in a position to dispute it, so he lived — and to some extent we all lived — in the afterglow of great events.

Of the brothers only my grandfather, Alan, returned to Canada. Having grown up, I think, as a Methodist, he had gone to Woodstock College — the acorn from which McMaster University grew — close to his home village. In later years he seemed prouder of having played baseball for Woodstock College than of having graduated and been ordained as a Baptist minister.

He was obviously gifted, but somewhere along the way he either lost his faith or rebelled against the politics of his church. For a few years he had a parish in Racine, Wisconsin, where my mother was born. Then he was in Boston, the brilliant young pastor of the fashionable South Street Baptist Church. And then he gave up — walked away from success — and returned to Toronto to a succession of humiliating white-collar jobs and periodic bouts of drinking. When later I knew more of the story I didn't wonder at my permanently sad little grandmother, and at my mother's horror of alcohol.

The return to Toronto must have been a sad retreat for the Putnams. All three of my grandfather's brothers had remained in the States, prospering as doctors; he had neither occupation nor living.

Presumably they might have escaped the full hardship of their circumstances, because my grandmother's father, Thomas Lailey, was a successful businessman on the way to being rich. But they were proud and fiercely determined. While my grandfather looked for the satisfactory employment he was never to find, my grandmother, who was a superb cook, undertook to supplement family fortunes by running a sort of board-

7

ing house, providing lunches and dinners for young men working as bookkeepers and accountants in some of the new businesses opening up near by. My mother, then a pretty eighteen- or nineteen-year-old, undertook to help as waitress and dishwasher. Apparently with her cheerful high spirits she was a success, though she didn't like the work.

Into this hospitable haven one day came young Morgan Gray, starting work with the Canada Foundry. Between him and Helen Putnam there seems to have been love at first sight. Sharply disapproved of and discouraged by his family, however: a waitress and a Baptist — could anything be so unsuitable or more unacceptable?

Just what my mother endured I don't know, for it was years before we learned the circumstances of their meeting, and even then it embarrassed her to speak of it.

With her upbringing in pioneer Wisconsin, her scanty education, and the noisy over-exuberance she was never to lose, it was years before the Grays accepted her into the tribe. The result made her by turns watchful and aggressive, flourishing her great gifts as a good organizer, a devoted mother, and a talented musician with a beautiful singing voice. She could be quiet but she could not be put down. If any of this perplexed my father, I never saw him waver in his loyal support of her. Affectionately she called him Sammy, and he could always tease her back to laughter — which was never difficult — by calling her Mrs. Dooley.

I still wish I had listened more closely, or had been old enough to question my grandfather. But he had his good and his bad days, which I could recognize but didn't understand. His good days were very very good, but his bad days could be grumpy, and intimidating.

We didn't live in Toronto at this time before the Great War but in Cornwall, and our visits were not frequent. My Putnam grandparents lived on Blythwood Road, in what was called North Toronto, then almost in the country; they kept chickens and a horse, and had a considerable garden and an orchard. It was a joy for my brother and me to go with my grandfather (inevitably called Granpa Putty) to feed the chickens and gather eggs. Because we loved games above all things and longed to be stars, he talked about his modest baseball triumphs. But when once in that connection I spoke of Americans he said sharply, "Don't call them Americans, they're no more Americans than you are." I asked, "What do I call them?" "Call them Yankees," he said. Apart from traditional old Ontario attitudes, his bitterness had probably a large element of grief over the loss of his only son, Frank, an adventurous boy lost in the Spanish-American war from yellow fever and, it was said, bad doctoring.

In the winter of 1922, Alan Putnam contracted pneumonia, part of the treatment of which at the time was fresh air so that the windows of his bedroom had to be wide open, though it was bitterly cold. At the end, near delirium, he insisted on sitting up, supported by my father. Wrapped in his overcoat and wearing his bowler hat, he repeated the Apostles' Creed in a strong but gasping voice, punctuating the recital by thrashing the bedclothes with his stick; and then he died.

One thing about the Blythwood Road house stands in my memory as a kind of growth milestone. The front room was a very stiff little parlour seldom used, but it contained one marvel, an ostrich egg. Like many small boys of the time I collected birds' eggs, but knew I would never have one so splendid as this; and I would sit and stare at it, and just occasionally with nervously moist hands I was allowed to hold it. I yearned for that egg. And one day, without preamble, my grandmother said I could have it. I hadn't asked for it, hadn't knowingly even hinted. Suddenly, it was mine and for a few days I could hardly contain my joy. But of course as part of a birds'-egg collection it was absurd. Even invitations to little girls to come and see my ostrich egg didn't do much good. Sadly I put it in the museum that my brother and I had, and lost my pleasure in it. Did I learn then that to travel hopefully is better than to arrive? I doubt it. I'm not sure I have learned it yet, though I know it is true. But I learned something.

In late 1907 my father and two of his brothers moved with

their wives and children to Cornwall, Ontario. It was a dying wish of my grandfather's that "the boys" should go into business for themselves, and the estate set them up by buying the Ives Company, an old and respected firm from Montreal and the Eastern Townships making metal beds, together with the Modern Bedstead Company of Cornwall. The three — Charlie, Fred, and Morgan — though they knew nothing about making metal beds had between them a good deal of business experience. It was a rather bold venture, and, though they probably had insufficient capital, it might have succeeded but for one tragedy.

Charlie, the brother whom all seem to have loved and admired, came after the others to Cornwall and had not yet secured a house; meanwhile he and his wife and two children lived at the Rossmore Hotel. On a bitterly cold night in 1911, so cold that the hoses would not function properly, the hotel caught fire. Judge O'Reilly, who also lived in the hotel, came out into the corridor and through the smoke saw Charlie Gray emerging from his room. Charlie called that he would bring his wife and children through the Judge's rooms to the fire-escape. He went back into the room and did not reappear. All four, along with several other people, died in the fire.

I was only four at the time but the horror of the event and its effect on those around is still vivid. Its effect on the business was very serious. Just at first, in spite of sadness, all seemed to be well. Young Fred and younger Morgan, owners of a substantial factory, with their attractive young wives cut something of a figure in the town. My father was twenty-eight when they went to Cornwall, my mother twenty-three. For a few years business went quite well. These were the years just before the First World War when immigrants were pouring into Canada and markets were expanding. All seemed to be right with the world. After three or four years in modest houses, both families moved to larger houses — probably larger than either needed or could afford. Both houses had a good deal of lawn and garden and a small barn or stable, perfect for small-boy games.

One of my few vivid memories of the time hasn't to do with

the barns but with a piano box, left in the garden as a children's play-house. In our innocent play we stumbled on perhaps the oldest and most elementary sex game, "you show me yours and I'll show you mine". My girl cousin didn't really welcome this, but we all got excited and involved for reasons we couldn't have explained and didn't begin to understand. We even brought in some neighbours' children. And then the heavens fell; we were caught. We had known, I've no idea how, that this was forbidden fruit but we weren't prepared for the wrath to come. My aunt, so far as Bob and I saw, was merely chill in her disapproval, but my mother found us horrible, disgusting, and sinful. "God doesn't like little boys, God punishes little boys who do things like that." We hadn't realized. The cousins were forbidden to play together and my brother and I were made to understand that we were in deep and shameful disgrace. We settled down at the ages of four or five and six to bear the burden of a terrible guilt. I can't imagine how my mother, who had a lively sense of humour and boundless affection, could have them so completely quenched by her stiff puritan background. That she thought she was acting for our good I've no doubt, and there were to be many more such fierce battles for our virtue in the years ahead. Since we had no real evidence of God's disapproval, my brother Bob and I must have concluded in the end that either God didn't care, or mother was wrong about what concerned Him.

Apart from these struggles with original sin, the next few years appear only through the filtered and hazy memory of a happy childhood, except for one event. In 1911 there was great secrecy and excitement in the household and one morning it was announced that we had a baby brother brought by the doctor. A year later more secrecy and stir of a more frightening kind, and the baby we had just begun to play with and to make chuckle was dead. My poor mother, comforting us over her own need of comfort, assured us he was in heaven and happy. That helped, though my father when questioned on the subject of where little Alan had gone didn't seem quite so sure; but he was very quiet and gentle with us.

Our first encounter with the automobile was in 1911 or '12. We must have seen them before, but no one we knew owned one. Now the word passed like smoke under the door of every house on the street where there were children. Mr. Kyte across the road had bought a car that was to be delivered that evening. It was incredible but infinitely exciting.

In due course the car arrived from Warner's livery stable and stood panting and vibrating. My memory is that it had a blanket over the bonnet, like a horse, but that may not be true. What is certain is that the children from blocks around crowded the sidewalks, staring and hardly able to contain their excitement. As Mr. Kyte emerged to take possession and climb into the driver's seat we cheered madly. He lifted his straw hat slightly and gave a little bow. Behind us the curtains of the houses stirred discreetly as parents acknowledged the great event.

The car had brass everywhere and a mighty hand-brake and bulb horn set somehow, I think, in the running board. Mr. Kyte listened to last instructions and then suddenly shot forward like a bucking bronco. Our cheers could not be contained as the car settled down and noisily disappeared in the distance. Our excitement had not evaporated when we would hear the car returning, having rounded the block in a practice run. Again we cheered and ran alongside as the car went by. Mr. Kyte looked serene and confident enough to loosen one of his clutching hands from the steering wheel and salute us once again with a quick lift of his hat. Then he was gone again and did not return for some time, making a big sweep through the town. Once more, hearing him approach, we rushed out, but something had happened to his calm glory. He just barely sketched a lifting of his straw hat, and it was clear that he was wrestling in desperation with the controls. We couldn't guess what was wrong, but even small boys and girls could see that all was not well. It wouldn't have occurred to us that Mr. Kyte had forgotten how to stop the car.

He disappeared again and we were put to bed. When he came by at longer and longer intervals, circling the town in desperation, we were asleep. And when the car finally ran out of gas, coughed, and died, nothing disturbed our rest. The car was a mile or more north of the town and the humbled Mr. Kyte had to walk home in the early morning.

Even before the new house, my father had bought a cottage on the banks of the St. Lawrence a mile below Cornwall. The great Courtauld plant now spreads over the fields that surrounded us, and the old farms that ran back from the river east of the cottage have been subdivided and built upon. Before the first war most of them were still in the hands of the families who, as Loyalists, had drawn the land from the surveyor's hat in 1784. We can't have spent all our time swimming and eating strawberries and ice cream, but so I remember it. And at night, the murmuring of the river was only broken by the clumping of horses in the dusty road behind us, the splash of a jumping fish, or the boom of steamer whistles calling the Cornwall canal.

Into this idyllic scene burst war in August 1914. I don't think my brother and I had much idea what the word meant, much less that it could change our lives. But my father, who had always been active in the militia, was now a captain in the 59th Highland Light Infantry and within days he was in uniform with his regiment, on guard at the Cornwall canal. It was all still vague and glamorous, the streets full of soldiers wearing tartan trews or kilts and scarlet jackets. But by the autumn my father and part of the regiment were in Kingston, converted with contingents from Brockville, Peterborough, and Kingston areas into the 21st Battalion. Though we missed Dad — both as a playmate and as a kindly guide — I don't believe it seemed possible to us that he might be killed.

That autumn we were to start school, Bob having been held back a year so we could start together. I was just seven and school was both mystifying and a little frightening. There were fights between the bigger boys, and it was said if you were bad you would be sent to the Principal for a strapping. My most vivid memory of those few months was of the delicate neck of a little girl who sat in front of me. Suddenly I realized it was completely adorable and determined that we must be friends. I fol-

13

lowed her home from school. She ran and I chased her and caught her, to no purpose. She was too shy to talk and would only hang her head and dig her toe in the grass. I went home with her and appealed to her mother, who said Jean could come out to play if she wanted to; but she didn't — she never did, though I maintained pursuit for some weeks. Had she come out, would it have been like the case of the ostrich egg?

Fortunately I was whisked away. In the winter sixty years later, she remains like the girl on Keats' Grecian urn: "She cannot fade, though thou hast not thy bliss,/For ever wilt thou love, and she be fair!" My mother took us to Kingston, where all the talk was army and war, and small boys played at being soldiers. In the spring the 21st Battalion embarked for England and early in the summer we followed, in an American ship sailing from New York for Liverpool.

It was an exciting time, filled with the quickly alternating joys and sorrows and fears of childhood: joys in the strangeness and charm of England, fascinating to one fresh from an Ontario small town; above all, joys when my father had a few hours' or days' leave or we could go to see him in camp; sorrows at separations or when the strange country seemed hostile in some way; fears always there because a longer separation was coming from which we half understood, but couldn't believe, my father might never come back. In retrospect that summer of 1915 seems to have been beautiful. We had rooms at Hythe on the Kentish coast with a kindly English lady who I am sure had never had paying guests before and seemed to regard helping uprooted Canadians as a patriotic duty.

I can remember long afternoons on the beach with destroyers moving back and forth in the Channel, a silver dirigible hanging in the air near the coast of France, and occasionally in the distance the muffled thunder of the guns. And I can remember standing with my brother beside the road in complete little khaki soldier outfits, stiffly at the salute as the 21st Battalion marched by, with my father on horseback smiling and returning the salute; the men, looking hot, called out to us as they marched at ease singing "Pack Up Your Troubles in Your Old

Kit Bag" or "Tipperary" or "There's a Long, Long Trail A-winding". Our playmates on the beach and elsewhere were usually the children of other Canadians stationed at Shorncliffe Camp or Sandling.

With brutal suddenness the summer was at an end, my father's battalion was in France and we were in London. Bob and I were to go to a prep school in Hampstead and my mother was going to do war work and take singing lessons — anything, I suspect, to keep her mind off the casualty lists. "You must pray," she said to us, "whenever you think of it — even crossing a street — just ask God to keep Daddy safe." We knew about praying in church and at bedtime, but this was a novel idea, and we threw ourselves into the work with great enthusiasm.

A strange school in a strange land seemed very alarming. It was worse than that, though considering how cruel little boys can be it was not a cold or heartless place; but we started very badly. The school, called Heath Mount, had provided my mother with lists of the clothes we must have — grey flannel suits with short pants, white flannel shirts, Eton suits and collars for dress occasions and Sunday, green school ties, paddy-green peanut-scoop caps and blazers with the school crest. Everything was duly ordered from Harrods but the day school opened the clothes hadn't arrived. We thought this a reason for not going to school, but my mother thought otherwise, and she could be fiercely determined. What followed was a battle royal with tears, threats, and tantrums, as a result of which we all arrived late, exhausted, and tearful just as the school was finishing prayers at morning assembly in the gymnasium. The boys were formed in a U around three sides of the gym facing the main door near which stood the masters. Into this open doorway strode my by now flustered mother towing her two wretched sons, dressed in sailor suits. Our arrival was something of a sensation, and though pushed quickly into the most junior form, we could not miss the malicious smirks on all sides. What sport! They hadn't yet discovered our Canadian accents, but at intermission they did, with a vengeance. I came out to the playground a little late, to find a crowd gathered at one end. Cautiously I went in that direction and found the crowd surrounding my white-faced brother Bob, taunting him with questions about the sailor suit and his naval career. And when he answered, everyone took up the Canadian accent. Equally white-faced, but nearer to tears, I got in beside him and we did our best, and presently the older boys, who had watched without taking part, broke up the rough little game.

The first and probably the worst of the ordeal was over, though the effects lingered, but I was to have one more confrontation with the school. A few days later at school lunch I was faced with suet pudding, which I had never encountered before. I didn't like the look of it and a first taste confirmed my worst fears — I hated it, and sat without eating. Toward the end of the meal the master at my table called down, "Gray Minor, eat your pudding." I said I didn't like it, and was ordered again to eat it. I didn't answer and didn't eat. By now the whole table was watching, and the master was angry. For some minutes I sat in mulish silence not eating, but I had begun to cry. There was quiet throughout the dining room now except for the master's repeated commands "Eat your pudding." Broken at last I tried, but the miserable pudding, bad enough before, had become cold and gluey and I gagged, and vomiting and crying was rushed from the room.

Yet in a surprisingly short time, dressed in grey flannel and having learned to speak like English boys, we had settled in. There was little outward sign of our having had a hard time but we were undoubtedly nervy and watchful. I had a tendency to cry easily, and was called in by one of the masters and lectured coldly about being a cry-baby. On another occasion when in sheer excitement or joy I flung an arm around the shoulders of another boy in the group, I was taken to the Prefects' locker-room and shown a gym-shoe. "Any more of that," said the Prefect, "and you'll get this on your backside." Inexorably we were taught to conform, in dress, in speech patterns, in the control — even suppression — of all emotion. Bob managed better than I, perhaps from being a year older. My conformity, like my high-spirited mother's, kept coming apart.

On one occasion we were invited by one of the boys to a party at his house. After a rather stiff beginning it was suggested we should dance, which was comparatively new to me, but I entered with enthusiasm. Finding the Lancers rather sweaty work, I went out into the hall and got rid of my Eton jacket in order to get seriously down to business. My reappearance in shirt-sleeves and braces caused a mild sensation; some of the mothers I think found it cute in an eight-year-old, some clearly thought it what might be expected of a wild Colonial boy. But I was still hard at it in my shirt-sleeves when my startled mother arrived to take us home.

The days were busy for all of us but the evenings and even more the week-ends were often aimless and lonely, with time for worrying. The 21st Battalion had been in action and some of the officers and men we had known were dead. My mother, aided by a kindly distant cousin, worked hard at keeping us happy. We saw the sights again and again: the zoo, the Tower of London (I could spend all day looking at armour), Madame Tussaud's Wax Works, Westminster Abbey, and many more. The English cousin, Alice Simpson, who had had some romantic connection with my father long before, had a beautiful reading voice and was tireless. Sitting before a fire being read to, away from the rain and fog of a London winter, was bliss, and even the thought of war could be shut out.

And then during the battle of the Somme in April 1916 came the dreaded telegram. My father was coming back to hospital in England. We didn't know it for some months, but his war was over and he was never to be a completely well man again. For eight months he had commanded an infantry company in the line — and now he was out with shell-shock, what in the 1939 war was called "battle exhaustion". Proud to be a soldier and determined to be a good one, he had been broken by eight months of seeing his men killed and hideously wounded. There followed months of convalescence, of walking and bicycling in the quiet parts of England with my mother. He wanted only to get well again, to return to his men. A final Medical Board declared him unfit for further active service. He argued, broke down and cried; it only proved their point. He had the option of returning to military service in Canada, of becoming a colonel at a training centre, but he wanted active service or nothing; he asked for and was granted his discharge.

During the months of convalescence, two small boys were a problem. My father could tolerate no noise, and noise was our element. So it was arranged we would go into Heath Mount as boarders. Though by now the school was no longer strange, the idea of life away from both parents, of sleeping in a dormitory with other boys, of not seeing our parents for weeks at a time, brought back all the old fears. Long after, cousin Alice told me that when the decision on boarding was made, I marched up and down the room, in characteristically dramatic fashion, holding my head and saying, "I shall go mad, I shall go mad." But those of our friends who were boarders were delighted and gave us a welcome that comforted our homesickness. People were kind; cousin Alice sometimes came for us on week-ends and occasionally we went home for a meal with one of the boys. But there were week-ends when from Saturday noon until Sunday evening Bob and I were the only boys in school.

It was lonely but it wasn't so bad. By now we knew Hampstead well and the Heath, and ran about it happily. It was still a London with almost no cars but with plenty of horses and bicycles, a rougher and friendlier London. Immediately back of the school was a blacksmith shop and we loved to hang in the doorway watching the glow of the forge and the sparks flying up as the bar iron was hammered on the anvil, and to smell the burning as the shoe was hammered onto the great hoof held firmly between the blacksmith's knees.

One Saturday, my father and mother came to take us out overnight. We were suddenly shy and quiet, bottling up our happiness as required by the "good form" we had learned so painfully, and partially. In the taxi rattling in to the West End we sat on the jump seats facing my parents, unsmiling and correct, answering their questions in clipped tones: "Yes, thank you, Mother," "I think so, sir," "Yes, jolly good." My parents looked and listened with mounting dismay, as we learned later.

18

When we arrived at our hotel — the Regent Palace, which was a kind of headquarters for Canadians on leave and seemed to me very grand — Dad led the way up to our room, then my mother took over. "Take off those jackets," she said, "and your Eton collars." She ruffled our hair fondly looking at us, trying to understand what had happened to her children. "Jack, I wonder whether you are still ticklish." I squirmed in anticipation and began to grin, and presently we were all three rolling on the bed laughing uncontrollably, while my father watched smiling. Bob and I were soon chattering away, happily — but it was all very bad form.

On another week-end something of lasting importance to me happened; presumably it would have happened elsewhere, sooner or later. I only know the moment of revelation. It was a fairly free Saturday morning and I was wandering around thinking of all the wonderful things I might do. In one of the study rooms two or three older boys were talking and working together with great concentration. One of the boys was Evelyn Waugh. I crept closer and finally dared to ask what they were doing. I was told firmly though not brutally to buzz off, they were writing a book.

I buzzed off, in immense excitement. I had suddenly decided what I wished most of all to do on that glorious morning: to write a book. And I did. Seated on my tuck box, which contained paper and pencil and all my treasures, I wrote an eager, untidy little volume entitled *The Percuywiaratees of Birds and Thier Eggs*. Birds were my passion at the time, and over Christmas with our cousins in Durham we had caught some birds without injuring them and later let them go. My narrative was a good deal less fascinating than the stories I loved to listen to, but the writing of it was a great happiness. From that moment on when any interested or patronizing elder asked what I wished to do when I grew up I answered always that I wanted to be a writer, without really knowing what the term meant or what I meant by it. I can't explain this sudden certainty. No doubt the joys of being read to had much to do with it. I only know that it reached me in that way. Though I was never in fact to reach my apparent goal, I was, like a blind puppy, moving toward it by some sure instinct from the age of eight.

2

OMING BACK TO CANADA in the late autumn of 1916 was coming home, to a loved house, to friends and relations, but in some dimly perceived way it was more than that. It was returning to a way of life we knew, to familiar scenery, to a place where one hadn't to be forever on guard — more than the young had always and everywhere to be careful at that time. The trip was rough and I was a little sea-sick, and we were always in fear of submarines — especially as terrifying darkness came down and the ship was blacked out; and yet, tramping around the cold, wet decks with my father, it seemed that every day was a joyful day. It was a contrast to the trip over in summer in an American ship, when the sea was calm and the days were sunny, and at night after we entered "the danger zone" great American flags on the side of the vessel were brightly lighted all night. On an overcast wintry day we landed in Halifax. We landed not far from the spot at which, just a year later, two ships colliding in the harbour produced an explosion that tore the old city apart. If I had had a grown-up's sense of symbolism, I would have kissed the historic and rather unsavoury earth of Water Street before being bundled onto the Intercolonial train for the long ride home. Ours was a troop train with an assorted cargo of wounded and widows, war brides, and soldiers' children. Each of the adults no doubt carried emotions as mixed as the train's company, but the children played happily in the aisles until exhausted, then climbed into some friendly lap to sleep it off; one of our merriest playmates was a younger boy, too young to feel, except briefly, the quiet sadness of his mother; his father had been killed in action a few months before.

In Cornwall we stopped for a few days with my aunt and uncle, since our house had been rented and was still occupied. We had a joyous and boastful time with our cousins, Elizabeth and Howard, while my parents collected clothes for winter and for civilian life; then on to Toronto and Christmas with grandparents.

Bob and I had assumed we were returning to the old pattern of life in Cornwall, to picking things up just where we had laid them down. We were in for a shock. Some time over the Christmas holidays, in family conferences about my father's health and his unfitness to return to business right away, our course for the next ten years was rather casually arranged. My father must have rest and quiet, and these were not to be had in our presence; he and my mother and grandmother Gray were going to California for the winter and we had to be taken care of somehow. Uncle Frank had heard well of a small school in the country that he referred to as Mackenzie's school; he undertook to find out more, and especially whether they could take two boys of nine and ten on two weeks' notice. He did, they could, and we went; it was all as quick as that. Once again the shopping list of clothes; this one allowed either a blue suit for Sunday best, or an Eton suit. Well, we had Eton suits but, great misery, we were to be almost the only boys in the school who had. Suddenly the joys of Christmas and New Year were behind us and we sat quietly with our parents on the train bound for a school none of us knew anything about, a school called The Grove, or simply Lakefield. Round about us boys romped and told stories of imaginary adventures over Christmas while we sat silent in mounting dread. Our parents would do little more than deliver us and then, once again, we would have our way to make among these wild and noisy kids. We had just got our safe and happy world together and it was again beginning to come apart.

The trip was at once endless and alarmingly short. We

changed trains at Port Hope and again at Peterborough. During the cold, long waits there were tentative approaches from some of the boys, "Are you guys new kids?" It was not unfriendly, perhaps because there was a certain amount of wary circling round my father, who was still in uniform. Came the last slow and bumpy ten miles from Peterborough on the Lakefield Bullet — butt of endless schoolboy jokes — and we were piling out at the little red frame station — Grand Trunk Gothic — that we were to love and hate by turns for many years. It still stands, now unused, and empty but for the load of memories it carries.

The boys, who had been noisy enough before, now became happily demented. A big flat-bed sleigh was drawn up near the baggage car of the panting Bullet and for the next few minutes of organized confusion trunks were shifted to the sleigh and roped in spite of boys who would help, boys who insisted on lying on the trunks as they were piled until other boys pushed them off, boys who climbed to the top of the mounting pyramid of trunks and, uttering weird cries, plunged into the snow piled up beside the track. Somehow the teamster, Billy Stabler, strong, quiet, good-natured, and patient, moved through the tumbling bedlam, assisting those who were trying to help, checking the load, picking up the wounded, and calming the over-excited. His team of white horses, sharing his patience and strength, stood quietly through it all, breathing jets of steam into the cold, clear air.

At last we were on our way, the big team pulling steadily up the long rise out of the village while boys tumbled off and scrambled on, pelting each other with snowballs. Bob and I joined tentatively in the fun but we had back of us an understanding of the pack of wolves we were playing in; small boys can be playful, then suddenly turn on an intruder in the pack; for the moment we were protected by the presence of our parents, with my father riding beside Billy Stabler. Besides, with every ring of the sleigh bells through the mile-long ride we drew nearer a frightening gap. We would be at "the school" —

hardly to be imagined — and then our mother and father would be gone and we left alone with these wild characters.

There was a final hard pull up a hill past a house called Ashelworth and in through stone gates into which were chiselled the words *Porta Itinera Longissima*. This was the first formal lesson the school intended to teach; freely translated the message of the gates was *Starting Is the Hardest Part of the Journey*. Doubtless this was one of the accepted proverbs of the day, but like most clichés it offered us the proven wisdom of the experience of the race. And more than once since, facing the cold water of a difficult decision, the memory of that motto has come to my aid.

But a little while later, sitting on the floor in the big living room, in front of the Headmaster's fire, a sense of the desolation to come swept over me. Above and around me were the sturdy legs of masters and their wives, of some neighbours, and of my mother and father. Suddenly crouched in my warm but alarming cavern I began to cry. I had a companion, Florence Mackenzie, one of the Headmaster's four daughters. I was to learn in time that, from birth, the Mackenzie girls' duty and joy in life was to help lonely new boys. They were devoted to their parents but in the world of children and grown-ups their loyalty was with the children, and they were one of the happy elements that made a human and remarkable school. But at that moment Florence, a pretty and sympathetic little girl in a middy and skirt, couldn't do much for me. I was grateful for a friend but I was facing a loneliness no one could share and I could not explain.

My father, the too gentle soldier, took me out into the hall, trying at once to understand and to comfort. Bob, white and quiet but dry-eyed, standing by and with the brave and quavery confidence of a ten-year-old, assured my father he would look after me. And then they were gone; a quick, surreptitious kiss from my mother which threw us into an agony of shyness, and produced more tears and clinging from me, a firm handshake from my father, and they were whirled away in a jangle of sleigh bells and of flying snow from the horses' hooves. Someone suggested we might like to skate, and with a guarded joy I dried my tears. We didn't know just how badly we skated by Lakefield standards until we found ourselves on the outdoor rink, already growing dark by late afternoon. We had been too young to skate much before going to England and now we were well back of boys our own age who skimmed around us, with what seemed the grace of seagulls, as we shuffled along on our weak ankles. But in the clear, cold air, caught up in the general mood of sheer animal joy, we moved around in a series of desperate teetering lunges, our loneliness for the moment forgotten.

Our induction was not over and was not easy, though in a few weeks we were almost indistinguishable from those around us. This bliss was reached over a bumpy and sometimes painful road, but once attained it brought with it a sturdy confidence worth, I think now, all it cost. It is possible — though I can't think of cases — that it destroyed or permanently maimed the confidence of a few. Sensitive and very young boys flung into this vigorous struggle sometimes learned to survive by becoming cute and sly and taking no risks, and some never really outgrew these attitudes. Lakefield in 1917 was a hard school, and intended to be, but it was not cruel. It was too small — thirty-five boys in all, ranging from age eight to fifteen or sixteen — for cruelty or persecution to remain hidden for long, and the Headmaster, though capable of rage, was a kind man. To become a received member of the club was to complete a kind of obstacle race, and Bob and I had an extra obstacle; without being aware of it we spoke like English boys, and having been persecuted in England for a Canadian accent, we were now mildly persecuted in Canada for the reverse. That was soon fixed, superficially, though to this day some trick of accent or manner has caused people to think I was born in England.

At Heath Mount we had lived with three or four others in the smallest boys' dormitory. We were now assigned to a long, narrow room containing fifteen small cubicles, each barely big enough for one narrow iron bed, a set of shelves and some hooks for clothes, and a window which had to be open at night; this was not a school rule but a dormitory tradition, enforced on newcomers if necessary; in January it was like sleeping outdoors. Down the narrow aisle between the cubicles there were bureaus in which each boy had a drawer or two and in the centre of the floor stood three iron radiators spaced down the room, cold all night and only beginning to warm as we dressed in the morning. At the end of each radiator stood two or three jerry pots which someone was always kicking over, and into which it was our great forbidden joy to pee from the top of a nearby bureau. The result was that one of the really homey things about Number 2 dormitory was a welcoming smell of urine from the permanently impregnated floors, and since with our climbing, crying, fighting, and laughing we were like puppies in a basket, it was not an inappropriate aura.

In the mornings, in winter, the jerries were usually frozen solid and the floor was like a skating rink. We were wakened by a school bell at seven and the new boys had to close all the windows. Those who had been there a year remained huddled beneath the bedclothes with only a nose showing while their woollen underwear warmed on their particular coil of the nearest radiator, placed there by a new boy. The new boys, if they had a coil, had it at the jerry-pot end of the radiator, which didn't get warm until after we had gone to breakfast. This was the law, accepted after the first shock by all; new boys would one day be full members of the club and enjoy the perquisites of that exalted station.

But from one ordeal no one was exempt: everyone had to have a cold bath to start the day. It didn't involve soap or any pretence at cleanliness, the object was hardiness. Since there were only two tubs in the communal bathroom, one was filled with cold water, the other with naked and shivering small boys. We were chased through in relays by the prefects into the icy water, into the other tub to shiver and towel, then back to the dormitory through the chill hall to scramble into long woollen underwear and clothes and rush down to morning prayers with hair half brushed and sticking up spikily, and a hastily knotted tie, more often than not under one ear.

It was all a very long way from stiff and orderly Heath Mount; the setting alone guaranteed that. Lakefield Preparatory School had started in 1879 as a school for the sons of Anglican clergymen. The Grove was the name of the Headmaster's house and for many years it provided all there was in the way of school facilities. One large room adjoining his study, which in our day was called the Reading Room, was at first the sole classroom, and above it the only dormitory. The Reading Room contained a fireplace, a long table with benches, a small locked cupboard holding "the library", an old piano, and a case of stuffed birds, animals, birds' eggs, and Indian arrowheads. A friendly room, but not seriously suggestive of or conducive to scholarly or intellectual effort. It was more a room in which tired boys might rest happily after a strenuous game of football or hockey or a long day in the woods.

For the outdoors, games, Lake Katchewanooka, gardening, and the woods and fields had more of our time — and much more of our interest — than the schoolroom in 1917. To my brother and me it was wonderful beyond belief. This country, on the edge of the great Northern Shield, was wilder than the tranquil and long-settled valley of the St. Lawrence near Cornwall. Here on half-holidays, instead of a walk through the streets of Hampstead or on the Heath, we were turned loose. The village south of the school was out of bounds, but we might go north or west as far as we could and still get back for supper at six — unless we owned a hut and had "tea-leave". Here was another wonder! The woods below the school were full of huts belonging to the boys and on Saturday those with "tea-leave" might draw food from the kitchen and cook their own meal in their hut.

Living as it seemed on the edge of the wilderness awakened an old dream of mine, to have clothing made of skins like Robinson Crusoe. As usual I didn't do anything effective about it except to study the Hallam catalogues with their pictures of traps and guns, to watch older boys skin the rabbits they snared, and to catch one groundhog whose skin even I didn't think very suitable.

27

But one early morning my dream seemed to come a step closer. I was out before school breakfast sniffing the delicious air when I saw two big boys coming up out of the woods carrying a long pole on which a black and white animal swung between them. At once I was dancing around them, full of excitement and eager questions. The animal, they said, was a skunk that had got caught in one of their snares. Jeez, what were they going to do with it? As to that they seemed a little uncertain. "Would you like to buy it?" they asked. The prospect dazzled me but I knew I could never afford such a prize. They suggested thirty cents. To me that seemed a wonderful bargain, though beyond my means. Miraculously the price came down, after a suitable hesitation, to twenty cents. I couldn't really afford that, but neither could I let the bargain go; it simply meant pledging my pocket-money for two weeks, going without chocolate bars and jelly beans and licorice whips, but oh, it was worth it!

And suddenly to my joy, tinged a little with dismay, I owned a dead skunk. Behind a high board fence adjoining the barn was the rubbish heap. Here later in the day my dismay grew as I skinned the skunk and the rich perfume of its secret weapon made my eyes water and almost choked me. With the wretched job done, some joy in my prize returned as I tacked up the skin on the outside of the barn. Then I washed up, small-boy fashion, and went into the Reading Room and sat down. Almost at once someone lifted his head and sniffed audibly. "Pew," he said, and held his nose. Others joined in and I tried to pretend I hadn't noticed. Then they were all holding their noses and pointing, then chanting, "Gray Minor stinks."

I fled and washed my hands again and even my face. But the mark of Cain wasn't to leave me for weeks. People sat as far away from me as possible in class and at meals. The only ones who came close to me of their own choice were the big boys to collect the purchase price. Periodically I peered into the rubbish heap at the tacked-up skin, but without going close I could tell it hadn't turned into a luxuriously soft and sweet-smelling garment. Came the day when the Headmaster announced that whoever owned that skunk skin on the barn wall was to take it down and tan it or get rid of it. Fifteen or twenty heads swivelled around toward me with furtive grins. Later I crept out to the rubbish heap and with a long stick detached my precious skin, carried it on the tip of the stick to a quiet corner, and buried it.

As the year went on we penetrated further into the school's special qualities. The boys were encouraged to snare rabbits in the woods, and the catch could be cooked in the school kitchen and served with pride to one's friends at supper. When March came we tapped the maple trees and boiled down the sap in a perpetually boiling cauldron in the carpenter shop; and more than one small boy broke his mother's heart by proudly carrying home at Easter a precious but imperfectly sealed quart of his own maple syrup packed in his clean clothes.

In summer those who could swim might borrow a school canoe on half-holidays and spend the afternoon on the lake, cooking the evening meal somewhere up the shore. Periodically Indians from the nearby reservation used to visit the school with supplies of sweet-grass or birch-bark baskets decorated with porcupine quills; parents of boys who were at the school for some years tended to acquire rather more of these than they could use or even hide away. And sometimes the Indians brought splendid cedar bows and blunt arrows so desirable as to rock a small boy's judgment. In all these transactions money was the big problem, for our 10¢ weekly pocket money, even with the embezzlement of our 5¢ "church money", didn't go very far. Then some genius discovered that the Indians enjoyed barter, and one could get a bow and arrow in exchange for a pair of boots or spare trousers, and there was brisk trading. However, the trade fair was always in the Headmaster's front hall and the whole economic system was disclosed, and promptly collapsed, when one of the youngest boys was caught hurrying in with his Sunday suit. With regret on both sides boots, pants, and bow and arrows were exchanged once more.

To Bob and me, to whom it was all so exotic and free, the happiness of this new life more than balanced the fears of the unknown still to be encountered. By the end of winter we had almost learned to skate. In the spring we each had a little garden plot as part of the war effort, and though my interest in this didn't run to weeding carefully, my more patient brother grew quantities of lettuce, radishes, nasturtiums, and onions. Since many other plots were producing much the same fare, our physical systems must have been kept in good if windy shape; our aesthetic systems continued emaciated.

Coming in January we had missed the great social event of the school year, the Football Supper. We heard again and again about the glories of this event, which took place not long before the Christmas holiday. The chief splendour for the boys, of course, was the great feast — of turkey, I think — washed down with quantities of cider made from the school's apples, gathered by the boys and pressed in our own cider mill. The prospect of this glittering occasion, though months away, drew us through the year marred only by one thing: we were told that at the Football Supper New Boys were required to make a speech, and until the following January we would still be New Boys. Reports varied; most said all New Boys must speak, others said only a selection. My dread told me that of course I would be called on, and it returned to torture me throughout the year. I remember the fear so vividly, it is strange that I cannot now recall whether I was eventually called on or not. Since then I have made many speeches, even some good ones, but I have never overcome the preliminary nightmare, and, just before speaking, the nerve storm that sometimes seemed so severe as to threaten a breakdown. When, a generation later, as parent and Old Boy I made a speech at the Football Supper, my son, John, sat at the first-team table (and that made us both nervous). The captain of the team, Tom Ryder, was the son of my friend and comforter of long before, the little girl in the middy and skirt, Florence Mackenzie.

The independence, the physical rigour, the vivid new terrain all contributed something to a rounded growth; the academic side of our lives was much more haphazard. The masters at the boys' private schools in Canada, and I suspect in England, a generation and more ago must always have been a chance lot; in wartime the mixture was thinned even more. I'm sure none had any training as teachers and I suspect most had little academic qualification. The Headmaster, Mr. Mackenzie, was both a fair scholar and a born if unorthodox teacher, but in a small school there are many things to call a headmaster away and his classes were often left to "get on with the work", unsupervised. In addition those boys who were well up in their work — the very ones who should have been pushed on to greater efforts and higher standing — would often be rewarded by being allowed out to chop wood or hoe potatoes, or to go on an errand to the village. Some boy went to the village for mail every day — in summer by bicycle, in winter on foot or driving a horse and cutter, and he had always food shopping to do for those who had withheld money from the school bank; food that might be wolfed on arrival or hoarded for Saturday supper in "the hut" — a tin of pork and beans, or a tin of Reindeer Cocoa or Coffee Syrup.

The Headmaster, tall, quiet, with a weathered face and rimless glasses on a big nose, was a formidable figure; but we came to know that this rather stern appearance covered immense warmth, a kindly understanding, and a love of fun. A less predictable and welcome aspect of the warmth was a temper that could flash out, sometimes woundingly unfair, though afterwards he would make generous amends.

My impishness amused him but my wool-gathering, and my almost complete inability to be on time for prayers or for meals, sometimes exasperated him beyond amusement. The outside bell rang at seven every morning and at seven-twenty-five there was a shrill inside bell. When "second bell" went we were usually clattering down the stairs, doing up buttons and ties and combing hair as we hurried to our places for morning prayers; there some would surreptitiously lace their boots. At seven-thirty the gate at the foot of the stairs was locked but sometimes, if there were too many late arrivals, the Headmaster would stand at the foot of the stairs calling, "Come along, boys, come down as you are."

This was a kind of challenge we never took beyond perhaps carrying down a tie or a pair of boots. Most of us could dress after a fashion in two or three minutes and we usually had that interval after the "come down as you are" call. But dawdling, fighting, arguing, thinking took time, and one morning I had been dreamier than usual and was quite unprepared when the call came; I was still in pyjamas. When it came again insistently, I had struggled into my long woollen underwear, and obedient to the command, in my bare feet, I went down as I was. My arrival at prayers created the mild sensation I hoped for, and even the Headmaster cocking his head at me in mock reproof could only send me up to dress properly after prayers.

But there was a quite different day when in arithmetic class I somehow arrived at a right answer by an entirely wrong method. When Mr. Mackenzie asked who had the problem right I alone, eagerly, proudly, held up my hand. "Good boy," he said, "good boy." He then set out and worked the problem through on the blackboard and I saw with dawning horror that though somehow I had the right answer, my working out of the question was quite wrong. I sat paralysed, not knowing what to do, though I knew what I should do. As we worked away at another problem I knew better than ever; the Head was strolling up and down the aisles looking at people's work and presently he was nearing me. I felt him back of my shoulder and I knew he was looking at my exercise book. Something wretched was going to happen but even my misery didn't prepare me sufficiently.

In a loud, angry voice he said, pointing, "You didn't get that right. Why, you little liar you." In terror I tried to explain. "Get out," he said. "Go and sit by yourself in the Reading Room. We don't allow liars in here." In dragging wretchedness I left the room while everyone watched. Once in the Reading Room I gave way to my despair and cried inconsolably, taking out my book and staring at it with swollen eyes, trying to understand what had happened and how.

Some time later I heard the classes go out; there was to be a practice for Sports Day. At last, timidly, I crept out and joined the others. I was not welcomed but there was a more or less kindly moving over and making room for me. I began to recover, and then the Head arrived and saw me. "You're not supposed to be here," he said. "We don't like having liars around."

I fled back to the Reading Room and sat in silent misery, dried out and empty. Perhaps an hour later the Headmaster came in. I said fiercely, "I'm not a liar." He sat down then and put his arm around me. "No," he said. "Jack, what happened?" In tears again and gasping, I tried to tell him while he comforted and reassured me.

It was characteristic of Mr. Mackenzie's unorthodox system that when later he found me insufficiently challenged in English literature he arbitrarily jumped me ahead two years at the age of eleven or twelve, because I seemed to be ready for something with more body to it. For the rest of my subjects I stayed with my own class, but for that one I was with the big boys, excited and hard-pressed as I needed to be.

The second master, the Reverend Henry Brittain, known as "Jimmy", was not a happy figure. He had a good Oxford degree and had done some graduate work in Germany. Mr. Brittain was a shy and awkward man given to flashes of temper that we learned to find comic rather than chastening; it was too easy for boys to make his life a misery and we never let up. And yet with his well-stored mind, on his few good days, he taught us better than we realized, for when he was at ease and happy he could and did talk well, on many subjects. The study in Germany, as ignorant little war-mongers, we could neither understand nor forgive. It was evident that he had learned to be guarded in his admissions, but there was much about the Germans he admired, and we could always break up a class by making some artless reference to the Germans as barbarians. The very fact that he questioned some of the propaganda about German atrocities, and let us know it, was enough to produce the recurring rumour that he was a German spy. We felt no need to wonder what in the world a German spy would find to do in Lakefield, but if some German agent had thought it worth while to blow up the locks on the Trent Valley canal near Lakefield, Jimmy Brittain would have had twenty-five or thirty accusers at once.

With his marked Oxford speech and a nervous habit of clearing his throat every few words, Jimmy Brittain was a natural mark for mimics. We all tried our hand and since I longed for approval, I tried harder than most. This earned me my first caning and a measure of popularity within a few days of arriving at school, and set me on a course of behaviour — as a professional naughty boy — that held me for a long time. There had been few spankings in my life and never one at school. In the next few months I learned the tricks of the trade — tightening the buttocks, putting on extra underwear, and a thin scribbler or newspaper in the seat of the pants — but that day I was unprepared and vulnerable. For the balance of the school year I was in a contest with a dormitory mate to see who could get the most spankings. We kept score in the back of a scribbler and I claimed I won with a total of 32; 1 from the Headmaster, 29 from Jimmy Brittain, and 2 from the most junior master, Philip Ketchum. This is the same Phil Ketchum who in later years was for long the popular and respected Headmaster of Trinity College School in Port Hope.

I've only the vaguest memories of other masters who came and went, some very quickly. Some could not control us, and some no doubt could not stand us. We were turbulent and barbaric, going eagerly to play and reluctantly to work, brawling like cubs with brawls often turning into serious fighting. It was taken for granted that men must know how to take care of themselves, which meant with their fists. So everyone had to box. Every spring there was a boxing tournament in which every boy in the school who was physically fit had to take part, boxing in classes graded by age and weight. We had little or no coaching; we had to be energetic and brave and gentlemanly — no hitting below the belt, win or lose gracefully. But outside the boxing ring the need to win was more important, more depended on it. New boys could only be sent on errands or made to "fag" by those who could beat them in a fight and we sized up our oppressors, gathering our courage for a challenge.

It was not as brutal as it sounds and it was perhaps inevitable in war-time with all its false emphases. The way of 1914 had been launched and still travelled, though barely, on a mythology of glory; the warrior was still king, and appropriately in a primitive society we were in training to be warriors. From pillow fights and pile-ons which began as play and often became more serious, we graduated to dormitory raids in which the weapon was a knotted towel, or a towel wetted so that it could be flicked like the lash of a whip — and for these fights we were always stripped to the waist.

On the winter roads, unploughed in those days, we stole rides on the great bob-sleighs that came bowling along behind steaming horses and a jangle of bells; here too the innocent rider enjoying the swaying rhythm in peace might be set upon by a boarding party and flung off in the snow. It was all rough fun, on the edge of sweet danger. When later in Greek history we encountered the Spartans, I think we recognized ourselves — though no one talked of "identifying" with them.

And yet — were we growing up? was I? — the Athenians were in some ways more attractive, more admirable. I trembled on the margin of an elementary but important discovery. The Spartans might be trained to behave like extraordinarily brave men but they were stuck in their mould; they were brave but nothing else. And what was bravery alone for?

Along with the animal spirits, the horseplay, and the cult of the warrior — "be a good soldier" had become an admonition of my father's — there were softening influences in our lives. In spite of the wretched library, which was no worse than that of most schools of the time, the Grove stimulated our reading. Before we could read well, and after, we were read aloud to. On Sunday after evening service when we were often tired and sometimes sad, in the dormitory before bedtime, especially if we were quick in undressing and quiet and had brushed our teeth, we were read to. In the Reading Room in front of a fire the Headmaster would read aloud while fifteen or twenty boys sat in the available chairs or squatted happily on the floor. We were after all little more than a large family and the feeling of

35

closeness was important to boys who had often to hide a loneliness. Here we were read *Huckleberry Finn* and *Tom Brown's School Days*, *Westward Ho* and *Dead Man's Rock* by Quiller-Couch, and the stories of P. G. Wodehouse then appearing in the *Strand Magazine*. Sometimes he would shut the book at an exciting point and say, "Now that's all I'm going to read of that book; if you like it you can read it for yourselves." In the dormitory, perched dangerously on a bureau with a foot braced against a radiator, one of the other masters would read Sherlock Holmes or from Robert Louis Stevenson while we hushed each other lest any fooling or inattention might break the spell and stop the reading. And afterward the questions tumbled out of us, and the talk went on excitedly after lights-out until the last questioner found there was no one to answer; in the manner of children we were suddenly asleep.

Even more than the reading, religion, directly and indirectly, touched our lives. The day began at seven-thirty with prayers which, since we had no chapel, were held in the big schoolroom. In spite of the dulling effect of repetition the opening of each day with a General Confession had a quietening effect on us — "We have followed too much the devices and desires of our own hearts" — didn't I know from many tellings that I was selfish? — "We have left undone those things which we ought to have done, And we have done those things which we ought not to have done" — and it was true of me; I knew it, and would know it better as time went on. So we went to breakfast rather humbled, and after an hour or so of eating, talking, and frantic rushing — to make our beds, shine our shoes, submit to inspection — we started the school day with a period of Scripture, which consisted of reading the Bible and sometimes reciting a psalm or one of the great passages that we had been required to memorize. We objected to Scripture on principle, but I think many of us really enjoyed it as we enjoyed being read to, for the wonderful stories and the splendid expression; and if it did little for our souls I'm sure it did something for our sense of language. Day after day we heard some of the finest writing

36

in English and, however unwittingly, acquired that frame of reference which surrounds much of our standard literature.

If the content of other courses had had as recognizable a relation to our lives we might have enjoyed them more. But spelling — except when we had a match — arithmetic, English grammar, geography, even history struck little excitement from us. To memorize the names and dates of the kings of England and the names of the counties in Ontario was meagre fare, but it was considered good for us; it was building a framework — and perhaps it was. More important was the conviction of educators at the time that memory was a muscle that could be developed with use. But as in physical training we enjoyed some exercises more than others. To have to memorize "Ode on the Death of the Duke of Wellington", or "The Burial of Moses", seemed both wearing and pointless, since much of it bore no relation to our experience and couldn't even be understood without long explanations. And to repeat the poems aloud after memorization was meaningless gabble. I can still hear the class chanting:

> *By Nebo's lonely mountain,*
> *On this side Jordan's wave,*
> *In a vale in the land of Moab,*
> *There lies a lonely grave.*
> *And no man knows that sepulchre,*
> *And no man saw it e'er,*
> *For the angels of God upturned the sod*
> *And laid the dead man there.*

Even now, almost sixty years later, I am sure that is close to an accurate quotation, lying unwanted and unused in some brain cell all that time. Has it been taking space that might have been better used? I hope not; I had none to spare. At Lakefield I came to like memorization, for I found I had a good, almost a remarkable, memory, and we like what helps us to shine. Besides, there was so much that did not even produce a dull glow from me.

37

After supper and a little time for play or reading, the day closed with evening prayers. This was the reflective moment of the day and the moment for homesickness. In addition to repeating the Confession: "We have erred and strayed" (as we often had), "We have left undone" (as it seemed I always had), we sang the Nunc Dimittis, "Lord, now lettest thou thy servant depart in peace", and one of the gentler evening hymns, "Abide with me" or "The day Thou gavest, Lord, is ended". The sense of guilt and inadequacy produced by the Confession settled over tired small boys. The suggestion of a refuge in God which we couldn't really understand was readily transferred to a refuge in our distant homes, warm, protected, and unattainable. Quite often as prayers finished there were reddened eyes and sometimes a new boy, crying openly and inconsolably, was hushed or led out to cry himself to sleep. We were gentle with each other's homesickness; it was something we all understood. After prayers the smallest boys went straight up to bed and the rest of us were released in relays by age; until our turn came we all did homework (or surreptitiously read books) in the big schoolroom. Then, up to bed with half an hour to brush teeth, undress, wrestle, and say prayers before lights-out. The new boys had an added chore. In warm weather and cold they had to run out to the pump with big granite jugs to be filled for the dormitory. Forgetting to go for water before undressing was no excuse; it was "tough cheese". Anyway, only sissies minded running through the snow in bedroom slippers, and we knew that even Spartans hadn't done that.

On Sundays the day was only more formidably framed by religious exercises. Each service was enlarged by a sermon and additional hymns. The hymns we liked, and with the noisier ones our enthusiasm for salvation or mischief mounted so that the service was sometimes turned into a sort of pep rally if the formidable Mac was away and Jimmy Brittain in charge. But the sermons, which the Headmaster used like a pair of reins to control a team of spirited horses, we faced with trepidation. Sometimes they were little parables, stories about boys like ourselves, with difficulties like ours; these we enjoyed. Others, though they might dwell gently on the great love of God for us, were also a constant reminder that He knew all our sins; "Boys, God is watching over you every minute; God knows everything you do." It was a terrifying thought, for under the constantly tapping hammer of the Confessions our sense of guilt and inadequacy was daily riveted on.

Sex never came into the open as one of the sins in which God took a special interest, but we knew. Indeed, I think most of us believed he had time for little else — sex, by what was said and not said, being the greatest of all sins. And since with growth and increased vitality the terrible and magnificent drives of sex enlarged in us, the armour of guilt grew tighter. Heath Mount had been a school for innocents, perhaps because the boys of Heath Mount had been kept unspotted from the world by a phalanx of nannies making sure that their little ones should see no evil, speak no evil, and hear no evil. In Canada there was no such barrier, and Bob and I coming to Lakefield knowing no "dirty" words, nor where babies came from, nor anything of forbidden sex games, had in a few months learned a great deal — or thought we had, and trembled at the knowledge. It seems to me now that what we chiefly learned was the terrible certainty of our wickedness. It was a certainty so great that it might either destroy one's confidence or, being challenged and its absurdities recognized, would in time destroy the doctrines that had given it force.

Those who have never known boarding schools are convinced that they are sinks of homosexual activity, and in this I think they show their own essential ignorance of such schools and of human nature. Boarding schools like all youthful society are feverish with activity, much of which is sexually directed. But in so far as the sexual activity could be called homosexual, it is probably for most *faute de mieux*. At any rate I know of none of my confused and excited schoolmates who in after life appeared remotely interested in homosexuality.

Remembering it like this I have suggested a very narrow focus to our lives at Lakefield in the nearly seven years that I spent there. After the first few frightening months, and with my

39

father somewhat better and back at his work, life settled into a pattern. Long summer holidays were spent at our cottage on the St. Lawrence below Cornwall, swimming and fishing and running over the old farms that lay all around us. And just as we couldn't wait for the holidays to begin, so by September we couldn't wait to get back to school. Football Term — Christmas holidays — Hockey Term — Easter holidays — Cricket Term — Summer holidays; as though in growing from nine to sixteen my whole life was play. But to fix the seasons by the games played in them was merely to frame the year conveniently for those who chiefly lived for games, and I was one. As I grew up a little the terrible need for approval and applause became somewhat less desperate. I had had some moments of glory on the playing fields which gave me a swelled head, and enough disasters to restore sanity. I had climbed the ladder from captain of No. 2 dormitory football team at the age of ten (an honour that seemed to me so great it almost rocked my reason and certainly made me objectionable), to captain of the school hockey team and a Prefect at fifteen.

It was part of growth and education but it was out of balance, and even I could see that it hadn't much to do with being a writer. In the classroom I was only occasionally excited by what we were studying. Outside class I read endlessly but without plan or real attention. I went on saying I was going to be a writer because nothing else seemed attractive (except occasionally soldiering or playing professional hockey), but I knew no better than before what I meant by it.

I had already been stimulated when in class Jimmy Brittain, perhaps as bored as we, or trying to strike sparks from us, asked what each of us intended to be when we grew up. I said sturdily that I intended to be a writer. After the class he stopped me. "If you are going to be a writer," he said, "you must get to work." I had struck a spark from him; and perhaps provided one of those moments for which teachers live, the glimmer of hope that they may be shaping an important life. His idea of how I must get to work mystified me a little, but I was grateful for his interest and glad of anything that nourished my vague and half-forgotten ambition. I was to begin by memorizing some of the great passages of Shakespeare and later to recite and discuss them. So for a time we played at being teacher and disciple, and one or two evenings a week, after I was ready for bed, I would run over to his cottage and recite "To be, or not to be: that is the question", or " 'Tis a common proof that lowliness is young ambition's ladder, whereto the climber-upward turns his face", or some other passage. Afterwards Mrs. Brittain would reward us both with milk or cocoa and biscuits and I would try with the gravity of ten or eleven to tell him what I thought the passage meant. Was this a good approach to the problem? I've no idea, but I'm sure it was a good small step toward an awakening, and I remain grateful for it. Presently our interest flagged and the game of author-making was dropped.

But it had been a cup of cold water in what was nearly an intellectual desert; a desert in which we hardly knew we were thirsty, for it was so general a condition. On Friday evenings we held debates and recitations in which we took turns arguing such subjects as the pen is mightier than the sword, or the horse more valuable than the cow. The topics required no one to stretch himself intellectually, and though the occasional attempt at wit or polish would be praised by the master in charge, a pedestrian performance was quite acceptable. Debates were new and exciting to me and in my role of naughty boy and dormitory funny man I struggled up from my snorting contemporaries to say, "Mr. Chairman, the sword is better than the pen because at least it doesn't get ink on your fingers." Mr. Brittain in one of his flash rages said, "Sit down, boy, don't make a fool of yourself." I was a little quenched but rewarded by feeling that at least the other little boys thought it quite funny and a daring remark.

The recitations tended to be of no higher level. We enjoyed the works of Robert Service and W. H. Drummond, or the occasional song. An English boy who had been bullied or teased roughly for his accent won instant popularity by singing "As We Go Marching Through Germany". Occasionally we took our blunted perceptions to an entertainment in Lakefield

41

Town Hall or even to the Grand Opera House in Peterborough and found it all wonderful. Bob and I had seen several pantomimes in London and even one or two musical comedies, but we were quite uncritical of these performances. Whatever they lacked, they had some of the magic and glamour of live theatre, and for several nights after hearing Dorothy Stone sing "An Old-Fashioned Garden" at the Grand I lay awake long after lights-out wrapped in an innocent enchantment.

In amateur dramatics my various roles and ambitions seemed to come together. For a moment the stage beckoned. We did *Charley's Aunt*, scenes from Shakespeare, imitations of the Dumbells, and skits featuring the Peterborough district accent, very similar to that of Parry Sound, almost fifty years before Charlie Farquharson appeared. There was some talent amongst us but more ignorance and misguided enthusiasm; no one to direct from experience nor any suggestion of books that might have made good our appalling deficiencies. It delighted the school, which deceived us as to just how painfully amateur it was. The acting life seemed alluring, but as a way of making a living in Canada it was said to be even more desperate than writing.

During our years at Lakefield we didn't see much of Cornwall — three weeks at Christmas and two at Easter; for the long summer holidays we were at our cottage on the river, a mile below the town. In the days when the automobile was still poised between being a curiosity and becoming impressive, a mile set us apart; a trip to town was an expedition not to be taken lightly or often. Within ten years everything changed! Cars became almost commonplace (though we didn't have one), roads improved, and we had bicycles as well as longer and stronger legs.

But there was always the river, first thing in the morning and murmuring against the bank below as we went to sleep. In front of the cottage it lay a mile wide to Cornwall Island, part of the St. Regis Indian reservation; across the Island was a narrower channel and beyond that the shore of New York State. It was not spectacular country, running back in a flat plain be-

hind the cottage all the way to the Ottawa River, a plain broken only by the line of bush (woodlot and sugar bush) that
backed every farm, but it never occurred to me that it was not
beautiful. Perhaps that was because we didn't look back; we
sometimes played there, wading through fields waist-high and
sweet-smelling with hay and daisies and buttercups, and fence
lines glowing with wild roses, columbine, and morning glories,
but we looked over the splendid river, and that was our main
playground.

Once we had learned to swim we were free to move out, to
fish and to explore. First with a sturdy skiff — called simply a
rowboat — then we added a canoe and finally a little metal
tub, a one-cylinder inboard motor-boat, bright green with a
red trim, which Bob and I called the *Helen G.* — after my mother.

The playground, we learned, had to be treated with respect.
In the steamer channel the water was deep and cold, and a
powerful current swept the strongest swimmer downstream, so
that once or twice in a summer we had to answer calls for help,
to row out to bold and reckless young men whom the river had
turned into shivering and frightened boys. This had for centu-
ries been the highway to the heart of the continent and to some
extent was still. There was a constant shuttle of cargo steamers
moving up and down stream, and tugs towing strings of barges,
calling to each other in greeting with great booming whistles or
calling to the lockmaster as the river narrowed above us nearing the Cornwall canal. When we were small boys the whistles
at night were at first terrifying, but with time they became a
kind of lullaby, a reminder that the river would be there in the
morning, lapping gently against the shore, sliding by; ready for
the swim before breakfast or the fishing trip.

Of all the river traffic the most glamorous was the group of
Canada Steamship Lines Rapids boats, the *Rapids King*, the
Rapids Queen, and the *Rapids Prince* — dazzling white with red
and black funnels. Every day in the summer one of them came
into sight around a curve in the river to be greeted with cries of
"Here comes the liner", as children scrambled into boats to row

43

or paddle out to "take the swells" as the gleaming ship swept past with tourists crowding the rails to wave at small craft. And every night one of the liners went up through the canals from Montreal to Prescott, to return to Montreal the next day, shooting the Long Sault, the Cedar, and the Lachine rapids on the way with the aid of leathery-skinned old river pilots, scorning the canals.

Once we went to meet the liner, with bizarre results. This was not to take the swells but to greet Aunt Elsie, who was taking the rapids trip to Montreal. The liner usually tied up briefly at Cornwall to take on and discharge passengers. Hoping to see Aunt Elsie, "the boys" had to be dressed up, which meant chiefly a clean shirt and scrubbed and blancoed running shoes, which my mother insisted on and inspected like a sergeant-major. We were going in the *Helen G.*, usually run by Bob or me, but to be handled on this special occasion by my father, who now stood poised above the fly-wheel. He faced the stern, where my mother sat with our cousin Dorothy Putnam, both of them in crisp white dresses, a vision of summer. Behind my father I lolled beside the little side steering wheel and Bob in the bow held us at the end of the diving-board. My father took a last look around, surveying his field, and reminded my brother not to let the current nudge us under the spring-board, to hold us out so as to push clear when the motor started. It was a golden day with just a ripple on the water as he turned back and bent over the fly-wheel.

The *Helen G.* was temperamental and the fact that she had no neutral gear made her doubly unpredictable. Just occasionally the motor would fire after one or two spins of the fly-wheel, more often there would be a long process of teasing, fighting, priming, and muttering. Bob, having pushed us out, fell to looking at the sky and thinking of other things in the way of twelve-year-olds. It was the normal start-up moment: the wheel being spun, a certain amount of black oily water being flung around the cockpit in spite of our pumping in advance, my mother and Dorothy getting ready to giggle. Bob was now surveying another quarter of the heavens and the boat had

44

swung gently under the spring-board, without any of us noticing this fact. My father advanced the spark and with grim determination bent once more to his work.

This time on the first spin the motor exploded into life and the boat shot forward. The spring-board tore itself from Bob's hands and the end of it struck Dad above the back of the knees, hoisting him up; in seconds we were shot toward a black comedy or disaster. My father, who might have been knocked forward on top of the engine, drew his feet up, dragging his oily shoes over the white dresses of my mother and Dorothy, who had flung themselves backward and were lying almost flat as the board swept over their upturned faces. The boat swung out into the river, leaving my father sitting alone, bouncing gently on the end of the spring-board. In the boat as the shock passed, we were reduced to almost uncontrollable laughter, not helped by our having to go back and face my father — and to apologize and lament, and explain the unexplainable. We made a wide circle and came back slowly and reluctantly. The women had tidied themselves but still looked as though they had encountered a Blackfoot war party. Bob and I had stopped laughing beyond a nervous snigger and concentrated on running the boat and bracing ourselves for the wrath to come. My father, who had crawled back off the board, was pacing the dock and appeared to be composing his reprimand. As we tied up he greeted us all in silence, my mother as usual barely containing a giggle while watching my father apprehensively. At last, when we were crushed by his silence, he said slowly and with quiet emphasis to us boys, *"I hope that some day you will learn to do as you are told."* In time we laughed together over it all, but not that day.

My father seldom raised his voice to Bob and me unless we had driven the whole house to madness by our bickering that often became fighting. But even at his quietest he had things to teach that he was determined we would learn. Many of them doubtless were the received wisdom of his generation, and before, perhaps reinforced by his own experience; let sleeping

45

dogs lie; don't start anything you can't finish. Things to which we only half listened.

But sometimes his own quick comment could cut deeper and leave more mark; a scar, in the sense that it never disappeared and might even continue to hurt a little, years later. Two such comments stung and curbed me, if they didn't cure (perhaps because I was incurable). Once when as a small boy I was carrying on, talking too much, making unfunny jokes; even my patient father could have too much, and he suddenly said sharply, "Now, stop, we've never had a clown in the Gray family and we don't want one now." I was not only silenced, I think I was even crushed into reflection. I wasn't quite sure of the difference between a wit and a clown — but I wanted whichever would win my father's approval.

At another time, when I was older but still a boy, he tossed out a comment in a letter: "I think perhaps you have always wanted too much to be popular." It hurt, I realized, because it was at least partially true.

It was two or three years later that we came suddenly to a realization that we had outgrown Lakefield. Bob and I were senior boys, Prefects, officers in the cadet corps, playing on all first teams. The school had grown considerably in our years there, but we had become big toads in what was still a small and too comfortable puddle. We had taken a partial matriculation and that only by the skin of our teeth; it was time to go. We talked it over with my father. Of the schools we knew from our games with them, we preferred Upper Canada. My father, remembering wistfully that he had hoped as a boy to go to Upper Canada, was clearly tempted, but the prospect of the expense worried him and there was doubt of our being accepted. Somehow, miraculously, the doubts and problems melted away. My father was clearly caught up in our excitement but my mother was concerned about our move to the dangerous and wicked city; we knew only the joy of adventure, of fresh and splendid worlds to conquer.

I don't remember that we made any last sentimental journey around the borders of our kingdom at Lakefield; once the decision was taken we were eager to be gone. Yet it was filled with memories and associations. Places had shrunk as we grew up; mysteries had peeled away, but they remained deep-etched in us and dear for the parts they had played in that growth.

Downhill, three hundred yards from the school, was still "the lake" — Lake Katchewanooka — where we had timidly learned to swim and paddle a canoe; the lake we had seen from our windows first thing in the morning and over which the sun went down nightly behind the surrounding hills, bouncing its red light off the bathroom taps as we brushed our teeth. Up the shore behind Third Island lay the Channel, where Gavin Rainnie and Carberry Christmas and I had dashed in naked through shell ice one April 9, eager to boast of being first in swimming that year. We were in and out of the water so fast we were barely wet, but we had earned our boast.

Near by on the channel shore was the spot where I had first slept in a tent and had wakened in the morning to find my eyes almost closed by mosquito bites. It had been as a result of Mr. Mackenzie's instinctive teaching. One morning in my first year during a Scripture lesson, we had been reading about Noah in his tent. "You all know what a tent is," said the Headmaster; "have any of you not slept in one?" Six of us had not, including Bob and me. It was settled at once that three of us were to camp one night and three others the next. We were instructed to take a school tent and draw food from the kitchen for our supper and breakfast. The early evening had been a joy as we crouched over our fire in front of the tent cooking sausages after a swim. During the evening the Headmaster just happened along to wish us good-night. Before bedtime we had a game of chase in the woods; but as darkness came down the woods were suddenly full of strange sounds, and we crawled into our blankets, glad of each other's company. As our fire died at the water's edge we fell heavily asleep, unmindful of the cloud of mosquitoes pouring out of a nearby swamp, looking for three tenderfeet who had no repellent and had built no smudge. In the morning we could scarcely see; moreover, our precious matches had been left in the dew and we could light no fire.

Cheerlessly, eating raw sausages, we crouched at the door of our tent, not so sure that camping was fun. We had been rescued by Winifred Mackenzie who appeared, rowing the school punt, just to see how we were getting on. She looked at this spectre of misery and between laughter and tears said, "You poor kids; you silly geese." It was a fair comment.

The group of buildings close around the school — the barn, the gym, the root house, the woodshed, and the giant privy — were all to be swept away in the next two or three years, making way for a new wing. The barn had housed a horse and Florence Mackenzie's Shetland pony, Tommy, as well as cows that supplied the school's milk, and chickens. All brought pleasant memories except the horror of the privy, and even it gave back one echo of laughter. It had nine little stalls, the ninth being a barely separate room for masters. In cold weather the squalid pit underneath froze and one year a chicken arrived on the ice, introduced either by its own curiosity or by a mischievous boy. The chicken strolled about on the yellow ice, liking its environment less and less. Apparently it had used up its patience just as one of the masters visited the privy and lifted the cover off the magisterial seat. The chicken, seeing its chance, flew up just as he settled into position. The result was a noisy and shocking and hilarious invasion of privacy.

We were leaving behind laughter and tears, triumphs and heartbreaks; the pains of growing up. We were never to get Lakefield, our home for almost seven years, out of our blood, but for the moment we were like children setting off for camp. The future beckoned excitingly and we were eager to meet it.

3

THE MOVE TO UPPER CANADA COLLEGE and to Toronto was more of a watershed in our lives than coming of age was to be. It was as if we felt that between June and September we had grown up. We were no doubt over-impressed with both the school and the city, and over-pleased with ourselves at having arrived there. We saw Toronto through my father's fond accounts of it and the streets were full of friendly associations. It was a shock to learn later that to many people it was a stuffy, small provincial city. To me with its theatres, with Massey Hall and smart new movie houses, the great football and hockey teams I had read about in the sports pages, its numerous cars (as it then seemed), its beautiful girls and smartly dressed men and women, it had the splendours of phantasy. Set against the occasional debauch at Hooper's Tea Room in Peterborough after an evening at the Grand Opera House, or our tame little house dances at Christmas and Easter in Cornwall, our skating and snowshoeing parties and the flickering movies at Cornwall's Wonderland and Starland picture palaces, this was LIFE. It was the era of Rudolph Valentino and *The Sheik*, of D. W. Griffith's *Four Horsemen of the Apocalypse*, of Lillian Gish and Gloria Swanson. Both my head and my heart were in a continual whirl; I loved both the pure beauty of Lillian Gish and the dark exciting promise of Gloria Swanson.

Against the excitements of the city, the school probably took second place, but it too had interests and delights of which we had been starved, without knowing it. After years of living in crowded dormitories we now had the privacy and dignity of individual bedrooms. Having always done my homework in a crowded schoolroom, I now worked alone, in quiet, under a small desk light, and was so unnerved that I had to go wandering about asking legitimate questions but staying to chat because I wanted company. Our fellow pupils seemed much more sophisticated in dress, and manner. By comparison my excitements and enthusiasms were small-town, and seemed "hick".

Though we were New Boys, we were hardly treated as such. For two or three years we had been playing games against Upper Canada teams and this gave us a place and friends before most New Boys had earned either. We were senior boys, but had shed all the responsibilities of being Prefects at Lakefield. For the moment it appeared we had the best of all worlds.

The classroom seems in retrospect to have been less important than games and social life both inside and outside the school. Yet even with my casual approach to education, I had to recognize a more bracing atmosphere. There were some outstanding teachers as well as some less than good, and even the latter could be valuable to those who really wanted to learn. I thought I did, but then I wanted so many things; everything seemed to be calling to me at once; look, enjoy! and I answered greedily. The position wasn't helped by the arrangements for partial matriculation. Until a few years before, Junior Matric, which consisted of twelve examination papers, and provided entrance to university for a pass degree, had to be taken complete in one year. This had been changed so that now the examinations could be spread across two or three years or more. This had led to a rather casual attitude and I had behind me only six successful papers, none of the results brilliant, and most of them in the subjects I enjoyed or was good at.

This meant I could devote a whole year to half a year's work. With my flickering enthusiasms and erratic abilities this could spell disaster. Someone more mature would have read the warnings. I could read them, but as usual I couldn't believe they meant me. Only an incurable optimist could shrug off my dismal record and be confident that he would be all right on the big day, for in all my years at Lakefield, from little boy to big boy, I had won one small bronze medal for a hurdle race and nothing else, nothing. And yet year after year at the school closing and prize-giving I would sit sweating with excitement, believing that by some miracle my name would be called. Many prizes I knew I had not won, having seen the marks posted, but Mr. Mackenzie had a way of saying, "And now we come to a special prize, for a boy who has done outstanding work." I would blush and sit forward on my bench — now it was coming; but it never did. I'm not sure now whether I really didn't understand the simple message or chose to disregard it. I believed, indeed I knew, that I had more ability than some who won prizes; it shouldn't have required great brilliance to see that the difference lay in work and concentration and in taking care. Since I was eight years old I had been subjected to supervised study, out of which had grown a kind of habit of mind: to put in the time was to have done the work, though I had ample proof to the contrary.

Though I elected to repeat some papers at Upper Canada for my own pleasure or enrichment, my time-table was almost half spare periods. For the spares I was supposed to work at the back of the classroom, or, with permission, in the library. If attendance was taken and one was not in class an explanation might be called for or it might not. Finding that no one seemed to worry much about people with spare periods, I grew careless, always too easy a course for me. There were other congenial souls in the same category and we found it pleasant to go for a walk, even occasionally to walk several blocks to Yonge Street at St. Clair Avenue for coffee and cigarettes and long talks about life. It was valuable, but not what we were supposed to be doing. We felt really liberated, and grown up. Suddenly my sins began to catch up with me; several absences were noted and I began to accumulate Punishment Drills (which involved marching smartly up and down for half an hour after school under the sharp eye of Sergeant-Major Carpenter) and Gatings (which meant curtailment of leave on week-ends). It was

51

discovered that I had accumulated more Gatings than there were week-ends left in the term. I was almost as shocked as the Principal.

Dr. W. L. Grant, known as "Choppy", was a short man with a military moustache which he would puff through in a moment of reflection or perhaps stress. His manner sometimes seemed pompous and it was said that he had to struggle against the overpowering image of his father, who had been Principal of Queen's University and a national figure when Canada was young. Choppy Grant had been appointed Principal of Upper Canada College soon after his return from the war with the task of re-establishing discipline and academic standards, both of which had deteriorated. He had accomplished these things and won respect for himself, though not yet liking.

Against such experience my offences, though I found them complicated and unmanageable, were swiftly dealt with. Choppy heard my specious explanation — that I couldn't work properly at the back of a room in which a class was going on — and gave his ruling. He would cane me and cancel out all accumulated punishments. I would then have permission to work in either classroom or reading room during spare periods, but if I were to be found in neither, and without a satisfactory explanation, I would be sent home — expelled. "Is that clear, and is it fair?" Through tight lips I said it was both. Then I had my caning; not savage but efficient enough to remind me of my misdemeanours whenever I sat down during the next two or three days. I was something of a connoisseur of caning and to this one I gave high marks; it was to be almost my last.

For a time I was subdued and though I didn't work much more effectively I read a great deal. Also, I was in love, though — sad to say — I have now forgotten with which girl; there were so many in those years, so sweet or glamorous or bewitching; and such elevating love had nothing to do with sex — that was merely a guilty secret that periodically made me ashamed and wretched but couldn't be connected in any way with these lovely creatures. And in the intervals in that first year I played football for the College's second team, hockey for the first team, joined the dramatic club and had a part in the school play, and joined the Curfew Club. This was a reading and discussion group that usually met on Sunday evenings and in retrospect seems almost the best part of life at Upper Canada for me. Much as I loved and lived for hockey and football, I could recognize a greater value, even the beginnings of a greater excitement, in the Curfew Club. In addition to our reading we had prominent men come and talk to us about matters of current interest.

Different masters took turns in leading the Curfew Club, though to a large extent the members planned the program and managed the modest administration it involved. But for a period I still remember with pleasure two young masters — "Wyly" Grier and Geoff Bell — who gave a good deal of time to it, initiating discussions and just occasionally guiding them a little, helping us to learn to think. Crawford Grier, nicknamed after his artist father, was an Old Boy of Upper Canada, recently returned from the war after doing graduate work at Oxford. Geoffrey Bell was an Englishman, also a war veteran and an Oxford graduate, destined much later to become Headmaster of a British public school — I think Highgate. I suspect that the war had left both men ready to question the values of the world we were growing up in; at any rate they were stimulating company for us. The Curfew Club was perhaps more attractive to those who lived in the school — the Boarders — than to the Day Boys who lived at home. The Boarders were usually happy to have their Sunday evening taken up so enjoyably, or I was; to Day Boys it often meant forgoing a tea-dance or supper party or some home activity.

On the whole we thought the Day Boys spoiled, self-indulgent, making only a limited commitment to what we all called "The College"; we were The College, we the ones who kept things going. Monday morning they rejoined the school, coming in from all directions, walking, bicycling, a few driving their own cars, and just a few being delivered by a chauffeur. We envied and teased them, and occasionally listened round-eyed to their knowing, worldly talk about girls and parties, and their repetition of grown-ups' gossip. This was especially true of the Day Boys who had had all their schooling at Upper Canada, having entered the Preparatory School as small boys and in process of time moved automatically into the College. Many of them were almost like sleep-walkers, they seemed so much at home, so comfortable, so pleased with themselves. In the summers they went to the same camps or to Muskoka or Georgian Bay, where they saw the same people they had seen all year. If they were bored they didn't appear to know it; they were not unattractive but, with a few exceptions, I thought them unaroused and uninteresting.

Though we tried to think them a poor lot, many of them were kind and generous, inviting Boarders to their homes for meals and parties. I know now that some of them envied us, for a kind of freedom they didn't have. When school was over they went home and their parents looked over what they were doing and with whom. We could apply for leave to go to a grandmother's or uncle's for Saturday or Sunday afternoon and supper, and then spend the time roaming the town; as long as we weren't seen at a race-track or coming out of a brothel, and provided we returned on time, it was unlikely that anyone would worry much about where we had been. And there was not much reason for them to worry; our liberty was often a burden. Our modest allowance was soon spent, on a movie or a meal, so that it was sometimes difficult to scrape together the price of an ice-cream soda at Rector's or Hunt's, and then to make it last long enough for a satisfactory session of girl-watching. Sometimes if one had been reckless early in the month the choice was between a cheap movie and a cheap meal, and then the application for leave to go to a relative's was as genuine as it was necessary.

Our circle of relatives, though large, had shrunk a little. Grandfather Putnam had died hurling defiance during our last year at Lakefield, and my Grandmother Gray a few months after him, before we reached Upper Canada. She had seemed thin and poorly the last times we had seen her, but still sharp and impatient of weakness. Sitting close to the fire and with a

54

shawl around her, she had roused herself at the mention of someone who had had a nervous breakdown. "Mercy," she said with a harsh little laugh, "when I was a girl we never had time for such things. We just had a good cry and got on with our work." She had never been a favourite of mine, perhaps because I believed she thought me soft and a show-off, and I agreed with her, but the house on Elmsley Place (which still stands) was not as warm without her. My unmarried Uncle Frank, eldest of the family, still lived there along with the youngest, my Aunt Elsie, her husband, Jimmy Rich, and their small children. It couldn't have been easy to welcome two hungry boys likely to call up on short notice to hint that they were free for a meal, but it seemed seldom inconvenient and we sometimes worked our passage by baby-sitting.

Aunt Elsie was perhaps the nearest thing to an eccentric in our kind but unremarkable family. She carried on a vast and amusing correspondence, mostly by short notes scribbled during the sermons at St. James' Cathedral on Sunday mornings. She off-handedly admitted to getting some of her cut flowers from neighbours' beds while walking her dog at night. She wore rather extraordinary hats which my mother and Uncle Fred's wife, Aunt Ada, claimed she could only have bought at rummage sales and trimmed herself. As his younger sister, she was a great favourite of my father's (and later of mine), which practically guaranteed she would not be a great favourite of my mother's, nor was she of Aunt Ada's. The three lived in a kind of armed truce, nicely balanced since my mother and Aunt Ada agreed on almost nothing except Aunt Elsie — and Morgan, my father; I think all three loved Morgan in their different ways.

On one occasion Aunt Ada, shopping for Aunt Elsie's birthday, found just the thing, a set of "darling" little linen shoes for cocktail glasses; they were very reasonable, since she bought them at a church sale, and were of a distinctive pattern; the only drawback was that there were only five of them; still they were just the thing. The following Sunday in church Aunt Elsie wrote a thank-you note, not effusive but suitable. At Christmas time she gave them to my mother, who was duly grateful and a few months later gave them to Aunt Ada for her birthday. They still had a distinctive pattern and there were still only five; and since Aunt Ada in thanking my mother asked bluntly whether she had received them from Elsie, the position was clear to all.

There were other kindly houses to help ward off loneliness, for the school on week-ends if one had no money and no invitations or was "gated" could be very big and empty. We went often to Uncle Bert's, the R. A. L. Grays', on Pine Hill Road in Rosedale, where there were four girls and two boys and where as the song went they "never had very much money but always had lots of fun". It was a home where there was always life and music and laughter, and where last-minute arrivals seemed always welcome and manageable.

In spite of all the good influences, the more orderly life imposed by Choppy Grant, and my own good, if wavering, intentions, I grew up very reluctantly; though, as usual, I enjoyed the process. At the end of our first year at Upper Canada I passed only one of my six remaining matriculation papers and my brother Bob didn't do much better. I was almost as embarrassed as I should have been. My father was obviously puzzled, worried, and deeply disappointed, but he didn't say a great deal. He questioned us about our work and our attitudes without knowing where to take hold or press the question. My mother for the rest of the summer missed no opportunity of delivering a little lecture about working hard in order to justify the expense and sacrifice Upper Canada required of my father. We felt guilty and swore to do better, without much idea of how to go about it.

When we returned to school in September my new Housemaster, Billy McHugh, called me in and asked me what plan of work I had for the year ahead. Having none, I improvised gaily, saying I thought I would take some honours work as a form of enrichment while I knocked off the remaining five papers. Billy McHugh, a kindly, experienced man and a notable teacher of mathematics, sat listening behind his desk, occasionally poking his glasses, which were normally askew, back into position. Though he was never far from a laugh, he could be serious, and for a few minutes now he was. He reminded me that this was probably a last chance. If at the end of the year I had passed only four of my five remaining papers, even three successful honours papers wouldn't help, I would not be admitted to university; either my schooling would be over or I would have to repeat a whole year for whatever papers remained. He went back over the point to an extent that I would have found tiresome from almost anyone else, but we respected and loved Billy McHugh and I knew he was right; he had set out the problem with the unanswerable logic of a mathematical proposition.

I knew the advice was good and by my standards I followed it. There was still time to play football and hockey and to participate in the Dramatic Club, with a major part in a Pinero play, the Curfew Club, and as a junior editor of the *College Times*, which accepted two of my informal essays and some verse — a triumph that excited me more than all the rest. And there was time for a little lawlessness as well — of a kind that I persuaded myself the Principal's ruling did not cover. On a beautiful autumn afternoon with windows wide open and outdoors calling more loudly than a dreary extra Latin class, Johnny Ellis and I crossed the classroom, one row of desks at a time when the master turned to the blackboard, then finally out the window as he turned to parse a sentence. Attendance had been taken, so there was no doubt that we were there. Those left behind said the master, "Doggy" Mills, wore a slightly puzzled expression on his face during the latter part of the class, and afterward when we met in the hall he developed a little frown as though there were something about me he was trying to remember, or to forget.

And with some of my livelier friends I took to "skipping out" of the school at night; not usually for any purpose, just to be out and to feel free. There was a way in and out through the furnace room which involved slipping by the furnace man when his back was turned. Once Graeme Gibson (due to become later a dignified major-general) and I slipped out and ran all the way to Rosedale and back in order to eat a cake and giggle with three girls whose mother and father were in Florida. Another time Powell Bell and I skipped out and ran across to Bishop Strachan School, climbed the fence, and wandered in the grounds, thinking of all the beautiful girls inside. Coming up close to the building we found a narrow little gothic window open. In the half dark I could see Powell's eyes wide with excitement. We shook hands and I climbed in. Powell followed and we stood in total darkness, our hearts pounding, trying to get our bearings and afraid to move, and with no idea of what we were there for or how to exploit so brilliant a success. Apparently the idea of a souvenir occurred to both at once, and one of us struck a match. We were in a small sitting-room and in the glow of the match we moved around looking for something with a BSS crest on it. There were two doors to the room, one open and the other closed. Suddenly as we crept around whispering, a hoarse voice from beyond the open door called, "Who's there?" We froze, our hearts hammering almost audibly. To get out of that high, narrow window in a hurry was out of the question, so with no idea of the geography of the building we went through the closed door into a hall and raced westward along it into what proved to be the dining room and across it to the windows. We opened one and then, hanging from the ledge, I looked down into a kind of cement pit surmounted by a metal grillwork that looked formidable. I whispered, "We'll never get out of there," and Powell, answering "We can't stay here," launched himself on top of me and we both fell into the pit. Fear solved our problem, and by boosting and hauling we were out and running along the street. Finally, gasping for breath and laughing we crawled behind a hedge and lay still until calmness returned, then circled back to the College, giving Bishop Strachan's a wide berth. It was reported later that someone had tried to set fire to the sitting room of the formidable Headmistress of BSS, Miss Hattie Walsh. By then we had some sense of how foolish we had been and how lucky, and we resisted the temptation to boast about our adventure.

The year seemed now to be rushing to a close. The finality of what was upon us came home at last and I worked hard, even taking extra Latin Composition, that subject having been a special hurdle to me ever since Heath Mount, where I had encountered it first at the age of eight taught by a grumpy and terrifying master. But of course I shouldn't have needed hard work, having covered every paper at least once before, and some of them twice. The conclusion that I was not very bright was almost inescapable, and only my ebullient cheerfulness and perhaps my father's stubborn confidence prevented my accepting such a verdict. Bob and I were going back to Cornwall for two or three final weeks of quiet study and then to write our papers at Cornwall High School. After exams we were to separate for the first time in our lives. He was going north as cook on a geological survey, and I with four others from Upper Canada to work in a lumber mill on Rainy Lake near Fort Frances, not far from the Manitoba boundary. It was to be our first venture into the world of men, and the excitement of the prospect was almost enough to make me forget the high hurdle to be cleared first. For two years now we had been agitating to be allowed to take a job in the summer, but my father had patiently and convincingly argued against it. We were conscious of more energy than we could use in a lazy summer of golf, fishing and reading aimlessly, shooting, or dressing up like lounge lizards to dance and flirt at the nearby summer hotel. Doubtless if my father had been less preoccupied or better equipped to guide us, the summers might have been fruitful; as it was they had become pleasant and aimless and ultimately unsatisfying.

I am more conscious now of what a puzzle and worry we must have been to my father, though I sensed it then: was he doing the right thing? How could he help prepare us better for life? Above all, how could he help us to a wise decision on what we were to do with our lives. Doubtless he hoped that university — if we got to university — would help us to choose. Meanwhile, men from the Ives Bedding Company had come in turn to teach us carpentry and how to run, repair, and maintain the little one-cylinder engine of our motor-boat, the *Helen G.* Each holiday we had by his arrangement been taken over one of the local factories, from the Howard Smith Paper Mill to the Beech Furniture Factory. And in between times we had golf lessons from the pro. This was the day of Bobby Jones, and for the moment he was my hero; my ambition was to play golf for Canada in the Walker Cup and to play hockey for Canada at the Olympics.

It was while we were taking golf lessons that my father came out with us one evening to play a few holes. We had teased him into it, though he protested he had not played for years, and I think he had never played very much. Almost from the first he was in trouble, chopping away at his ball in the deep grass. It was agony to watch as he became redder in the face and more humiliated. He went on chopping and the ball squirted deeper into the rough.

Full of our professional instruction, we began offering maddening hints.

"Dad, if you could just keep your head down . . . "

Chop.

"Dad, if you could go a little more slowly on the backswing . . . "

Chop.

"Dad . . . "

Sensing another helpful instruction coming, he turned on my brother. "Dammit, boy," he said bitterly, "I was breaking golf clubs before you were born." Whatever merit the remark lacked, it was at least unanswerable.

The week of exams came on inexorably and one by one the papers fell behind us. I thought I had done fairly well, but then I had thought so before. One paper remained, English Composition; it was a favourite subject and yet I had failed it two or three times. When the day came I received the paper with that mixture of dread and pleasure that by now I knew too well. The test was quite simple and was readily passed by quite simple people, but my habit of flying at things and trying something that was not called for (leaving undone those things that

60

I ought to have done, doing what I ought not to have done) had been part of my problem. We had to do an essay or story of at least five pages in two and a half hours; there was a choice of subjects. My eye ran over the paper and fastened on the quotation:

> *Forget all feuds, and shed one English tear*
> *O'er English dust. A broken heart lies here.*

Write a story suggested by the poem. This was one of our choices, and I leapt at it, hardly pausing to think — as so often. For two and a half hours I wrote eagerly, pleased with the story as it worked itself out, sure that no matter how the other papers had gone this one would be a triumph. It must have been a hopelessly romantic and sentimental little costume piece — a pale version of Robert Louis Stevenson — but my heart sang as I worked. Time ran out just as I curled the tail of my story, ending it with the quotation being chipped on a marble headstone; then I went home in triumph. My father heard me out, smiling happily, then looked at the paper. "Did you know the poem well?" he asked. "I've never seen it," I answered happily. "Look at the question again," he said. My heart sank; with my habit of rushing at things, I had written a story suggested by the quotation, not the whole poem. For a moment I could feel only despair. My beautiful story would not only not earn me a triumph, it might undo all my work and lose the year. By morning, having reread the paper many times, I had persuaded myself that my original reading of it must be acceptable, that no one could fail such a piece of work; but the question would remain unanswered for almost two months.

We were leaving for our summer jobs with the future far from clear. If we passed our exams we would go to the University of Toronto, from which we had received a provisional acceptance; if we failed . . . ? "We'll just have to see," said my father, "and hope for the best." It was only recently that university had been regarded as our objective. For some years it had been thought that we would try for entrance to the Royal

61

Military College at Kingston. My father had admired the training and style of the graduates of RMC he had served with during the war, and as little boys in Kingston we had longed to be like the cadets in their smart uniforms. But even as we had cheered wildly at the Armistice in 1918 and paraded down to the village of Lakefield, beating tin cans and singing, the glory of soldiering was fading. The simplicities of 1914 — a cruel Kaiser, white feathers for those not serving, and the murder of Edith Cavell — had been replaced by question marks. I had heard Geoff Bell say in a class, choosing his words carefully, that some of his friends from Oxford, whom he regarded as infinitely better and braver men than he, had chosen to go to prison as conscientious objectors to war service. So, though at this point I couldn't doubt that if a war came I would be a soldier, I knew I didn't want my life to be soldiering.

But whatever the results of the examination, our schooling was probably over. We had been given a private-school education — an education for an élite, though if we knew the term we didn't use it. It was assumed that boys exposed to such an experience had been granted an enriched training, were fitted to join a superior group. I don't think Bob and I assumed we had been born or made our way or been pushed into a position of great privilege, or wished to be. Our life seemed more glamorous than that of many of the kids we had grown up with, but judged on progress in school, we didn't seem better prepared for life, if as well. Whatever had happened to us was an accident. The war had sent us to Heath Mount and my father's health had led on to Lakefield. When that was over it seemed less of a jolt to stay in the private-school stream. Only Uncle Frank had openly quarrelled with the decision. As Chairman of Ives Bedding and older brother, he knew all about my father's affairs and had criticized him for bringing us up, as he said, to be a gentleman's sons — which he couldn't afford.

I don't know how my father had defended his decision. He had too good a sense of humour and too much humanity to be a howling snob, but as joint owner of one of the town's factories, he was a leading citizen; he was an army officer and a Justice of the Peace; and if that were not enough, he was an Anglican and a Conservative. Having been born into the little Toronto of his day he divided Cornwall society into three: Our Sort of People, Working People, and Riff-Raff. We could play with the children of working people but not with riff-raff.

Had we been steeped in history we would have seen these attitudes as survivals from an earlier day; trailing wraiths of a feudalism that died hard. We might expect some privileges, but we must also accept obligations; a generous paternalism was thought to take the curse off social distinctions. We had seen my father have his batman as a guest all one summer after the war. Poor Barstow's leg was in a cast from a wound and he needed taking care of, so he came to our cottage. Barstow had been brave but he was an ignorant, bumptious Cockney, who had trouble keeping clean and even more keeping quiet; he was a smelly nuisance. My mother, who tried to be kind, finally lost patience and wanted Barstow to go, as we boys did, but not my father. "Barstow was a good, faithful soldier. He took care of me under conditions you have no idea of. Now he needs help and care. It's up to us." Barstow stayed on, spoiling family conversation at every meal, adding to everyone's problems. When in later years I came to wonder about the system, to rail against it at times, I could dislike many of its elements. I couldn't disapprove of them all.

But setting off for Fort Frances and my first man's job I cared little about the future. In any case it was a long way off. There would be four years of university, then somehow — by one of those miracles that the young take for granted as an alternative to gloom and despair — then it would be clear, then it would happen. In Fort Frances it began to happen fast enough, and hard enough to jolt us rudely awake. We were there through the arrangements of Tommy Mathieu from Upper Canada, whose father owned the J. A. Mathieu mill. We had two or three relaxed and kindly days at the Mathieus' cabin on Rainy Lake — a relaxation occasionally shaken by apprehensions, for we had been up to see the mill — and then we reported for work. We were accorded one privilege, that of sharing a bunk-house with the filers, the under-foremen, and the millwrights. Here we slept two to a small, bare room with an iron frame double bunk, one window, one chair, no table, and some hooks on the back of the door for clothes. There was in the building one basin with cold water for those determined to wash or shave, and outside a privy. We were to work ten-hour shifts at thirty-five cents an hour; from seven in the morning till six at night with one hour off for lunch. Every two weeks the shift would change and we would work from seven at night until six in the morning. For four hours in the twenty-four the mill was quiet, while the millwrights moved around in its echoing emptiness with hammer and oil can. In those hours, when the wild screaming of the saws stopped, the silence was eerie and unreal; hellish noise had become our element. Whereas at first it had seemed unbearable and an absolute denial of peace and sleep, it became the music to which we fell asleep, and we were more apt to waken when it stopped.

The mill fifty years later still lives in my mind as a kind of mad inferno of screaming, crashing, yelling activity. And I remember it most vividly at night when the naked dangling electric-light bulbs both lit up the scene and threw shadows through the haze of sawdust in that great looming shed. For the building was no more than a sprawling frame shed, partially open at both ends, covering a vibrating pattern of moving conveyors and transfers, of whirling saws, and of violently active men. I longed to become such a man.

One end of the shed hung above Rainy Lake (originally Lac La Pluie), in which floated a great boom of logs, all destined to be pushed onto conveyors by men moving about with pike poles, on the logs or at the water's edge. The logs with black, dripping snouts came bumping up to the saws, the small ones — the Jackpines — up a narrow trough to be cut into lengths as railway ties, the Red or Norway and the big White Pines to the band-saw to be sliced into boards. The boards moved away to have their edging of bark ripped off and then out to be piled ready for the planing mill.

At the other end the mill opened onto a platform above a railway siding. Here I was to work for the next few weeks, sinking a pickaxe into the ties that came lurching down the chain conveyor, dragging them out, and piling them. If I didn't get them out of the conveyor quickly enough they began to butt and climb and spill over onto the tracks below. When we were cutting a run of Jackpine the ties came down in an almost unbroken stream and I would fling myself at them frantically, hauling and pushing them out to be piled later.

One workman who stopped and watched me sweating and dragging at the clumsy ties remarked that it looked like a job for a man with a strong back and no brains. I knew I was not powerful in comparison with the men around me but I thought I was quick and strong enough to do any work given to me. But more than once in the first two weeks I almost quit, asking for something a little easier. The July sun beat down like a blowtorch on the exposed platform and when the noon break came I sometimes thought, dragging myself back to the bunkhouse, that I was too tired to eat; but after splashing cold water over my face and sitting quietly for a few minutes I found I could make the cook-shack.

There was nothing about the cook-shack to lift the spirits; the smell of sweat was almost as strong as the good smell of food. But we needed the food too much to let squalor worry us for long, and after the shock of the first few days we lined up at breakfast with our tin plates and pannikins in which bacon and eggs followed porridge, and coffee followed cold stewed tomatoes without even a rinse in between. A few of us carried our food outside to sit on a rock in preference to the crowded benches and plank tables. Dinner at noon and supper at night were no more delicate, but the food was of good quality and substantial and we ate greedily and with diminishing revulsion. The few sitting outside chatted together and laughed, but inside there was little talk as men shovelled in the food, stoking the furnace. But if the silence was partly hunger, it was partly for lack of a common language. The foremen and sawyers and their top assistants were all Canadian or American — close to the border, men moved back and forth easily in search of jobs. The main work force was made up of central Europeans who spoke little English and were mostly known as "Bohunks". In between the two groups were the Scandinavians, experienced loggers and lumbermen who took their place, as of right, at the top of the foreign pecking order. When someone took me for a Swede I was astonished and then realized that I had been paid a compliment. There were rumours of savage fights in the main bunkhouse, a squalid place, where powerful men without a common language nursed their loneliness and resentments, and kept a growling watch over their small properties and rights.

After some weeks, having developed muscles and gained experience, I was promoted to the job of tailing the resaw. The big outside slabs taken off to flatten each log came to the resaw for the thin slicing that could get small boards out of them. The slabs climbed up toward the resaw from two sides on moving transfers, then dropped into a trough where spinning rollers carried them to the resawyer. Wearing a thick leather apron and heavy gloves, and wielding a short pick, I had to marshal and straighten the slabs, then release them one at a time when the resawyer was ready to feed the next one into his spinning band-saw.

The resawyer, with whom I never had a conversation, since he spoke no English, looked like a brigand and carried an immense scowling authority. He had a fine moustache curled up at the ends, and a jaunty but battered straw hat which he occasionally pushed back to scratch his head with the pick he used to feed the slabs into his saw. He worked waist-deep in a sort of foxhole, which he left once in ten hours, and in which he half rotated continuously for the ten hours, feeding a slab into the saw and turning to reach for the next I was supposed to release — not too late, never too soon.

Once, never to be forgotten, it was too soon. A big slab had been spiked only lightly and dragged at by the rollers; it broke away and shot toward the resaw just as the resawyer with his back turned to me was relieving himself into his saw. I had only a second to realize with horror what might happen — a man cut off in his prime. The slab struck him squarely in the bottom and pushed him at the saw. His thick back stiffened and held off the slab until he got hold of it and fed it round him and into the saw, staring at me with such rage I was glad I could neither hear him above the scream of the mill nor understand (except in a general way) what his moving lips were saying. I pantomimed an abject apology and a promise to never never do it again and we went watchfully back to work.

In time we arrived at an almost amiable working relationship, starting and finishing the shift with a half-wave or a nod, and sometimes from him almost a smile. The day came for him to express concern when, as I reached far out over the rollers for a maverick slab, my sleeve was caught in the chain that drove the rollers and torn almost to the shoulder. Only a quick snatch saved my arm, and he stood there shaking his head and scratching it with his pick.

After the first days of crawling stiff and exhausted to bed right after work, feeling as though we would never wake up, we had all begun to cram some play into our evenings. There were girls and dance halls and the Mathieus' car often available, so that with new-found confidence and toughness we often started a ten-hour shift after only a short sleep. That was not the only result of the evenings out; I had somehow managed to spend most of my pay. Even now I don't understand how it was done — my $3.50 a day — since our entertainments were neither lurid nor lavish: food and soft drinks, very tentative experiments with alcohol, and eager investigation of what appeared to be a new sport known as "necking", though that didn't cost money, only sleep. Apart from that I had bought some work clothes — heavy Mackinaw shirts, work boots, gloves and pants, and a Mackinaw jacket. My weakness had never been splendid extravagance but rather a light-hearted carelessness. And the work clothes were necessary to the romantic role in which I saw myself, a tough logger.

It was inevitable that the smart-aleck comments I mistook for wit would get me into trouble in these surroundings. Much of our play-time was spent across the bridge from Fort Frances in International Falls, Minnesota. Built around lumber mills and a pulp mill, it was bigger and tougher than Fort Frances, with a roaring friendliness barely concealing a slumbering capacity for violence. It was a dangerous town, with many drifting, reckless men. Here in our innocent folly we often wore our Upper Canada blazers, an invitation to trouble among the Mackinaw shirts and jackets.

One night in the Chicago Café an affectionate pow-wow which included some drunks flared into a near row over some teasing flip remark of mine, meant to be harmless and funny. An angry and abusive American boy was thrown out of the café while six of us, all Canadians, sat together; others left and we sat alone, while out on the pavement a crowd gathered at the window, peering in and waiting for us. Three of our group were older and tougher and more knowledgeable, and I was warned to be quiet, whatever happened. But when the American boy burst back into the café and announced that no God-damned Canadian was ever going to put anything over him, I couldn't resist standing up and saying, "Come on over here and I'll put this table-cloth over you." Regrettably — or perhaps luckily — no one laughed and the boy was bounced again.

But we couldn't just sit there, pretending to drink coffee, while the crowd outside grew. Finally we paid our bill and went out in a phalanx led by a giant fire-ranger known to and liked by the crowd outside. He was drunk, but at that point not looking for trouble, and for a few minutes it looked as though we might be allowed through and away. A little man in a Mackinaw and lumber-jack boots came close to me and said, "Name's McLeod, I'm a Canadian. If there's any trouble I'm on your side. But I don't want to see any trouble, because if it starts they'll kill you. I mean that. I've seen men killed in the street here." We shook hands gravely and then somehow our group had moved through and out and we were on our way down the sloping street to the bridge, three or four blocks away. It seemed to be all over.

And then, halfway to the bridge, the fire-ranger turned stubborn. No sir, he wasn't going to be run out of town by a bunch of Yanks. The drink had suddenly clarified his loyalties; as a fire-ranger in the Canadian woods he served King George, and at this muddled moment he saw a further withdrawal as a dereliction of duty. He wasn't the most intelligent man in town, but he was about to prove he was the most stubborn. I hung back, pleading with him, but he was immovable. "No sir. I fight for King George all day long, and I'll fight for the son-of-a-bitch all night if necessary." Leaning against a lamp-post he stared back up the street at the crowd that had only just let us go. Our companions had gone, and I should have gone with them. The fire-ranger was really among friends and with some rough kidding they might have escorted him home, but I didn't see that we could leave him. I had had little to drink, but I had started the trouble by being a smart-ass kid. So we stood there looking up the street to the crowd outside the café.

It looked like a challenge, and twenty or more men moved slowly at first, and then came on like a regiment. I can still see them and hear the scuff and thump of the heavy boots as they came down on us, menacingly. I was very frightened, but nothing would move the giant. They came down and moved around us. The argument started again but not for long. Someone singled me out, "Aren't you the guy that started all this? Come on, you God-damned potato, go a couple of rounds with me!" Then he hit me. Shocked but not hurt, I went into a boxing crouch and he leaned back, hands on his hips, laughing. "Kid wants to have a boxing match," he said, and charged at me. I landed one or two ineffective punches before being knocked flat by his charge, and before a fist hammered my head against the pavement.

We went home then, with me crushed and dripping blood all the way. The fire-ranger hurled insults and obscene challenges, but there were no takers — "Your mother is a whore, now hit me." It had all been silly and miserable. In the morning one of the millwrights, an American, took a look at my face. "You got beat, eh kid, you're Goddam lucky." I said sourly I didn't feel very lucky. "If you'd beaten their guy they'd have killed you. I mean that. I've seen them do it." This, together with little

McLeod's statement, sounded convincing. Perhaps I had been "Goddam lucky". All I knew for certain was that I had been a fool, that I had asked for trouble that, when it came, I couldn't handle. The "fight" had been a miserable little brawl in which I had, as so often, played a feeble part.

As my financial plight became inescapable and the time to go home approached, I was left with three alternatives: I could wire home for money; I might even now, by living hard for my remaining time, almost save my return fare; or I could beat my way home on the freight trains. Pride ruled out the first of these at once, self-indulgence the second, and the attractions of danger in the third choice fixed the decision. There was time to reconsider, and plenty of time to be appalled at our own daring. I was to travel with Oswald "Mac" MacLaren, one of our Upper Canada group, and as we casually announced our plans, the warnings and the advice piled thick around us. We met many who had beaten their way and knew how to do it, and many more with horror stories of men who had lost arms and legs, or been killed falling under the wheels. Just then there was an account in the newspaper of a hobo who had become locked in an empty freight car and died there of starvation, and of another shot and killed in a railway yard, running from a policeman. Our pride and a mounting excitement held us to the plan, which daily seemed less attractive.

Within the last few days at the mill I was wakened from a deep sleep after a hard night shift. I sat sleepily on the edge of my bunk looking at an unopened telegram, and knowing as I rubbed my eyes awake that it must contain the news of matriculation results. The question had been put out of sight for weeks but never far out of mind. Now it was here and I stared stupidly at the envelope more than half afraid. Though I had persuaded myself that I would get through, I had doubts, especially about the muddled English Composition. But it wasn't in my nature to hang back now or to worry unduly. Still half awake I tore open the envelope and stared uncomprehending at the contents until at last with re-readings I was sure. All papers had been passed, adequately though no better. In English Composition I had a second-class honour; my father had added simply "Congratulations". If it was less than the splendour I had at first counted on, it was better than I had some reason to fear. I came awake to a flooding sense of relief and happiness. Until that moment I hadn't realized how heavy the weight of dread on my mind. Now what I was feeling was sheer joy. I was going to "Varsity". And sitting there I thought of all the splendours that were to be; I vowed to be a brilliant student, and exulted in all that I would learn and become. It was a moment to live for, though it was only a short one.

Our remaining time at the mill fled by and the night came when, with farewells said, we found ourselves crouching out along the tracks east of Fort Frances waiting to jump our first freight. We had had advice on this from a friend in the roundhouse, but from the moment we climbed up, we would be on our own. It was raining steadily and we were 1100 miles from home with the clothes we stood up in, an extra sweater, heavy gloves, a toothbrush in a pocket, and twenty dollars each. (Mac had saved his money but by our arrangement he had sent the rest home.) There was a warning whistle and the engine's headlight came toward us through the curtain of rain. Though it was a small train, it made a great noise, and to wait there knowing we must fling ourselves at the monster in the slippery darkness was like awaiting a cavalry charge. The train was gathering speed as the engine passed us shaking the ground, and we waited for only two or three cars to go by before we were up and running alongside. Then it was a grab and jump for the rung of the ladder and we had swung in between the cars, standing on the couplings and clinging tight to the ladders. As the first milestone marker went by we reached across in the darkness and shook hands. We couldn't ride 1099 miles like that, but anyone seeing us grinning exultantly at each other would think we were almost home.

We knew that it wasn't all going to be as easy as this, but we couldn't guess how much would go wrong. Within an hour, forty miles on our way, we were ordered off by a trainman and threatened with arrest. And then, ignominiously, after twenty-four hours of eating only biscuits, drinking lake water, and sleeping on the benches of the station waiting-room in Kashabowie, we used almost half our money to pay our way into Port Arthur. There for two days we haunted the docks, hoping to work our way home on a grain boat. At the gangways we were turned away briskly; no hands were needed for this last run down through the lakes. We had one good meal at a Seaman's Shelter near the waterfront — nourishing and warming stew with bread and coffee for twenty-five cents. That night we burrowed deep into hay in a half-empty box car near the lake and in the morning we stripped and, wading out into the freezing water, scrubbed ourselves with sand for lack of soap. We started the day feeling brisk and confident, big husky fellows, but by evening we were boys again and facing failure. At the Seaman's Shelter in Fort William, lining up with our tin plates, we felt and were beginning to look like the other down-and-outs.

And then slipping into Port Arthur station for a wash we met a little Cockney sailor, a short ferret of a man who claimed to have been in every port in the world and to have been sunk in the Battle of Jutland. In the world of the hobos he moved with easy confidence, had been everywhere, and seemed to know every angle. If we wanted to get to Toronto quickly, he said, we were in the wrong place. The thing to do was to get up to the Northern Line at Long Lac and there we would find a daily cattle train going right to Toronto. It sounded perfect, almost too easy.

The little man didn't press it, but to our every question he had a ready answer — not always easy to understand because his broad Cockney was punctuated with hisses, whistles, and expletives rounded out by chopping gestures with his small, hard hands. He himself was going to Long Lac in order to get a freight going west. Where we had timidly asked questions about freight trains of people who brushed us off or didn't know, he marched up to the nearest trainman and, cigarette hanging from the corner of his mouth — one thumb in his waistband the other hand chopping the air — asked his questions. "They cawn't arrest yer fer awskin'," he said afterwards when we expressed amazement; and indeed they answered as helpfully as they could. He reported that there might not be a freight to Long Lac for a day or two. He was going to wait for it, but we were running out of time as well as money. Uneasily, feeling as though we were cheating, we bought tickets for Long Lac. It was an alarming decision as well as humiliating, for now we only had five or six dollars between us, eight hundred miles from home.

After a jolting overnight ride we arrived at what seemed to be the cold roof of the world. Across from the station was a small unpainted building with a café sign; and nothing else to be seen but scrub trees reaching it seemed to Hudson Bay. Over coffee and toast we learned that the cattle train for the east had just gone through. We bought a loaf of bread then and climbed up into the woods above the tracks, and there for the day we walked in the cold morning and slept when the sun had warmed the pine needles.

By nightfall the café was deliciously warm and cosy with good smells, so we sat as long as we could over big plates of bacon and eggs with mugs of tea, and all the bread we could eat and stuff into our shirts. Sitting back, content at last, we made friends with two tough-looking but easy-going hobos who had also arrived to go east on the cattle train. Outside, the night had turned bitterly cold and the four of us broke into a small railway shack above the station where we found a Quebec heater and some empty wooden boxes. Soon we were snug beside a roaring fire. But our firewood wasn't going to last; we found all the boxes weren't empty, and the full ones were marked "dynamite". This toned down our exaltation a little but we dozed, sitting on the dynamite, dreaming about getting home as the fire died down. A knock on the door and the sailor walked in, just off a freight train. Somewhere outside a wolf howled and was answered across the clear, cold stillness. Our experienced mates talked about tomorrow's train as though travelling on it was as easy and predictable as going first class on a transcontinental. Mac and I were excited and happy for the first time since we had crouched in the rain beside the tracks outside Fort Frances. It seemed to me a great adventure, and we were going to make it. The sailor was repeating his directions ("Get a free meal with the cattle 'ands at 'Ornepyne", "Watch out for the police at Foleyet"). Outside the wolf howls had died down and dawn was breaking. Tomorrow had arrived.

At the first curl of smoke from the café we were across the tracks teasing the sleepy and good-natured proprietor into action. He was cook, waiter, and dishwasher combined, but he didn't have many customers and our high spirits seemed to cheer him up. His fat, sleepy face all smiles, he hurried around filling up coffee cups, making more toast, assuring us that we had lots of time.

Then from far off to the west came the long, shaking whistle of the huge approaching locomotive and we ran out to see her in the distance racing toward us, still soundlessly, through a rock cut and trailing a long white plume of smoke. On she came and we were already down below the embankment, running to meet her, then crouching in the scrub as she thundered by, travelling at such a speed that it seemed she couldn't stop. Then came a screeching of brakes and gradually the immense train became still but for the cracking of hot metal and the bawling of cattle; cautiously we crept toward an oil-tanker car, then sank into the bush as footsteps came along beside the track; hammers tapped at wheels, metal lids were lifted and dropped, hoarse voices called. At last came the whistle, above us the wheels began to move, and a sharp cracking ran down the mile-long train as couplings took the strain. As the train gathered speed we scrambled up the bank, grabbed for ladders, and swung on. Rolling past the café I saw the sailor standing in the doorway with his crooked grin; one thumb was in his belt, the other jerked upward.

We settled down in the sunshine on the narrow catwalk surrounding the oil tank — the hobo's sun parlour — sitting with our legs hanging down and one arm hooked around the guard rail above our heads. And so we sat throughout the day and far into the night, getting up occasionally to stretch or walk around the car to keep ourselves awake, as the train drove relentlessly on through the endless rock and scrub country. Following the sailor's directions, we jumped off as we approached our few stops and moved through the towns to pick up the train as it gathered speed going out. At Hornepayne, looking like cattle-hands, we had a free lunch and at Foleyet near midnight we bought loaves of bread which we tore apart and gobbled as we ran.

It seemed our only problem would be to keep warm during the cold night, to endure one more jolting day, and then we would be in Toronto. That left aside the hazards of jumping off and on, at which we were becoming old hands, though in the dark it remained very dangerous. And there was to be one scare. Mistaking another hobo for a policeman as we left Foleyet sent Mac and me in a chase along the top of the box-cars in the dark, running along the catwalk and jumping the gap between the swaying cars where one mis-step would have ended it all. When finally we settled into the empty ice-compartment of a refrigerator car we were so exhausted that the bare zinc-lined box (insulated against the cold) seemed as comfortable as a bed. We slept heavily until a man climbed our ladder with a pail of ice in the morning at Capreol.

A quick wash and breakfast at a Chinese restaurant on the main street and we were out and running as our train started to move. Through a long day crouching on a flat-car we ran down along Georgian Bay and through the Muskoka country. And then, at last, near midnight the train was running slowly through the outskirts of Toronto. Mac had to get to Whitby and I on to Cornwall, but we were home. We hadn't managed all we set out to do, and even this much had needed help and luck, but we hadn't given up. We were absurdly pleased with ourselves. We began to see landmarks and then the train began a slow, quiet run down the Don Valley. We said good-bye to our friends, swung down the ladder for the last time, ran a few steps, and let go. In the strangely quiet darkness we watched the lights of the caboose disappear. We climbed up the side of the Bloor Street viaduct and stood waiting contentedly. Between us we had just enough money for a night streetcar.

4

THE GREAT RESOLUTIONS that I brought to university, or that I intended to bring, seem now to have been lost on the way. That moment when I sat sleepily on the side of my iron bunk in Fort Frances, reading the good news with doubt suddenly swept aside by happiness and great resolves, what happened to it? There appears to be no answer. All I know is that having fumblingly and painfully made my opportunity, I then threw it away. Perhaps I expected something quite different, thought that as I entered the portals of the university there would be a great light; and there was none I could recognize. All I found — or seemed to find — was a great opportunity to have more fun. No doubt, fifty years later, I make too much of it, because for fifty years I have been wondering what I missed, as well as why I missed it. Mine is so common a story as not to be worth detailed repetition or elaborate explanation. Boy Meets Life, or what he mistakes for life — something like that will do, though perhaps it should be Boy Misses Boat.

It was 1925 and we were in the midst of what would later be called the Roaring Twenties: the era of Prohibition, of bootleggers, of hip flasks and coon coats, and sports cars with rumble seats, of the Charleston and College Humour, of big bands and little flappers. The "Lost Generation" were our immediate seniors and they were whooping it up. Bob and I were living in a fraternity house to which in our innocence we had pledged ourselves two years before. Since the university didn't recognize

77

fraternities officially, it did not attempt to regulate them. This left them free to "rush" schoolboys, which meant inviting them down for Saturday lunches or Sunday tea-dances — all very flattering — and then popping the question: "Would you care to pledge?" What did pledging mean? Well, just indicate your intention of joining when you come to university. Meanwhile, you will be free to use the House, come to parties, drop in for meals any time — find yourself part of a group of attractive and sophisticated friends. It seemed too good to be true. Of course, as an afterthought, there was one little point: to break a pledge once made would stain one's honour and blight a whole university career. No one mentioned that two years hence many of those who made the fraternity so agreeable would be graduated and gone. Also, in two years' time one's school friends might join a different fraternity or none at all. No doubt we should have asked advice, but we didn't. The people who loaned themselves to this system — and in due course I was one — were not bad people, but it was a bad system. To boys who didn't live in the city the idea of belonging to this pleasant club was too tempting. To be fair, the objection was not that school-boys were led into dissipation; in the two years of our pledge we were neither offered drink nor aware that upstairs there might be drinking going on.

In retrospect the pervading atmosphere of the university seems to have been anti-intellectual, but that may only be the perspective from our closed little society. Indeed, to someone coming from ten years of boarding-school life the whole thing was too big and impersonal and exciting to be seen and ex-plored coolly, as it ought to have been. The first sad let-down was to find that most of the work in the General Arts course seemed no more stimulating than the last years of school work. There was little challenge in it, but rather a sense of its being an endurance test. If you could survive the boredom of the first year the university would take notice of you later; perhaps something might be made of you. Meanwhile, over fifty per cent of the General Arts freshmen were plucked by the end of their first year, many of them by Christmas-time. The students

78

in professional schools — medicine, engineering, law, and so on — had fewer problems. They knew what they were after, and their professors saw to it that they got to work and kept at it. But the Arts students — many of whom were still groping, still trying to decide what they wanted to do and be — had trouble in seeing that the course they were embarked on led anywhere. That kind of fumbling uncertainty was a poor defence against the multitude of competing interests that crowded in and claimed attention. The idea — the ideal — of simply being an educated person was neither beyond our grasp nor unattractive, but it was hard to see that we were moving even a step in that direction.

And always there was the alluring clamour of the fraternity house: clever young men arguing a point of law; bright and amusing men arguing about politics, about manners, about love or football, and doing it with what to a schoolboy seemed to be wit. And there was nearly always a group playing bridge or hearts amid roars of laughter. In the afternoon there was football practice and the glory of being able to trot up Devonshire Place to Varsity Stadium behind the great star Warren Snyder, until now a distant hero. Then, as autumn wore on, a good part of the day was used up in going downtown to the Mutual Street Arena to practise hockey with the Varsity juniors. Sometimes coached by Connie Smythe, we practised with the seniors, who as Varsity Grads were to win the Allan Cup, and a year later the Olympic Games. To be on the same ice as these giants was to me worth more than all the Latin verbs and all the calculus.

And at week-ends the fraternity house was a whirl of cheerful, mindless activity. There were always alumni dropping in, to park their cars, to play bridge, or merely looking for playmates. Most of them were war veterans and their talk was fascinating, though many of them were not otherwise impressive, even to someone as ingenuous as I. And always there was singing around the piano and a great surging in and out of people in high spirits. It was all pretty innocent, even simple-minded, fun but it was not an atmosphere in which to work.

79

It's not for knowledge that you come to College
But to raise Hell all the year.

Those who lived at home or in residence could slip away into quietness, but we in the House lived in the path of the storm and had little defence against its amicable power. In any case the attitude in the House was that no one was expected to get excited about work until the spring; six or eight weeks before exams was soon enough to "get at the books". It wasn't enough for me. Besides, hockey went on well into the spring and left one too tired and excited at the end of the day to settle down and do good work. And I was in love: deeply, desperately, joyously, and was always ready to skip lectures or give up reading in the library in order to wander around the campus where I just might meet the girl and be able to persuade her to take time for tea or coffee. Against such competition work ran a bad third.

Meanwhile, an important event had taken place at home. My parents, having had three sons, had for a long time clung to the hope of having a daughter. As we grew up it was clear this was not going to happen and, moreover, they would soon be alone. Ready or not we would be trying our wings in the big world. They began more and more often to talk of adopting a baby girl. We argued against it. Perhaps unconsciously we begrudged sharing their affection, but our argument was against their taking on ties and heavy responsibility just as they won the freedom to travel and relax.

But my mother, who didn't argue effectively, usually got her way, and it became clear she intended to this time. One day she arrived outside the fraternity house with a basket on the seat of her car carrying a six-month-old little girl. She was transparently happy and lifted out and displayed the baby with joy. We stood there agreeing, yes the baby was pretty, was adorable, but oh dear she looked fragile. My mother already handled her with easy confidence; we weren't yet ready to touch anything so breakable.

This hesitation passed quickly enough after our first term

80

break at home. She was adorable and every day grew more so as we learned to help to take care of her and make her laugh. She was suddenly part of the family and was never to be anything else; not a plaything but a much loved little sister.

In the fraternity-house atmosphere of hustle and distraction and laughter my vague dream of becoming a writer was put away. It wasn't altogether lost, thanks partly to my father, who cherished it for me, and tried in his sometimes embarrassing way to bring it a step nearer realization. During the summer at Fort Frances I had written some lively letters home and these had been copied and sent off by him to Sir John Willison, publisher of *Willison's Monthly*, and to "Choppy" Grant at Upper Canada. They were not submitted as publishable but as evidence of talent, and with a request to knowledgeable acquaintances for advice to a young writer. Both were kindly, courteous, and brief; they saw some promise, but a writer must find his own subjects and develop his own style; no one could teach him, he must teach himself; above all a writer must write and keep on writing. To my father, this seemed both sound advice and easy to follow, as his letters would remind me. I was sure the advice was good, but it was fixed in my mind that a writer must have peace and quiet coinciding with the moment of inspiration; in the House I lacked both.

This was to be for several years a task for my father, to help me realize what he thought of as my potential. Against the background of his own neglected education and uncongenial work the idea of being "a writer" — whatever that meant — shone out like a star. In the years ahead, wherever I might be, I would be overtaken by a book — usually Canadian — of which he had seen a favourable review, or a clipping that related to my interests. It was to be a continuous and touching reminder of his quiet support and hope for me, and though it was always warming, it was also a reproach.

I think he was a writer manqué, as I was. I came in time, however, to think of his case as painful, while mine was quite different. His education had been neglected, whereas I had thrown away the opportunity which, at a sacrifice, he had provided. When, in later years, he was old and ill and bored with forced retirement — making his life out of reading newspapers, long walks, and other people's conversation — it was my turn to urge him to write. Would he not come to Toronto and live with us, or in rooms if he preferred? He could do research and write at the Central Reference Library, filling out his memories — always vivid — of the Toronto of his boyhood: a Toronto of horse-drawn streetcars and clean beaches, of picnics on Toronto Island and bicycle trips to Bond Head and Lake Simcoe, of the Huron and St. George Street Gang that called itself the Bloody Brotherhood; a Toronto in which the horse-car would wait while my grandmother picked up a parcel at Mr. Eaton's. I offered to help with the writing, and I think he was tempted. But it was too late; he was tired and had lost his jaunty confidence.

While we were at Varsity his hopes for us were still high as ours sank below the horizon. Late in our first year my father was in Toronto on business. After lunch on a Saturday we walked around the university with him — it was a short walk in those days — and then settled down to talk in a corner of the Debates Room in Hart House. Suddenly our fears and sense of guilt tumbled out; we were costing him a lot of money and doing no good. Bob in particular couldn't see that it was leading anywhere; he was ready to stop then and go to work at Ives Bedding. I wasn't quite so certain but was equally clear that I had not found what I expected and hoped for. I believe we blamed some lack in ourselves and not the university in this, but either way the result was bitter disappointment. Though it did not come as a complete surprise to my father he was not prepared to accept it yet. He produced quotations from friends on the subject of education and its importance, and cited examples of the early falterings of great men.

One of his pet examples was Sir Edward Beatty, president of the Canadian Pacific Railway, with whom he and Uncle Fred had gone to the old Model School in Toronto. Sooner or later in any conversation about prominent men, or the path to greatness, the name of Eddie Beatty was certain to be batted back and forth between them; "You remember Eddie Beatty at school?" one would say, "Oh sure, Eddie wasn't a good student" or even "Of course, stupidest boy in the class". They had between them a puzzled and tentative grip on one of the mystifying truths of the educational process, that people develop at different rates, respond to different stimuli. This was produced now, though I couldn't see its point, unless it was to suggest that one of us must be well on the way to becoming President of the CPR. And there was another pet reminder of my father's to prove that everyone must work for his rewards: "There is no Royal Road to learning" — a warning once to a young and idle Egyptian prince, which seemed to have little enough to do with me. In the end our talk became a circular and exhausting argument. We all had a good deal of north-of-England stubbornness in us but little anger, and in the end we parted on a note of affection and sad defeat. We promised to see the year out and to do our best.

And up to a point we did, but it wasn't good enough. Even the House settled down, and along St. George Street — Fraternity Row — quiet prevailed in the evenings. In our little group of houses, where the Robarts Library now stands, people broke off work about eleven o'clock and drifted down to the kitchens for milk or coffee and distracted chat, then back for a little review before bedtime. We became, briefly, a model community, except on Saturday nights. But it was spring, and I was in love and prepared to count the world and the university well lost for a late walk or coffee, and just occasionally an innocent kiss with a dazzling girl. She was a little older than I and much more sensible, and though flattered and pleased, was not in love. Her third-year work was well in hand and she was quite able to afford an occasional hour of relaxation, which I could not; but I was well content to rush on my doom.

After exams we went quietly back to Cornwall and, after a short holiday, to work at Ives Bedding. Bob was to work in the office, keeping gentleman's hours and learning the business. I was working in the factory and learning the beginnings of welding and how to run the lathe and the shaper, bending metal tubes and using punches and drills. I found the factory a thrilling place; noisy against the dull red glow of the foundry and the occasional flame and tangle of sparks as men with blackened faces filled their pots and then poured the molten metal. Over-all from the floor above came the smell of paint and the sharp lemon-sweet smell of shellac. It was understood that this was a temporary arrangement — a useful killing of time — for if I passed I was to go back to Varsity. When work finished at the factory for the day we cleaned up in the machine shop by dipping our arms almost to the shoulder in a deep tub of liquid soap and sluicing off the top layer of grease, then hurried home for a bath and to wait for the evening paper. From early June the *Mail and Empire* on most evenings carried long lists of examination results — remarkably and symbolically like the casualty lists of a few years before. When at last our class was reported and our names were not there it was a disappointment but not really a shock. It was decided that I should apply to repeat my year, and I wrote a careful letter. My failure was explained as being in part due to my having played hockey and football, "a mistake I shall not make again".

Life settled into a pleasant pattern while we waited the result of the appeal. Every morning I was up at six and by six-thirty I had eaten my breakfast, made my lunch, and was on my way to the factory, which lay near the old Grand Trunk Railway station about a mile north of the town. It was pleasant to walk on a summer morning along the tree-lined streets past the still-sleeping houses. Cornwall was a comfortable, quiet town and one of the oldest in Ontario. Being just above the Quebec border it had been the first collecting and dispersal point for the Loyalist regiments demobilized after the American Revolutionary war. Here for some years were the government stores and land offices. Here in 1784 men had lined up in their already travel-stained uniforms and drawn their lots from the Surveyor's hat, then trudged off into the bush with axe and blanket in search of their lands. Here many of their descendants still lived on streets named after the family of George III

(Cumberland, Adolphus, Amelia, Augusta, York), rather severe and careful people. Five generations of work had made them comfortable, even rich, but they behaved as though they didn't believe in their good fortune and half expected to see it snatched away — probably by the Americans, whom they by turns admired, distrusted, liked, and found appalling. They were guardedly polite, even rather formally kind to strangers, and they watched each other to see what people were getting up to — you never knew, they said and "you can't be too careful". The Presbyterians and the Methodists kept an eye on the stuck-up Anglicans, and all kept an eye on the Catholics.

Arriving at the factory I was in a different world. Here on a summer morning the men would be sprawled comfortably on the grass, their backs against the factory wall, enjoying a last cigarette before the factory whistle blew. My arrival, for the first few days, tended to check conversation, for though I had known many of the men all my life — and with Bob had played in the factory since childhood — I was now in a different role, grown up and the boss's son. But the slight chill thawed after a week or so and I joined in the chat, kidding and being kidded, which my raw clumsiness on the job laid me open to. At noon and after work we played softball together in a vacant field across from the factory.

The whistle we waited for had regulated my life since childhood and must have had the same expanding echoes for the others. As children we had listened for it at noon and at five o'clock, distinguishing it from the whistles of the paper-mill, the cotton-mills, the McGill Chair Factory, and the Beech Furniture Factory. It meant running to meet Dad and fighting, with Bob, to hold his hand. But now under the chat and banter we waited for the whistle, slightly bracing ourselves for the day, for the moment when switches were pushed home and belts began to revolve and machines to turn; men had now to be alert and strong. I enjoyed these moments as I enjoyed the tension before a hockey game; it was like the little tingle of excitement as one skated into place just before the puck was dropped and everyone exploded into action.

The summer moved pleasantly on. To have won a place among the men at the factory had soothed my battered self-respect. In the evenings I read a good deal and even wrote some poetry. At week-ends we played golf or fished. It began to seem that one might be very content with such a life. Could I be a bed manufacturer or salesman and be a writer in spare time? There was no one of whom to ask such a question. Everywhere I found good-will and incomprehension. The only kind of writer that came within people's definition was a newspaper man. They knew of Ralph Connor and Stephen Leacock as Canadian writers, but one of them was a parson and one a professor; and anyway was I aiming that high? I didn't know how high I was aiming, indeed I wasn't aiming at all. Perhaps that was my trouble, I was drifting aimlessly, hoping to be carried to a point of land marked "writers".

Once at the fraternity house I had let it out that I hoped to be a writer. One of the older men, showing a mild interest, said, "You should talk to Dunc Bain, he's going to be a writer." This sounded both impressive and intimidating. Here was a man who didn't just hope, he planned and intended. I longed to meet and talk to him but was shy of trying to arrange it; he sounded too much older and surer. When, some years later, we did meet he was teaching school, and inquiries about his writing were answered by a sad and resigned shrug — "Youthful aspirations," he said, "I don't do any writing now." This was as close as I came, knowingly, to a writer at university. Yet down on Queen Street in Toronto at that moment a young graduate in law, Morley Callaghan, was running a book shop and writing stories that were to give inspiration and the beginnings of confidence to a generation of writers in Canada. And a few blocks from the fraternity house, on Yorkville Avenue, Mazo de la Roche was finishing her novel *Jalna*, which was to win her the $10,000 *Atlantic Monthly* prize and to have an electrifying effect, out of all proportion to the book's importance.

That summer marked a milestone in my life. My brother Bob set off to live in Quebec City to learn French. As a little boy he had been held back a year so that we might start public school together, and we had moved side by side through four schools and into university. We had fought each other, like wolves, but presented a united front to outsiders. From now on, with occasional reunions, we would go our different ways, though we didn't then recognize it. The Quebec venture was my father's idea. He was always brimming with ideas for us; once it was a plan for our taking out homesteads, doing our settlement duties, and owning a piece of land in return for a few months' work. (Since the now popular resort area of Haliburton was just then being opened up, we may have turned aside from a fortune.) Another idea was that he might stake us in a prospecting venture. This had probably grown out of Bob's experience with the Geological Survey the year before; he had worked around Kirkland Lake and Rouyn and the earth seemed to be full of gold mines. But once again we turned a deaf ear to the call of fortune.

But the wish to have us learn French was not just a passing whim of my father's. I think he had always regretted his own inability to communicate better with the men in the factory, though they all spoke English. For several summers we had been sent as small boys to take conversational French from a Mademoiselle Blondin, a French teacher who lived near us. We liked the idea of speaking French, and wished we could, but we dodged the extra lessons when possible because they cut into play time.

I have never known how useful the lessons were, but certainly they did something for our accents. Doubtless the small, quiet Mlle Blondin did not enjoy them any more than we did, though just occasionally I could make her laugh, which seemed always to be my objective, with everyone. But even on a mutually precious Saturday afternoon she was unfailingly courteous and dignified and rather formal: "Bonjour, Jack, comment allez-vous?", "Très bien, merci, Mlle Blondin", "Qu'est-ce que vous avez fait aujourd'hui, Jack?", "J'ai joué au baseball, Mlle Blondin". And so it went with inquiries after our parents and her invalid mother being exchanged across the stiff little parlour, in which drawn blinds shut out the hot summer, and muffled the distracting sounds of fun.

Above the normal considerations I think my father's plan for us to spend time in Quebec had a special reason. An almost passionate Conservative, he had always been deeply interested in politics. The politician he admired most, Arthur Meighen, had been defeated at least partly by his inability to win favour in Quebec. Meighen was sending his eldest son, Ted, to Quebec to live and study to become bilingual. So my father's ambition for us was given point and force. Though he had resisted a suggestion that he might try for nomination as a candidate, I think he secretly hoped that some day one of us might.

Just as Bob left for Quebec I heard that my appeal to the university had been granted; I was to be allowed to repeat my year. Once again I went to Toronto, filled with good resolutions. Why these did not include living outside the fraternity house, or why my father did not insist, I don't know. The result might not have been better but it couldn't have been worse. I started well, choosing a serious-minded room-mate (who accepted me with evident misgivings). I bought my books, tacked up my time-table, and organized my desk. Breakfast found me at my place in good time to be off for a nine o'clock lecture. I even went to nine o'clocks on Saturday and listened to the venerable — almost legendary — Principal of University College, Maurice Hutton (known inevitably as Horace Mutton), teaching Horace in the College amphitheatre; his pink bald head distracted us from whatever his great drooping moustache did not smother. One Saturday morning he sat on the forward edge of the long desk, dangling his legs and reading aloud from *Stalky & Co.* to show us that even English schoolboys had amusing problems with Latin.

Occasionally the revered old man was to be seen drifting gently along the corridors tugging at his gown, but his appearances in class were spasmodic and infrequent and, having decided that Saturday nine o'clocks were not worth the great effort, I encountered him directly only once more. On that occasion I had been summoned to the Principal's office. Though I did not know the specific reason, I could guess. The old man hunted through the papers on his desk and then, having found what he was after, said in his thin, tired voice that he dared say I was having an amusing time, but I really ought to consider what I wished from university. He had a depressing record of my non-attendance. I was respectful and contrite, but the contrition did not have any lasting effect. There were to be other warnings and reproaches as the year went on. One was from a young graduate student lecturer whom I knew later as a gifted and inspiring teacher of drama in the schools, Billy Milne. Having given me a high mark for an essay on Rupert Brooke, he sent for me and asked why I was repeating my year. My answer was muddled and lame, and being a Scot he cut me short with the brisk but encouraging comment that there was no excuse for anyone who could write such any essay failing the course. I said I intended to do better; and indeed I always meant to.

But by this time I was mounted high on the merry-go-round of fun and what I took to be an entrancing sophistication. I was reading a lot, but much of it in Hart House Library — Balzac and Maupassant and Flaubert — instead of other books, more to the point, in the University Library. And I was spending almost as much time learning to play bridge, and to drink and to pursue girls — especially *the* girl, now in her last year, still glamorous, charming fun to be with, and cool (and there were occasionally some who were not particularly fun, and not a bit cool).

I had become part of a little group that provided much of the gossip and entertainment of the House. We affected a style between a detached and amused cynicism and outrageous fun; and becoming trapped in our role we had periodically to cap our performance with something more amusing or outrageous. There became less and less time and energy for the things we pretended to recognize as more important. "Look, you guys, we've really got to get down to it." For the moment we would nod in serious agreement, and then someone would say, "Week after next?" It was enough to touch off a burst of high spirits,

89

and to muffle any serious intention. The doctoring up of escapades into amusing stories was the chief artistic interest of the fraternity house. As an art form it had serious limitations and did not even call for a high level of execution. We laughed readily and joyously, so that during all the years that I have looked back to that strange and embarrassing time I have been grateful for the laughter. Not that I have ever been short of it, but that was the period when it spilled out, bubbled up, burst around us most copiously and continuously. The laughter and the singing. It only needed someone to sit down at the piano — and we had one really accomplished pianist, Hughie Wilkinson — and people would gather from all over the house. Again, our performance had no artistic merit, only animal spirits and joy.

The older and more serious ones would join in, but briefly, then away to do what they had to do. A few of us would stay as long as the pianist would go on, and Hughie, a laughing, effeminate, dear little man, was easily persuaded to continue. On such, and on most, occasions I went reluctantly to bed. One day one of the seniors said, as we shaved together in the community bathroom, "Why don't you ever go to bed?" I shrugged. "You just can't bear to miss anything, can you? You enjoy things too much for your own good; never seen anyone like you."

One day in the spring I encountered one of our more reckless spirits, and a close friend, Bobby Grant. He was studying the schedule of approaching examinations. "Hey, do you see what those crazy bastards have done?" he said. "They've put Trigonometry on the same afternoon as the King's Plate." I said it was bad luck. "But I always go to the King's Plate," he said, "always." "Oh, come on," I said. "You can't mean you are going to miss the exam and throw away your year." "But I have always gone to the King's Plate." By this time he was between an aggressive truculence and a giggle. He could see that this could be erected into a final and splendid gesture. "They can't expect me to change the habits of a lifetime just because they do a stupid thing like that, now can they?" I said grumpily and priggishly that I didn't know what "they" could expect, but I knew what he could. In the event he went to the Plate and then, having decided that he had lost the year, didn't bother to write the rest of his examinations. In spite of his coaxing I stayed and wrote Trigonometry and, it subsequently proved, might just as well have shared his gesture.

Long after I was shown clearly how all our careless high spirits and reckless posturing had looked to others. I was lunching with my wife and the Alan Macleans at the Park Plaza in Toronto when across the dining room I saw one of my contemporaries of fraternity house days. He had been somewhat younger and much more serious; a model of good organization and sensible behaviour. I had not seen him for years, but knew he had become a successful and rather senior oil executive. I went over and he looked at me as though I had risen from the dead. "Can't get over you," he kept saying. "I've told my son about you." I didn't understand the remark and after a short chat returned to our table.

Presently he came over to greet my wife, was introduced to the Macleans, then threw himself into a crouch beside my chair and went back to staring at me. By now it was clear that he had had a good deal to drink, but the reason for his staring and wonderment remained a mystery. "Told my son about you," he said again, shaking his head slowly, "several times." Finally to penetrate the mystery I asked, "Told him what?" It was his turn to look astonished. "Told him how the stoopidest man I knew at university made a big success, of course." Laughing I told him I didn't admit either proposition, not all that stupid, not all that successful. His eyes widened: "You had nuthin'," he said, "less than nuthin'. Couldn't figure out how you even got to university. You and Bobby Grant and Billy Richardson — never knew which was the stoopidest." The more we all laughed the more he piled it on, and since Alan Maclean was a Director of Macmillans in London I was glad this testimonial was being presented at the end of my career instead of the beginning. At last he left us, smiling a gentle, puzzled smile and still shaking his head.

Not long before this I had been invited to give out prizes at Sedbergh School Closing by one of my great friends and good angels, Tom Wood, the Headmaster. Looking just before the ceremony at the beautiful lawns, set in a cup of the Laurentian Hills and soon to be filled with boys of all sizes, parents, and masters, I had a nerve storm. How could one spread a speech across such a group and have something for everyone? And yet having suffered through many such speeches I had worked hard at this one; had even wakened at five o'clock that morning in our Ottawa hotel room and sat by an open window staring over the sleeping town, memorizing and polishing. Now it seemed as though I couldn't deliver the speech; I felt as though I might just go to pieces, begin to scream. As so often in important moments, my wife Tony took charge. She begged a few minutes' quiet for me in the Woods' house. "Take off your shoes," she said, "lie flat on the floor, relax." Outside I could hear the cars arriving, the excited, happy voices. Relaxing, I realized that this was not a formidable occasion — indeed I knew there are very few such — it was a happy event; no one was going to listen carefully, or care much, whatever I said.

I was led like a sleep-walker down to the lawns, through a crowd of small boys in white trousers and mothers in bright-coloured dresses; a few curious glances at me, nothing more. And then, after prize-giving, which was delightful and relaxing, came an elaborate introduction of me — including every title and fancied accomplishment of my life. Then I was on my feet speaking and there was by turns laughter, attention, and interest. When it was finished I knew it had gone quite well. A number of people came forward to comment or congratulate, among the first being a young graduate student in psychology who told me that I was obviously a "verbalizer". I could only hope that was a good thing to be. Then, just behind him came an attractive woman whom I recognized when she smiled. It was *the* girl, the light and despair of my life at university thirty years before. I was delighted to see her but sad to realize that my heart didn't miss a beat.

Laughing, she asked, "Is it true what Woody said about you

in his introduction?" I said, "More or less, he made the most of it." "Well," she said, shaking her head in a bemused way, "I just said to Arthur, that stoopid boy." We laughed merrily over that, but afterwards I thought she might at least have given me credit for the essay that as a failed freshman I wrote for her in her fourth year, for which she was given a B plus.

One of my strange encounters at university was with the mayor of Toronto — Tommy Church. He was either a great hockey fan or an admirer of young hockey players, though in those days we would have been slow to come to any sinister conclusions about that. Tommy, an elderly bachelor, was a consummate politician; he was believed never to forget a name or a face, and to have met every troop train and greeted every soldier returning to Toronto at the end of the war. During my time he used to sit along the boards at Mutual Street Arena during hockey practices; often alone and unsmiling, sometimes talking to Connie Smythe, who coached in his snarling fashion when we were practising with the Varsity Grads. Afterwards Tommy Church would occasionally come to the dressing room and drift around chatting in his curiously hollow and nasal voice. He took to sitting down beside me, claiming to remember my father — "Sure I remember Morgan Gray" — though my father had not lived in Toronto for twenty years.

As mayor, Tommy Church doubtless received complimentary tickets to all sorts of affairs, and one morning in the mail I received a pair of tickets to a Saturday matinée of Sigmund Romberg's *The Student Prince* at the Royal Alexandra Theatre. With excitement and some trepidation I took my girl friend and found we were sitting in the middle of the front row. Even my cool companion was excited and impressed, and the candy-box-top confection of the show was beautifully suited to my mood. Afterward I wrote thanking Mr. Church and by way of reply he sent me two tickets to the boxing matches. I decided to bow out. As gracefully as I could I thanked him and returned the tickets. Only once afterward did I see Tommy Church and was treated to a demonstration of his complete memory-bank. After seven years as mayor of Toronto he had

93

run successfully for the federal Parliament and I met him on the street in Ottawa; he was wearing the bowler hat and flower in the buttonhole that I always suspected he copied from "Gentleman" Jimmy Walker, the mayor of New York. As we approached he began his slow smile of genuine friendliness. "Hullo-o-o" — the computer whirred — "Jack," he said, "how is your father?" The computer whirred again — "Still living in Cornwall?" By any measure it was an impressive performance. My father knew all about Tommy Church, of course, but wasn't at all certain that they had ever met.

Varsity finished with the same pre-exam hush, tantalizing to madness on soft spring evenings. Then came a rush of parties, of farewells, and of people drowning their sorrows. Our group of bold, bad lads, having hushed briefly, rushed into the final saraband with as much joy as if we had earned it. For my part I thought the exams had gone fairly well. I had worked hard for a few weeks in my erratic and sometimes foolish fashion — one night I had sat up the whole night through and by morning had memorized the translation of every ode of Horace; only to find none on the examination. Up and down St. George Street the parties swirled in and out of the big houses (now mostly demolished to make way for new university buildings).

As we broke up, two more earth-shaking events took place. A young unknown American called Charles Lindbergh flew alone across the Atlantic and electrified the imagination of the world. We knew only at the last moment of the attempt, but by late one afternoon there was a crowd around the old City Hall as news came through that he had landed in Paris. In a day of slow communication we took in the implications slowly, but overnight Le Bourget was a place we had all come to know, and the world had contracted to half its size. The other event was the ending of Prohibition in Ontario, and almost the end of the bootleggers; the end of buying a "scrip" from impecunious or unscrupulous young doctors or cadging from our newly graduated friends; at one blow much of the glamour, as well as the furtiveness and the silly boasting, went out of everything to do with drinking.

94

The act passed quickly in 1917, before the young men came home from the war; the act that reflected Ontario's deep and abiding fear of "the drink", echoing its memories of the crude horrors and brutalities caused by it in pioneer days; the act that had laid the foundations of some Canadian fortunes and produced rum-running and some minor gangsterism at most American border points; above all the act that had made almost a virtue of law-breaking, was swept away. It would be a generation before Ontario learned to treat drink without disapproval or a snicker, but it had bounded toward maturity overnight. All it meant to most of us at first was that one could get a bottle without a doctor's scrip, and since it was available there was no need to finish the bottle in a single session; but bad habits are not so easily broken.

I went home fairly confident that I had passed my year, though I had done little to deserve it. To my parents I gave only a half-truthful account of the year, finishing with a confident statement of the result. I still think that so far as the examinations were concerned my prediction was sound, but when the results came — the evenings when we grabbed the evening paper and scanned the casualty lists — my name was not there. Unbelieving, I went over the lists again — and again. Many of my friends' names were also missing. I tried to believe it was a mistake in printing. "It's probably a mistake," said my mother, and then a wave of shame and guilt swept over me and the gay blade, at nineteen — almost twenty — burst into tears. I started for my room and was stopped by my father. His bitterness must have been greater than mine, for he had not deserved that disappointment, but he was quiet and firm. "Whose-ever fault this is I want you to be a man about it." I said miserably, "It's my own fault." "All the more reason. Now wash your face and come downstairs." Somehow we got through the evening, though the ordeal was prolonged a little when an hour or two later there was a telegram from Bobby Grant, "Congratulations, 'J'" (the nickname I had truly earned). So there must have been a mistake; my name must have been in other editions of the paper. But a phone call to the *Mail and Empire* in

95

Toronto quenched that hope. I had failed and the wire was one last joke from Bobby; an impudent wave from one outcast to another.

I don't remember that we talked much in the next few weeks about the mess I had made of things and what I was to do with my life, what I might become. The atmosphere in which we all moved wasn't chill, but it was sad and full of unasked and unanswerable questions. I suppose I knew then that my father's experience had prepared him for almost any unlikely thing people might do. Somehow his broad humanity, for all the rigidity of a Victorian upbringing, permitted him to understand failure better than success. His own lack of formal education made him diffident, often when he had no need to be. Like many of his generation he had been put to work at fifteen, but unlike many of them he had done more to make good the loss than he realized. When his soldier friends came back to visit after the war, often travelling great distances "to shake hands with the old Major", they would say to Bob and me, "Be as good a man as your father." It was never "Be as successful", because by many measures he was not that. A discussion of problems with him usually ended up with his little wry smile, "We just have to do the best we can."

One evening that summer Dad asked whether I was free to drive him back to the factory; he had never learned to drive well, and in any case it was clear that he wanted company, felt the need of support. We drove the mile to the factory almost without speaking. He didn't tell me what our mission was, but he seemed unhappy and nervous; apparently what he had to do was unpleasant, perhaps even dangerous. On arrival we parked and sat for some time in silence in the darkness. It began to seem that this was a false alarm; nothing was going to happen. And then we detected some movement in the heavy shadow near one of the basement windows. With a sigh my father climbed out of the car and disappeared into the dark patch along the wall of the building. I stood by my door braced for action and trying to guess what was happening. There was the sound of a challenge in a sharp voice, then an exchange in a lower tone.

A moment or two later my father came walking back with another man, one of them carrying a small cloth sack that gave out a metallic clinking as they walked. The two of them sat together in the back and I drove, eavesdropping on their conversation. My father was gently reproachful, the other man quietly despairing. "I never done nuttin' like dat before, never." And there were references to his wife and child. I learned later that he had taken bits of scrap brass to make a doll's bed for his little girl, and had pushed them outside the window to be picked up later. Someone had seen this and informed on him.

We drove along quiet back streets to the man's home, a small, cared-for house that looked as though it too might have been largely made of scraps of material. There we all got out and the man shook hands with both of us. We seemed companions in misery.

On the way home I asked my father what would happen now. He said the man wouldn't be prosecuted, but he would have to go. As if in answer to some doubt in my voice over punishing such a sad little crime, he added with a kind of desperate firmness that you couldn't keep a man who would steal from you. But in the end he did, though he didn't tell me about it; I learned from my brother Bob.

༖ 5 ༖

ECISION TIME ABOUT MY FUTURE had been rushed forward by three years. My university days were over, and I remained half educated and totally unskilled labour; in Fort Frances I had been rated at 35¢ an hour, promoted by late summer to 37½¢. I still clung to the notion that I wanted to be a writer, but had shown no real evidence of talent or of a willingness to be serious about anything for any length of time. Had my father been inclined to insist that I start learning the bed-making business, I could not in my present guilty state have refused, but I think he held to my dream for me as tenaciously as I did, though with no better reason. At any rate it was decided that I should go to Quebec for six months, as Bob had done, to learn French. Once I had settled into a job, it was assumed, there could be no breaking away for a few months. One took on a job for life, and never looked up until a presumably unwelcome retirement. There had been hints about learners' jobs being available for both Bob and me in pulp and paper, in insurance, and I don't know what else, but I believe my father was unwilling to see that final gate close.

Though somewhat chastened by my university performance I went to Quebec in a mood of happy anticipation. There was also some apprehension — strange ways, a strange language — but the beautiful old city fascinated me, and Bob had enjoyed his time there. I expected some hostility, because hostility, or at least a sharp wariness, was always present in the relationship of the two language groups in Cornwall. As children we seemed to have inherited the almost primordial prejudices of our elders — or even of our ancestors — and little gangs would chase each other through the streets, the English chanting, "Pea soup and Johnny Cake makes the Frenchmen's belly ache." The French-Canadian kids (the Frenchies as we called them) replied in undoubtedly suitable terms, but perhaps fortunately we couldn't understand them. I doubt that these attitudes had much to do with conscious or subconscious memories of the conquest of Canada; we were the too-willing inheritors of tribal memories, product of the endless wars and mutual distrust of France and England, since 1066 and probably before.

If my first few weeks in Quebec were a little uncomfortable, they were full of the interest and the charm of the exotic. I was working, as Bob had, in a large furniture store, part of the empire of the P. T. Legaré Company. The store was on Rue St. Joseph in the Lower Town, not far from that part of the old Ville de Québec that lay between the foot of the great rock and the St. Lawrence River. I didn't have a well-defined job but was to help out; so I pitched in with the boys, sweeping floors and dusting furniture before the doors opened, and then waiting on customers — or at least greeting them, because my French was not equal to much more. Judging by the manager's astonishment I was apparently not expected to sweep floors, but he then looked pleased and it helped my relationship with the other clerks. Within a few days they were covering for me quickly and generously when customers found my inability to help them more irritating than interesting. And imperceptibly I found I was needing less and less help, except with complex problems. I hadn't suddenly learned French but by listening and watching I had acquired some of the vocabulary of my trade — I knew a *fauteuil* from a *poêle*, and I knew that for a *table* or a *cendrier* people had to *montez au quatrième étage; prenez l'ascenseur, madame, par ici.*

The other boys and I seemed poles apart in our backgrounds and interests — most of them had grown up on farms or in small villages — but we became a happy band. We seldom met outside the store except for a stroll in the sun at noon or just occasionally a beer together after the store closed. We had family jokes; we helped each other and lied for each other. We agreed on the departmental managers we liked and those we feared or despised. Against the latter we fortified ourselves by little competitions in mimicry, especially of the oily hand-washing manners reserved for beautiful women and important men: "Certainement, madame", "Justement, madame", "Comptez sur moi, m'sieu". For us the soft voice, the bows and smiles were often turned to a harsh bullying tone, "Mette ça ici, icit, icit", and "Dépêchez-vous", always "Dépêchez-vous", sometimes shortened in patois to "Pêche-tway". Since I was there in a special capacity and for a limited time — and apparently in some way connected with people in power — the full weight of displeasure seldom fell on me, though I deserved my share.

Outside the shop, life was quite different. I was living with the family who had taken care of Bob the year before, in the village of Giffard which linked the eastern edge of the city to the old town of Beauport. Morning and night I caught a tram that ran from Lower Town through Beauport to Ste. Anne de Beaupré, twenty miles down river. As far as Montmorency Falls the line ran at the northern edge of the flat and narrow fields that bordered the St. Lawrence. Just above it lay an escarpment and the old winding highway, along which Montcalm's thin and hard-pressed forces had marched and counter-marched as they defended the flat shore against Wolfe and the British through the spring and summer of 1759. The exhausted Montcalm must often have galloped on his black horse through the villages strung along the road, past old stone houses, still standing solidly, that had probably been strong points one hundred and seventy years before.

The Paul Girards had been chosen because they spoke no English, but they had other things to recommend them: they were friendly and kind, and they had a host of nephews and nieces who became our friends. It was still not easy to adapt to a way of life so different. It was a life based on warm family gatherings, often at the Girards' and always in the kitchen with

Captain John Gray, his wife Rachel, and the Widow's Pension Ticket which provided her with the sum of £2.10 per annum after he was lost at sea.

WIDOW'S PENSION TICKET.

This Ticket must be taken care of, and is no Security for Money.

No. *557*   18*40*

Rachel Gray   is reduced on the
MERCHANTS' SEAMEN'S CORPORATION PENSION-
LIST, to £*2.10*   per Annum, or   *12/6*   per
Quarter, commencing *Lady-day*   18*50*

The Pension is payable QUARTERLY, as undermentioned. AT THE TRINITY PAY-OFFICE, GREAT TOWER-HILL, on the Friday next before the 25th day of March, the 25th day of June, the 25th day of September, and the 25th day of December in each year, between the hours of 9 and 3, and on the Friday following between the hours of 10 and 1, and after the last of the above-mentioned days AT THE OFFICE IN BIRCHIN-LANE, any day within One Month, between the hours of 11 and 1.

Should the 25th day of the month fall on a Friday, then THAT DAY will be the first of payment, and not the Friday preceding.

The Money may be received by the Pensioner upon producing this Ticket; or in case she should be unable to attend, then by any person applying on her behalf, with a Certificate (according to the printed form) of her Life under the hands of the Minister and Churchwardens of the Parish in which she resides.

N.B. Pensioners failing to make application during a longer period than Two Years will be struck off the Pension List.

MARCHANT SINGER AND CO., PRINTERS, INGRAM-COURT, FENCHURCH-STREET.

(*Above*) Isobel Gray, Robert
Gray's wife.

(*Above*) Robert Holt Gray,
grandfather of the
author.

(*Below*) Samuel Morgan Gray,
the author's father,
shown here as Captain
of the 59th Highland
Light Infantry (later
the Glengarrys) in 1913.

(*Below*) Helen Putnam, the
author's mother.

Young "Jack" Gray,
accompanied by elder
brother Bob, in 1909.

Young Jack.

The Gray family in England in 1914. The author is on the right.

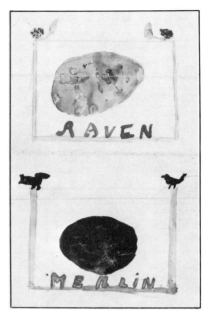

Soldier boys John (*left*) and Bob Gray.

John Gray's first book. Entitled *The Percuywiaratees of Birds and Thier Eggs*, it was produced in an edition of one in England in 1916.

The Gray family home at 238 First Street East in Cornwall, Ontario.

Lakefield School in the
1920s, where John Gray was
both pupil and teacher.

The Headmaster, the Reverend Dr. A. W. Mackenzie.

The young logger —
John Gray in Fort
Frances in 1925.

John Gray, the sole
English-speaker, and
his team-mates on the
Beauport hockey
team, 1927-28. The
author is seated,
second from the right.

John Gray, third from left, in Budapest, 1929, with the English Ice Hockey Association team and the Hungarian National team.

much chat; and for once, robbed of my language, I couldn't talk or understand the talk. The occasional question addressed to me, out of a mixture of courtesy and curiosity, would throw me into an inarticulate agony; even if I understood the question I could not frame the answer. But I was learning. The day came when I even made a pun in French, and one of the Vachon girls, a niece, called attention to this as some kind of a milestone.

Paul Girard, my host, worked on the docks at Quebec. He left the house in the early morning before I was awake and by the time I came home in the evening he had already eaten his evening meal and was rocking contentedly in the kitchen, filling the house with clouds of rank French-Canadian pipe smoke. At first he greeted my return with little more than a shy grunt, but within a week or two he would call out cordially as I climbed the stair, "Bonsoir, M'sieu Gray, bonsoir; entrez-dans, asseyez-vous." For a long time it seemed to me that Paul Girard had almost as little French as English, and since I had almost no French there were long gaps in our conversation.

Our talk, when it started, was like a chess game, with recognized opening gambits. M. Girard would open with, "Il faisait beau aujourd'hui." "Oui," I would reply carefully, "il faisait beau." After a couple of puffs at his pipe and a long, considering silence he would burst out with a kind of sigh of pure joy, "Il faisait tellement beau aujourd'hui, mon cher . . . " then words would fail him, the splendour of the day beyond recapture. "C'était magnifique," I would suggest. He would consider this and then say, "Justement, c'était magnifique. C'était tellement magnifique, mon vieux." Words failed again and he would push back the cap he invariably wore and scratch his head.

Sometimes these openings would be sufficient to launch him into a story, especially on Friday when he might have had a little beer, or on Saturday when he had had a lot. He would sit forward in his chair, pipe bowl gripped in his fist, and lowering his voice begin slowly, "Je me rappelle une fois moi . . . " It would be a story about hunting, or fishing, or politics. To his left front as he talked was a spittoon, which helped his punctuation, and to the right rear his black spaniel, Skidoo. The outdoor stories were enlarged with gestures and sound effects. He would slowly raise an imaginary shot-gun or deer-rifle and fire above the stove, or cast out a fly and we would wait for a tense moment until he got a bite; he would then lose the fish or reel him in to his own disgust or to chortles of satisfaction. "Tiens," he would say, and carefully removing the fish from his hook lay it on the kitchen floor. Occasionally these re-creations of the past were so real as to stir memories in the dozy old dog, who would come wiggling and wagging out from behind the chair, to be swept back by a slap on the snout as Paul Girard, his voice thick with excitement, shouted, "Oute-tway, Skidoo" and landed his fish.

Madame Girard, in the midst of getting my supper or washing up after it, would watch this performance, pausing in her work to fold her thick bare arms with a half-smile like an indulgent parent. If she thought he was getting too excited or noisy the smile would harden and she would quieten him with a word or two. He retreated growling like Skidoo, and with as little effect.

Madame was always a formidable figure, her sternness accentuated by the prominent bones that hardened her face; casual friendliness didn't come easily to her and the laughter and teasing of her nephews and nieces she tended to check very quickly when she thought it was going on too long or getting out of hand.

One morning during one of those tête-à-têtes that became a part of my breakfast she rushed into a sort of explanation — something that both amused and puzzled her. Standing at her sink, hands on hips, she began to talk about her childhood. She had never played as a child, didn't understand the pleasure children found in play, and wondered what she had missed. I believe that her mother died when she was very young and that her father married again; in any case she was left at the age of eight to look after younger brothers and sisters aged one, two, and four. There was no time or inclination for play. Life was serious and important and pressing.

When she was fifteen they all moved to Giffard to work in a match factory. The work day started at six in the morning and ended at six at night, winter and summer. For this, as the eldest, she earned 30¢ a day; the little boys of seven and eight earned 15¢. Every Sunday morning and afternoon in the year she walked two miles to Beauport Church and back — eight miles of walking on her day off.

In her harsh way I think she loved children, though she had none of her own. One morning with her eyes sparkling with an excitement I had never seen her show, she went to a hiding place and brought out six little pairs of pants for her half-sister's children. She had made over some of her husband's old clothes, but I wasn't to tell him, "parce qu'il n'aimerait pas ça." If life had made her hard, it had also made her very strong.

She was the manager of the family. She ordained that they should live in the upper half of their house and rent the lower. She received my rent money of seven dollars a week for bed, breakfast, and usually supper. She scolded me gently, but unmistakably, for opening my window at night because it cooled the house, and in her view was bad for health. She received Paul's pay packet and allowed him enough for a case of beer a week and a modest gamble at euchre with his friends. On Sunday mornings if I was up before they left for Mass I would share her husband's humiliation as he was cleaned up for the occasion. While he sat on a chair in the middle of the kitchen she would shave him, then briskly scrub his neck and ears. During this he sat with his pipe bowl clutched, a collar stud gleaming in his neck-band, and as his head was pushed around he kept up a steady rumble of protest like a rebellious small boy.

When I didn't waken until after Mass I had to emerge in my dressing-gown and hurry to the bathroom through a kitchen crowded with nephews, nieces, and friends finishing up the week-end case of beer. Sleepily, as I passed through the warm kitchen to the cold bathroom, I ran the gauntlet of remarks about the cold water. It had been reported in the village, though only half believed, that for lack of hot water I took a cold bath. My Lakefield training was in fact proving valuable, but on winter Sunday mornings in that freezing room it took all my Spartan background to step into that cold water and stay just long enough to rinse off the soap.

During the autumn on Sundays I played golf at the beautiful Kent House course above Montmorency Falls, but when winter arrived Sunday afternoon was given to hockey. Bébé Vachon, one of the Girard nephews, and I were playing for the village of Beauport, in a league that included teams all the way down river to Ste. Anne de Beaupré. Except for two or three young engineers who worked for the Ste. Anne paper company, I was the only person in the league whose first language was English. There was a good deal of English to be heard in our dressing-room, for the boys liked to practise their English as I did my French, and many English words associated with hockey had been adopted in Quebec. So people talked about *le goalkeeper, le puck,* and *mon pullover.*

Bébé and I changed into hockey gear at the Vachon house, then carrying our sticks and skates we piled into big sleighs. Buried under buffalo robes and to a jingle of sleigh bells we were carried along in the sunshine above the sparkling ice and snow of the St. Lawrence to St. Grégoire or Boischatel to find the whole village turned out for the game and excitement running high. I was the object of many a local war-cry — "Tue le Bleu" (kill the Conservative) — which was mostly good-natured fun. We played on natural ice in outdoor rinks and it was often bitterly cold, but I remember those games with a little surge of joy. There was the play itself and then the sitting around the Quebec heater in the warm dressing-room after the game, amid the smell of sweat and liniment, nursing a cup of coffee or chocolate or occasionally beer, and singing to salute someone who had done well, "Il a gagné ses épaulettes". Once or twice I received the salute and felt enough happiness flooding over me to ease all bruises.

But one Sunday was tragically different. As I went through

the kitchen in the morning I was conscious of the quiet. People were as always polite, but more subdued, and one or two of the girls had been crying. When they left early Mme Girard explained as she gave me lunch. One of the little Vachon brothers, René, aged I think ten or eleven, had been watching some hockey the day before and had heckled one of the bigger players into a rage. The older boy in a blind moment had thrown his stick or slashed at young René and broken bones around one eye. It was believed the injury was serious, but how serious was not yet known.

Having had no chance to alter arrangements I went to the Vachons' to change, though I disliked intruding. Marie-Ange Vachon answered the door, and took me in to see René, whimpering and twisting in his bed; the terrible injury surrounded the eye and disfigured what had been a bright and laughing face. As Bébé and I changed almost in silence, there was a cry from downstairs, followed by other voices and more cries. Bébé went to find the reason and came back looking stunned. The doctor had come and given his verdict: René would probably not live many hours but should he survive his brain would be permanently damaged. Ambulances and even hospitals were not readily available at the time and René could only be left to suffer and die in his own rumpled bed.

Quietly Bébé took off his hockey gear and put on his clothes. There was no need to explain, though he did. It would worry and upset his family more if he played that day. As I went out the Vachon girls tried to persuade me too to give up today's game; I would be killed. But with Bébé not playing I was needed, so I went to the game though in no mood to play.

We won the game, joylessly for all of us — for everyone knew about little René. Afterwards I returned and changed as quietly and quickly as possible. Wishing to slip out unobtrusively I took the open stairs down to the big kitchen, but I had gone the wrong way. There the whole family sat around a long table, silently making a pretence of eating; the lamps on the table shed only a dim light on the scene of deep sadness. It was too late to retreat and I could only say lamely, "Excusez." From the head of the table Mme Vachon dashed away a tear with the back of her hand and said in a firm voice, "Viens donc, M'sieu Gray, à souper avec nous autres" — come and have supper with us? For a moment I doubted my understanding of the French words; so unfailing a courtesy and dignity, in spite of so much sorrow! My French was hardly equal to the occasion. I thanked her humbly and perhaps clumsily, then saying I had to go in to Quebec I bade them good-night and hurried out.

Mercifully René died the next day, but there was one gratuitous horror reserved for the family. It had been a winter of deep snow and as the horses bucked and struggled up a little hill to the cemetery, the hearse carrying René to his grave overturned. The coffin was shot through the glass wall of the hearse and burst open, flinging René's body out in the snow. For the final stage of the journey into the cemetery the small body was carried on the knees of his father and uncles in a light sleigh.

There was much about these tragic events and attitudes in the people I worked with to make me aware of the influence of religion on their lives. Not that we talked about religion — "don't discuss religion or politics, it will only make trouble" had been my father's parting injunction — but it was so large and ever-present a factor to them that they seemed challenged to find out where I stood on these things. So far as they could see I never went to church, and indeed I went seldom in Quebec. Mme Girard, who acted as a kind of policeman to her whole family — scolding the girls sharply when they rebelled against a recent edict forbidding dancing and skating with boys — clearly worried about me.

As I ate my breakfast at the kitchen table, and her short tub of a figure moved around the sink, or the stove she was always stoking or polishing, she would pause and lead off with a question about "your church". Controversy at breakfast has never appealed to me and my natural inclination, reinforced by my limited French, must have made these occasions very unsatisfactory for her. She would give up in the face of the fumbling half-answers, clearly gathering her resources for another day.

In her, religion produced, when needed, comfort and a degree of resignation that seemed to me close to a supine fatalism. These things are stronger than we are — "c'est plus fort que nous, n'est-ce pas?" she would say, of grief over René and equally of fear of the dentist. But it was never used to justify idleness or waste. She cooked and cleaned and made do endlessly. In a little room off the kitchen she ran a kind of small dressmaker's-supply shop, but if a neighbour dropped in for a spool of thread and a chat, she was served the thread and had to carry on the chat against the clatter of Mme Girard's housework.

Part of this included the endless dusting of a stiff and shiny little parlour that was seldom used. I had to go through it to my bedroom, and for the first two or three mornings my breakfast had been served there. But once I had persuaded Mme Girard that I preferred the kitchen with its warmth and its friendly smells, the parlour returned to being a chilly passageway. I only sat in it one other time, to be inspected by the village priest. M. le curé's care of his flock included a look at all strangers in the village, and I suppose especially Protestants. He came for a stiff and over-hearty chat, an inquiry for my brother, and some general questions about my work at Legaré's. Paul Girard sat cleaned up and cowed. His wife, rigid as a sergeant-major, her dress blacker than ever, had her hair tightly drawn back in a bun that exposed her large, strong, and unsmiling features. She clearly regarded the visit as an opportunity for an interim report to the Almighty, and she didn't intend any careless answers to spoil the record. In a few minutes it was over, and after spraying a handful of religious medals across the table M. le curé stood up briskly. "Come and see me," he shouted at me in English with his almost overpowering heartiness, "I have some good ceegaars." Even as the curé went down the stairs Paul's confidence returned. He indulged in little bobbing bows, and touched his forelock as he repeated with mock humility "Bonsoir, M. le curé," "Plaisir vous voir, M. le curé," "A bientọt, M. le cure." For once Mme Girard's icy control failed her. "Arrêt, Paul," she said in a dangerously quiet voice and he slunk back to his rocking chair, growling. It was doubtless bad enough that he should behave like this; that it should happen in front of me was I am sure intolerable.

I never went to the curé's for a cigar, merely paying him a farewell visit when I left the village in the spring, but we occasionally met on the road for a cordial greeting. One such time I was waiting for my morning tram into the city when M. le curé approached. As we stood chatting and stamping our feet in the cold early-morning air, a line of sleighs came by. They were carrying cord-wood and hay and sacks of root vegetables, and each sent up little jets of vapour from the nostrils of the horses and of the men who walked beside them. Each man touched his tuque or cap to the curé, and, though there seemed to me no warmth and some surliness in their greetings, he called each man by name: "Bonjour Henri", "Bonjour Armand", "Bonjour Michel". As the line slowly went by, the curé said to me in English, "We don't like our people going into the city like this — Bonjour Jules — it gives them ideas; it unsettles them. But — " he spread his arms and shrugged, "they must earn their living — il faut vivre, n'est-ce pas? Bonjour Claude." The scene came back to me months later when I was telling my father that Quebec was changing, that the young people were questioning the authority of the church. "Yes," he said with a shrug like M. le curé's, "it was changing when I was a young man."

The boys in the store were as curious as Mme Girard about what sort of religion I practised, and when. But after a while the slightly loaded questions and the oblique references stopped, though I had a continuing sense of being under friendly observation. On one occasion when an undressed statuette had been placed in the shop window a passing priest stepped in the door and curtly ordered it removed. Someone attempted, mildly, to argue the point — this was art — but the objection was overruled peremptorily: remove it, at once — and it was removed. The boys, between irritation and amusement, watched and even asked about my reaction. Would such a thing happen in Ontario? I said probably not. Well, what did I think of it happening in Quebec? I grinned and shrugged.

Only twice was I drawn onto controversial ground; once

when I was taken to Paul Lachance's boarding-house for supper and a poker game. While he washed and changed his shirt I thumbed over a book from his shelves. As I paused over a picture of Voltaire, I realized he had come to look over my shoulder. "That's a bad man," he said in English and added with a comfortable chuckle, "I am pretty sure he is roasting in the Hell, now." I asked why, and he ran off a list of bad men, Diderot, Rousseau, and others, who had destroyed the church in France, brought on the Revolution, and ruined the country. He said they were all "fremasons". I didn't understand the term and had him repeat it several times. And then it dawned on me: they were Freemasons. "But Masons aren't bad men," I said incautiously, "my father is a Mason." Undoubtedly in the circumstances it was a shocking declaration, and as I made it I realized I knew nothing about what the Masons stood for, and nothing of their history. Paul said courteously that he was sure my father was not a bad man and, if I said so, not anti-Catholic, but nothing would shake his opinion of Masons in general — a bad and dangerous lot. We let the argument go with slightly ruffled feathers on both sides.

A few weeks later before morning opening in the shop we stood gossiping and joking in a group. My particular friend, Gustave Beaulieu, had just had news of the birth of a new baby brother and was strutting a bit. He was a loose-jointed, still clumsy, and endlessly good-natured boy who liked to march up and down like a soldier with his broom at the slope saying gaily in English, "I am Beaulieu, it is a fine place I am, eh Jack?" In return I called him Beau Geste. This morning he announced that the new baby was the nineteenth in the family, of whom eleven were still living. The group seemed to share his pride and approval of these statistics, and I said nothing until he challenged me directly in French. What did I think of that, he asked, was it not a fine family, nineteen children and eleven still living?

The size of French-Canadian families — the revenge of the cradle — had always horrified Ontario people, and some slumbering irritation or hostility burst out. I said I could never agree that such a big family was a good idea; it wasn't healthy for mother or children, and only a rich man could feed or educate so many children properly. I ran out of words and we all stood embarrassed. Then Beau Geste said very gently, "Listen, Jack, we work for our country — on travaille pour la patrie — if there should be a war . . . " He opened his arms expressively. Fearing that the harsh and bitter Ontario answer would come back quickly, that Quebec had not been eager to provide its sons in the last war, I backed away from the gap in viewpoint that separated us. I patted him on the shoulder — "Anyway, you're a fine place," I said, and we all laughed and the difficult moment was passed.

With the end of winter my time in Quebec was also ending, and perhaps it was just as well. I was coming to know too many people, making too many friends, and falling back into the too-familiar pattern of too many activities and too much fun. Some of my first fine earnestness about the work was being lost. In addition to Beauport on Sundays I was playing hockey for Legaré's in the Ligue Commerciale in the evenings; and since I was the only one from the store on the company team, this earned me some distinction and some privileges — the right to leave early occasionally and sometimes to arrive late. The members of the Fortier family who ran Legaré's had been kind and hospitable, and with some of the younger ones there were frequent parties and late hours. And I had made a number of English-speaking friends who were a wild lot. The one orderly point in my life was provided by the Basil Carters, an old Quebec family and friends since Lakefield days. With them there was always good talk, often Sunday-night supper, and — greatest blessing of all — a hot bath; they were the embodiment of peace, order, and good government. But my French and English friends lived in separate worlds and seemed to assume it would always be so.

A few days before my time to leave I witnessed a small historic event. It was the period of feverish and often ill-prepared attempts to fly the Atlantic — stimulated by Lindbergh's success. But the east-west flights into prevailing winds were still being beaten back, with some tragic results. One such attempt had just ended in a crash landing somewhere on the Labrador coast or in the Gulf of St. Lawrence. After some delay the survivors were brought to Quebec, one of them, an American, dangerously ill with pneumonia.

Somehow I heard that Lindbergh was going to fly from New York to Quebec with a special serum for the pneumonia case. It was a last-minute emergency decision and, perhaps fortunately, not widely known. Quebec had no airport at the time; there were only the historic Plains of Abraham, still partially covered with snow. A number of us made our way out the Chemin Ste. Foy, not knowing what to expect, or when. For an hour or so in the raw overcast afternoon we stood around the edge of the field watching the sky. And then, without warning, incredulously, we saw a small speck in the distance. The idea of long-distance flying was still strange, a near-miracle, to most people in 1928; and this emergency flight from New York was high drama. The two or three hundred spectators were herded back as the speck became unquestionably a plane. It circled the field and landed, then taxied toward us and stopped. A tall young man in the cockpit stood up, just as we had seen him do in a thousand pictures. He peeled off his flying helmet, and it was indeed Charles Lindbergh. We saw the famous shy smile as he waved and climbed down, and then was hurried to a waiting car and to the hospital.

My own farewells were undramatic but had a kind of desperate sadness. I was already learning that experiences can't be repeated or friendships picked up just where they were left. No one in English-speaking Canada would ever hear me speak of Quebec except with affection and respect, but neither could I return to the particular mood and happy relationships I had enjoyed. I said an affectionate and sad farewell to my friends in Giffard, had a last beer with the Beauport team, and made the round of the people at the store. We had laughed a lot together, worked long hours, helping each other out, and now it was finished. I shook hands all round, and openly kissed the girls from whom I had for weeks — with some co-operation —

snatched kisses behind the larger pieces of furniture. Everyone asserted that I now spoke French well — "Vous parlez couramment; parlez comme nous autres." Though I knew it was not remotely true, I had learned a lot, regained a little confidence, and enjoyed it all.

Beau Geste followed me to the front door as I left; he had for the moment lost his coltish high spirits and was suddenly shy. We made a little lame conversation. And then he blurted out a declaration. He had a romantic notion of the places I would travel to and the things I would see. When you need a man, he said, just to stand by you and help out — "C'est moi. Je serais ton homme. N'importe quand, n'importe d'où. Compte sur moi." It was a kind of swearing of fealty, and the generosity of it left me unable to respond. He waved away my embarrassment and choked thanks with little chopping motions of his hands. "C'est tout," he kept saying, "c'est tout. Quand tu as besoin d'un homme." He seemed to be offering to be Planchet to my D'Artagnan, but we were three hundred years too late. We shook hands for the last time and I turned away.

❧ 6 ❧

I N JUNE THAT YEAR Bob and I with Jim Little, a friend from
Lakefield days, sailed for England, which suggested that I
was the rich and pampered young man my friends in the
store believed me to be. But it was just my father being
consistent; better do these things, see the world a bit, before you
settle down (not that I had shown much sign of settling). Bob
and I had been left $1,000 each by Grandmother Gray — for
education or travel. One could do a lot in 1928 with $1,000,
and we intended to do it all. We sailed from Montreal and once
again I found myself at, though not in, Quebec. Our ship lay
out in the stream facing the city. To complete my frustration I
could see the twin spires of the Beauport church, and almost
imagine I could pick out the houses of the Vachons and the
Girards, while nearby a Cunard junior officer talked nonsense
about *my* Quebec for the benefit of the American tourists.

My last ocean crossing had been at the age of nine and had a
different kind of joy and magic about it. Now, travelling Tour-
ist, we were surrounded by young people, including a number
of attractive girls. Two days out I had fallen in love again more
gloriously and desperately and briefly than ever, and five days
out we celebrated my twenty-first birthday; a trip to remember
and yet I remember little, except that it was a happy time.

And so were the weeks that followed. Pooling our resources
we bought a car and toured England and Scotland, seeing the
things tourists had been seeing for a thousand years, and making the same penetrating comments. We were solemn but we

were learning more than we knew. Then we crossed to France and drove through Belgium to Amsterdam where the Olympic Games were in progress. I was to see it all again one day: Arnhem as a smashed city, the great bridge at Nijmegen, damaged and under constant fire. Now we rolled through it all happily, ignorant of the future. But crossing the German border at Cleves the shadow of an earlier war hung over us; we suddenly remembered it: it was August 4. Many of the people round us in the hotel had been enemies ten years ago.

A week later after travelling up the Rhine we had come through Metz and Verdun to Paris. That evening in a Montparnasse bar a Dutch student said I must be very proud of Canada's showing at the Olympic Games. Having not seen a newspaper in English for ten days I merely looked blank. Did I not know, was it possible I hadn't heard, that Canada had won the two classic sprints, the 100-metre dash and the 220? At first I thought he must be wrong, must have confused Canada and the States, as so many Europeans did. But no, he was sure — a young man called Percy Williams, whose name I didn't even know, had won two of the world's most prized gold medals. He appealed to someone else for confirmation while I held my happiness under control. (Earl Thompson had won the hurdles for Canada in 1924, but he had been a Canadian student in an American college, so it hadn't seemed to count fully.) But the wonderful news was confirmed and I hurried off in wild excitement to find Bob and Jim, to spread the great news.

Was it just a schoolboy enthusiasm in one who was supposed now to be a man? But Bob and Jim, both more moderate and orderly characters, were equally delighted and proud. Was it just a Canadian reaction of the period? We were proud of being Canadians but we didn't really expect our fellow countrymen to do well on the world stage, except on the hockey rink and the battlefield.

But in a first encounter with Paris, ideas about nationalism and inferiority complex couldn't hold my attention for long. Besides, the object of my great shipboard romance was in Paris, and abstract ideas were a vanishing miasma; this was what mattered. She was from Wisconsin, a devout Roman Catholic and slightly older than I. We agreed this was all too much for us (without even needing to mention that I had no job and, when the $1,000 was gone, no money). We must go our different ways. Meanwhile we clung together, feeling as desperate as Romeo and Juliet, and did all the sweet, romantic things that made up our generation's view of Paris. We ate onion soup late at night in the market of Les Halles and — she with an armful of roses — we leaned on the parapet of Henry IV's bridge over the Seine and watched the sun rise along the river and set Notre Dame glowing with delicate fire. We pressed money into the hand of a derelict huddled in a doorway and wandered home exhausted through the still-sleeping streets of the Left Bank. I dutifully left her at the door of her pension and plodded back to my hotel filled with a sense of the unbearable sadness of life.

A few days later, with a breaking heart, and a slight puzzling sense of relief, I saw her off on the boat-train for Cherbourg; and a few weeks later I had a letter telling me she was about to be married — to the boy next door. For the moment I chose to forget the relief and felt only injury and desolation. The faithlessness of women!

One evening I went into an American bar near the Luxembourg. It was pleasant and relaxed, like hundreds of such bars in Paris. Some people sat at the bar, a few couples at tables with red checked table-cloths, drinking wine or beer or Pernod and talking with a kind of relaxed intensity; though it was almost as comfortable as an English pub it also managed to feel exotic. At the opposite end of the bar a tall dark young man with a moustache was shaking dice with the barman as they chatted together in English.

Perhaps taking pity on my apparent loneliness — though I was quite happy, exultant, seeing life — he moved down the bar to me and struck up a conversation. Almost at once he asked whether I had read *The Sun Also Rises*. I hadn't, and he said most Americans who came to Paris these days had. A little bristly, I said I wasn't an American, I was a Canadian. His look said, "So what?" "I thought if you had read it," he said, "you might be interested to know that the dame over at that table is the dame in the book, Lady Brett. The guy with her — the guy in the pink shirt — isn't the guy in the book, he's another guy." I stole a furtive look. (Boy, was this ever life!) The look was a little disappointing, but I had no trouble believing that Lady Brett's air of weary sophistication covered enchanting mysteries.

And the tall dark young man who pointed her out, was it Hemingway? I didn't wonder then, but I did later.

By late autumn I was alone in a London streaming with rain. Jim Little was the first to go, back to university and the fraternity house, and I found I did not envy him. Nor, a few weeks later, did I envy Bob going home to "settle down"; only, with his going I was swept by a wave of loneliness, of homesickness. He would be home for Christmas. I could almost hear the train thundering into Cornwall station, and see my mother and father with little Joan in her bunny coat coming towards us along the platform through a light sparkle of falling snow. I was staying to confront London and Fleet Street; in fact to face squarely for the first time my glibly declared intention of becoming a writer. Unless I had some success and earned some money the confrontation would not last long, but for the moment the prospect was so exciting as to quench my homesickness almost as I walked away from the station.

As yet I had nothing to show in Fleet Street, but I went there often just to read the famous names and be jostled by presumably famous people. To sit in a pub or coffee-house and listen to snatches of newspaper shop-talk produced an illusion of having arrived, of beginning my real life. To be among writers seemed in my mood of innocent intoxication almost as good, indeed almost the same, as being a writer.

And for the first time in my life I settled down and tried seriously to write. An elderly Scots couple, Mr. and Mrs. Seton, had taken me in as a paying guest; their daughter, Mary, had married a neighbour of ours from Cornwall, John Relyea, who was now running a steel mill in Lincolnshire. Mr. Seton in his younger days had been a very successful business man, and before that in Edinburgh had shared the interests of a lively group of writers, artists, and booksellers. The prosperity was all gone now and he seldom made even a passing reference to it; but he loved to talk about books and bookmen, to declaim Shakespeare, to recite scenes from Dickens, and to talk about old London. We spent many evenings in front of the fire in their living-room, where I had usually spent the morning, and sometimes the afternoon, writing.

Mr. Seton's practical help included introducing me to a working journalist called Malcolm Mackenzie, who undertook to take me to various offices in Fleet Street, "where they will be glad to have your stuff." That airy statement was consistent with the style of one of the oddest characters I was ever to meet. Mackenzie, always hinting at his great connections, his adventurous past, and the important events he was superintending, looked like a slightly seedy impostor, often amusing, seldom to be relied on. And yet he was genuinely kind to me, and did open some doors as promised. It was not his fault that nothing came of it; I had nothing the people inside wanted.

We met first for lunch with Mr. Seton at Gough's Chop-House in the Strand. Mackenzie arrived late, with sketchy explanations and apologies, wearing an ancient frock-coat and top hat and twirling an umbrella. A small moustache suggested the old soldier, and he was always quick to suggest an interesting, if somewhat mysterious, war career; it was indicated as "special service" after a severe wound on the Western Front in 1914, inevitably serving with "the Guards". Almost any remark could launch Mackenzie on a fabulous story: "I was once waiting at a small railway station in the mountains of, shall we say, Eastern Europe, when the station porter shuffled up to me and slid a piece of paper into my hand. When the westbound express roared through the station a few minutes later I went with it, clinging to the footboard. I was hauled into a compartment, more dead than alive, and came around to find myself looking at one of the most beautiful women I have ever seen." He would pause there, and add, "What a story that would make if only I were free to tell it." He was always trailing these brightly coloured bits of his career, and I found them dazzling at first. But by the time I had heard him tell that story, that way, to that cut-off, three times, I had come to suspect the whole performance, though I continued to enjoy it.

Another story concerned his being sent by his editor to interview the French Foreign Secretary, who was on a quick visit to London to discuss disarmament. Briand (or Poincaré?) was to meet the Press briefly before going to Downing Street. On arrival at the French Minister's hotel Mackenzie was directed to a room where the Gentlemen of the Press were waiting. He went to the open door of the room and announced to the assembled newsmen (who didn't know him since he had just returned from Eastern Europe), "His Excellency will be here directly, gentlemen," closed the door, and waited in the corridor. Presently Briand appeared, hurrying down the hall nervously fussing with his gloves. Mackenzie stepped forward and said, "Your car is waiting, Your Excellency," and led the way out to the car, into which he also climbed. He interviewed the captured lion all the way to Downing Street, then hurried back to his paper to recount his triumph. His editor interrupted briskly to ask, "Where does he stand on disarmament?" Mackenzie would pause dramatically in his story: "Do you know I had forgotten to ask him. But I said firmly that he endorsed it, and we wrote the lead story that way." Again the pause, and a little laugh, "I was right, but it isn't a chance I would care to take now."

On one occasion he brought this remarkable style to my rescue. We were gossiping in a Fleet Street office with a magazine editor and a Captain Broadhurst, who had just won a bet by living for several weeks on very little money, and had moved around England from job to job to prove there was work available if the unemployed cared to bestir themselves. He was a small seven-day wonder, but seemed more impressed with what he had proved than I was. He was now in process of selling his story and, full of triumph, announced that he now understood the criminal mentality; having been hungry and cold he knew

118

how men came to steal and commit murder. This seemed to me posturing nonsense, and I was embarrassed to hear myself, hoarse with nervousness, saying that surely it wasn't as easy as that. I had been a hobo and hungry and cold and very dirty and frightened, but never dreamed of theft or murder; always knowing — as I suggested Broadhurst did — that a phone call would produce cleanliness and comfort. There was an embarrassed silence. Broadhurst stopped twirling his monocle round his finger and it hung limp as we all stared at each other. Mackenzie's clear, high voice cut across the silence. "You must remind me," he said to me, "to tell you about the time I stole the Austrian battleship."

I had been granted a little bonus for the months in London. A young man with whom I had fallen into talk over coffee at Les Deux Magots one morning in Paris became a guide to the London theatres. He was an American, Jimmie Dyrenforth, who had already had a musical comedy running briefly in the West End and he seemed to know everyone in theatre. Later, in London, we had dinner together and went to a play once a month, and afterwards went backstage to meet Marie Tempest and Marie Lohr, to have a drink with Jack Buchanan, and to shake hands with others who were charming the West End at the time. I came to realize that Jimmie didn't really know these people well but was trading on a nodding acquaintance and some trumped-up reason for our visit, but if I was embarrassed I was also delighted to be there. One day Jimmie proposed lunch with a young publishing friend of his and we went to collect the young man at a publishing office in Vigo Street, the Bodley Head. We had a fine lunch, though whether the food was good I have no idea; I listened enthralled to book talk. Jimmie's friend's name was Alan Lane and I wasn't to hear it again until he emerged as the founder of Penguin Books, a venture that was to change the publishing world and the reading habits of an age.

These fascinating weeks were coming to an end, though I didn't know it. The long hours at the Setons' living-room table had produced nothing salable, and indeed nothing good. Perhaps I was learning something about writing, but the evidence suggested I could not yet write or had nothing to say. In this mood of some frustration I heard that anyone who could play hockey well might find opportunities for travel in Europe. I sent home for my skates and equipment and presently my mornings were given to writing and my afternoons to hockey. I was signed to play for a team called United Services. Most of my team-mates were Canadians in the British Army or the Royal Air Force, and I was said to belong in that group on the basis of having a provisional commission in the Stormont, Dundas and Glengarry Highlanders in Canada. I was a fair hockey player in Canada but at that moment in England I had the superiority of the one-eyed man in the kingdom of the blind. When a team from our league was chosen to represent England on a European tour, I was picked to play left wing. There was just time to accompany the Setons north to spend Christmas with the Relyeas in Lincolnshire with enough carols, mince pies, and hot punch to help ward off thoughts of Christmas in Canada.

Two days later I joined the team in London and we set off for Chamonix in the French Alps. It was the first leg in a gilded odyssey; great fun but less than great hockey. Everywhere we were told that we were the best hockey team people had seen since the Canadians — meaning my friends, the Varsity Grads, whose picture was to be seen in many rinks. We were made too much of, wined and dined and asked for our autographs. It was nice to be treated as heroes but we hardly played like supermen. After Chamonix we had two glittering weeks in St. Moritz, where we behaved like members of what would now be called the Jet Set. We rubbed shoulders nightly, as we danced or gambled, with Michael Arlen, the Dolly Sisters, Gene Tunney, the World Heavyweight Champion, and assorted aristocrats — less impressive than their titles. The Oxford and Cambridge teams joined us in St. Moritz for games, Oxford captained by Clarence Campbell (later to be President of the National Hockey League, but then a rather awkward if gutsy and rough player). We moved on our triumphant way, feted and over-praised for our light-hearted brand of hockey; kings for a day in Innsbruck, Milan, Prague, Vienna, and Budapest. In this joyous and ultimately foolish carnival I had reverted to the playboy role of my university days.

At Budapest we turned back and travelled to Ostend; catching up on our sleep except when interrupted by customs and immigration officers at successive border points. As we crossed to Folkestone and returned to the grey skies of London, I prepared to get back to my writing. But on top of my mail at the Setons' was a cable offering me a job as junior master at Lakefield. My father, who had forwarded the offer, had added that he thought newspaper work in London better experience. But of course I hadn't been doing newspaper work; I had been hanging rapturously on the fringe, pretending that aroma was substance. I had overspent my money, and wasted some of my father's at the gambling tables of the Kulm and Palace hotels in St. Moritz.

The offer of a job, however modest, caught me in a mood of guilt. I had a return ticket to Canada, and a letter of introduction to Lord Beaverbrook that I had carried for weeks and been reluctant to present. What to do? For two agonizing days I walked the streets of London, leaned on the parapet of Waterloo Bridge and gazed at the Thames, feeling that this was a fateful moment. If I turned in my ticket I might live quietly for some months on the proceeds. Meanwhile I could swallow my pride and go to see Lord Beaverbrook and perhaps get a job, and a start. But if that led anywhere it led to living in England, and I knew now that, though I loved London, I wanted to live in Canada. Moodily I plodded down Fleet Street and ran into Malcolm Mackenzie, who had a streaming cold, "beed sleepi'g with a dap woban" he explained airily, waved, and went on. I never saw him again.

Walking the streets I made my decision: I would go back. As a schoolmaster I would have time to read, to begin to make good some of the great gaps in my education of which my travels had made me more conscious than ever. In the long holiday periods — so my dream ran — I would write. Meanwhile, once again the round of farewells and sad leave-takings, just as in Quebec the year before. I had a fine collection of rejection slips, a lot of experience, and happy memories, but apparently nothing accomplished.

Perhaps it was these solemn reflections that held me when, at the last minute, I was tempted to change my mind; once by the offer of a job at what seemed a lot of money and once to join another hockey tour of Europe being arranged by Clarence Campbell. He was gathering a picked team of the Canadians who were doing graduate work or coaching hockey all over Europe. I was to be left wing on a team with the resounding title of the European Canadians. For a moment the call of hockey, of all that glamour and fun, rocked my judgement. But I had decided, had sent my cable accepting, and perhaps I had also matured a little; gratefully and with regret I said no and caught my boat-train.

The trip home suggested that I had not entirely matured. A cigarette end which happened to touch a child's balloon during a solo almost ruined the ship's concert. The noise from the exploding balloon was nothing compared to that from the child, who lacked a sense of humour. So did the ship's captain who, very red in the face, shook an admonishing finger at us.

Once again I was to land at Halifax, and only as we landed did it occur to me that I might be assessed heavy duty on all I had bought in nine months away: clothes, gifts, and a trunkful of books — one of them inscribed, with my perpetual playfulness, "From John M. Gray to himself as a farewell gift, and as a token of esteem shared by few". I had no money for duty, indeed I had borrowed ten dollars from a Montreal schoolteacher on shipboard to pay for my meals on the train.

I faced the customs officer apprehensively and threw open my trunk. There, on the top, tossed in at the last minute, was a group of hockey pictures from all over Europe. He pounced on them. When were they taken, and where? He called one of his fellow officers, who left an old lady sitting in the ruins of her open baggage. The two went over the pictures with questions and exclamations. It came out that someone I had played with in Quebec the year before was now playing in Halifax. Regretfully the customs men remembered work and gave up hockey talk. One returned to the old lady as the other chalked my luggage without examination and shook hands very warmly. Clearly, I was home — and home free.

I was not well qualified to be a schoolmaster but inevitably, as the junior, I was handed everything no colleague wanted or had room for in his time-table. So I found myself teaching beginners' reading, and on up through every age and grade doing some arithmetic, Latin (my old bugbear), geometry, English composition, and modern history. The reading time I had counted on was swallowed in my frantic efforts to educate myself for my job, and to keep ahead of the class. And in spite of my disabilities I enjoyed it all. I found that I liked teaching and seemed to have some aptitude for it (if only I knew enough!), and I enjoyed my colleagues. It was not a powerfully intellectual community, but it was stimulating and civilized. Against the background of a harsh and beautiful countryside we were isolated. Television lay in the future and even radio was not far advanced; there were few cars and primitive roads. Life was quieter and more orderly than I had known it for years; it was even a little dull, and for the moment that was delicious. Since I had not arrived until March, the June closing came along altogether too soon.

For two months that summer I worked as a reporter on the *Evening Telegram* in Toronto. I checked daily prices at the fruit market and endured the wrath of busy men ("Look, kid, I'm goddam busy"); I checked police stations for news of crime and covered inquests at the morgue. Trying to live up to the stereotype of a big-time reporter I was torn between hoping I would uncover a crime ring and hoping I wouldn't. At times it seemed to me I could almost hear the city's heart beat, but having come close to what I thought was the core of a mystery I had been trying to penetrate — the writing world — I knew that this was not it. The more senior newsmen were at once cynical and capable, but just behind them marched the army of the tired, untidy, nicotine-stained support troops drifting towards middle age. Over coffee, in which they seemed permanently steeped, they talked unconvincingly about books they planned to write — and had planned, it came out, for years. But in spite of this chilling of my hopes I enjoyed it all and still believed it was in the direction I must go. Perhaps there was not a mystery, only a surround, a corral of letters, of which the newspaper world was a part.

When the summer ended I went to say good-bye to the Managing Editor — C. H. J. Snider. He was a genial, chatty man who had managed to make his hobbies — sailing and Great Lakes naval history — serve his paper, and had also published several books. I had reported to him on my arrival at the paper but had not seen him since. Beaming through his heavy-rimmed glasses, head cocked on one side, Jerry Snider asked how I had liked the work. I answered very much, tremendously. Would I like to stay on? The question floored me; I had been taken on as a temporary and for a very short term. I tried to express appreciation while I explained that I was committed to returning to Lakefield for the school year, that I couldn't back out now. He nodded understandingly. But did I think I wanted to be a newspaper man? Yes, yes. Very well, he said, when your year's commitment is discharged come back, and we'll take you on permanently. It was what I had thought I most wanted, and yet even as I thanked him warmly and walked out, I wondered. Was it to this that I wanted to settle down? Or was this perhaps another ostrich egg?

I was to circle around the question continuously in the months ahead. At twenty-two (going on twenty-three as my inner consciousness reminded me) it was time to stop this aimless darting about. Often the idea of going on with teaching was alluring. Sometimes a teacher of a residential school had rare opportunities for eavesdropping on small boys' expression of hopes and dreams that were perhaps not always granted to their parents; walking home in a group late and tired from a long hike, or in the pause with a hand on the switch at lights-out. Little troublesome questions would tumble out, or odd childish boasts,

and one was conscious of the listening group, the hunger for answers. There were questions about God and kings, about riches
and poverty, about life and death. Thomas Gray had cried out
in an agony over the blind innocence of youth, "Oh, tell them
they are men," and the impulse to stay, to try to help the grow-
ing-up process in these attractive children, was sometimes very
strong. But even if I had the temerity to think I knew enough
on my foolish performance to date, my horizon as a teacher was
severely limited. Lakefield would have me for a time, perhaps
indefinitely, but who else? I could go on doing what I was doing, as long as I could do it well: teaching kids games and
woodcraft — to swim and to paddle a canoe and use an axe —
reading aloud or telling stories; half big brother, half nanny.
But when they were older, or I was past enjoying it? I had seen
a number of schoolmasters for whom teaching was no longer a
pleasure, who were exhausted or hideously bored. Of course, if
I had a degree! I considered rather seriously working for my
degree through university extension courses; with a degree I
could at least move around, would have options where now I
had none. But my earlier failures were too freshly remembered
for me to have confidence in the outcome of so lonely and ardu-
ous a venture.

Meanwhile the year went happily along. Between coaching
and playing games (I had graduated from playing hockey for
England to playing it for Lakefield in the Intermediate OHA —
much less glamorous, but more vigorous), with the quieter moments going to teaching and reading, it was hard to believe
that I could be more contented. Perhaps it was all made more
precious by an inner certainty that it couldn't last long. I had a
few close and congenial friends on the staff, equally happy
when talking about great questions or school shop or nonsense.
This was the core of the school's life for me; but, though the
school had become bigger since I was a boy, it was still enclosed
by the wisdom of the Headmaster, now Dr. Mackenzie, and the
affectionate interest of his family. Beyond them was an outer
ring of people attached to the school and living in the Lakefield
area. Many of them were descended from that little group of

misplaced but gifted gentle-folk who had come to settle in the area and clear the bush a century before, the Strickland sisters (Susanna Moodie, Catherine Parr Traill, and Frances Stewart), together with their brother (who was still referred to as "old Colonel Strickland").

Into this tranquil pool, late in the winter of 1929-30, dropped a most unlikely pebble. At St. Moritz more than a year before I had become friends with a young Englishman, Lee Whitefield, recently graduated from Oxford. To him and a score of others I had given my address, saying the usual "If you ever come to Canada . . . ", that casual gesture that seldom results in anything and is seldom meant to. Now Lee wrote that he was coming to Toronto and would like to renew acquaintance. He said he had no idea where Lakefield was, but if we moved towards each other on an agreed date "we ought to meet before the pubs close."

I invited him for a week-end, and in due course he came, outwardly confident to the point of cockiness, and throwing away lines that sounded important to me. "I'm staying with my brother-in-law in Toronto . . . he is head of Macmillans in Canada." "You ought to go into publishing, suit you, just your cup of tea." It turned out that Hugh Eayrs, President of Macmillans in Canada, was Lee's brother-in-law-to-be, and that Lee knew no more of publishing and who was suited to it than I did. And yet — I think he was right.

On his return to Toronto Lee wrote suggesting that I spend Easter holidays there; we would have some fun, he said, and I could meet Hugh Eayrs. I don't know how seriously I took all this talk about publishing as a career, but it intrigued me. All I knew about publishing was that it involved working with books in some way, and that of itself was very attractive. So when I met the President of Macmillans I was on tiptoe, prepared to be charmed and impressed, and I was both. Hugh Eayrs in 1930 was thirty-six and had already been head of Macmillans for almost ten years. He was short, fair-haired, and on the way to being stout, with just a hint of Yorkshire in his speech, and more than a hint of confidence and authority in his manner.

He was one of the quickest and most entertaining men I have ever met, and though I was inevitably to see less attractive sides of him — and to meet people who had nothing good to say about him — those first brilliant impressions remain with me, and seem valid. During my stay in Toronto we met only socially, playing bridge and talking during a couple of evenings. I was conscious of being drawn out agreeably and tried to respond. I still knew nothing about publishing and I thought publishing knew nothing about me, but Lee assured me that Hugh Eayrs was going to offer me a job. The explanation was at once simple and mysterious: "He likes the way you play bridge," he said. Even to my inexperienced eye there seemed limitations to this method of personnel selection.

Back at school I waited uncertainly. Some weeks before, I had told Dr. Mackenzie that I would be leaving at the end of the school year, though with much regret. He had offered an increase and said some flattering things about me as a teacher; he had bolstered my confidence but in the end agreed with my reasons for leaving. So now I seemed to have two options, which I stretched to three: I might have a job at Macmillans; if Jerry Snider hadn't forgotten, I had a job at the *Telegram*. My third option was to take off and try to work my way around the world; this last had grown out of reading Joseph Conrad, inspired by my colleague Tom Wood.

Into this uncertainty dropped a letter from Hugh Eayrs asking me to come to Toronto for a talk about a possible job with Macmillans. I went and, as expected, the talk made a career in publishing seem infinitely attractive. But just at the end of it Hugh Eayrs said, "There is just one thing; if you come with us I would like it to be understood between us that you come to stay." I felt the trap closing on me. I was being asked to commit myself to a business I knew nothing about, one I might hate, though I didn't expect to. Late in the day, after talking with others in the office, I went back to Hugh Eayrs and said thank you, but no; I am going to take a year seeing the world. Hugh Eayrs insisted on leaving the door open: "Don't make a snap decision, I never do." (Though I was to hear him say

127

something like this many times, I was to learn that he seldom made any other kind.)

If I changed my mind I was to write him at once. But if I went around the world, come back in a year's time — a better man for the experience. Moreover, the way the business was going he could see the need for branch offices all across Canada, and would be looking for good men to handle them — so I needn't feel I was reading myself out of a part for the future. And then I found myself in Bond Street, in front of Macmillans, charmed and confused, and uncertain whether I had made the right decision.

As the train bumped its way back to Peterborough in the evening light I sat with a pad on my knee writing an account of the day to my father, asking for his advice. It was not characteristic but rather a measure of my excitement and uncertainty. The train ran through long stretches of wood carpeted with trillium and between ditches overflowing with marsh marigold and I barely noticed them.

For some days there was no answer to my letter, which was surprising, and then he telephoned, which was more so. Clearly I had posed a real problem, but his answer was sensible. I had had a better than average share of travel and experiences; if I had now found what I believed I wanted to work at I should take hold of it. As for the commitment required, he said, no one signs a contract for life. If you go into this in good faith, intending and expecting to stay, you do all that can be asked of you; if it doesn't work out, that is a pity, all round. I wrote Hugh Eayrs saying I had reconsidered carefully and wished to go into publishing, and I told all my friends I was going to work for Macmillans.

I waited for an answer to my letter, first for days, and then weeks; none came. The summer was going by. I had forfeited my job with the *Telegram* and said a fond farewell to Lakefield, welcoming my successor "Windy" Smith. During the weeks of waiting I went to camp at St. Johns, Quebec, and qualified for my commission in the Stormont, Dundas and Glengarry Highlanders. I was pleased to have found one examination I could pass, though I'm not sure that anyone failed the course. At least it suggested that I had some of the qualities of leadership. Discussion of occupations with some of my fellow officer-cadets from the Black Watch sharpened the sense of my predicament. I said I had been teaching but was going into book publishing — that is, I was waiting to hear — expecting.

On my return to Cornwall there was still no news and it was now late July. I wrote Mr. Eayrs at Macmillans asking for news. Within a few days came a letter from John Linnell, manager of the Educational Department, with whom I had lunched on my visit to the office. He wrote sympathetically saying that Mr. Eayrs had left for England without any decision on an appointment being made. It was not that I had been decided against but that "other considerations" had resulted in the question's being left open. There could be no decision until Mr. Eayrs returned from England about mid-August.

The course at St. Johns was still fresh in my mind and if it had done nothing else it had helped to sharpen a sense of the necessity to act boldly and swiftly if that was what circumstances required; not to be foolishly reckless but on occasion to be decisive to the point of recklessness — and that suited my temperament.

High diving had not been part of our training, but in the Richelieu River, in front of the camp, was a forty-foot diving tower. Inevitably, in the atmosphere of physical competition that pervades a military camp, we had begun to move up from level to level: a ten-foot dive, a twenty-foot dive, and on up. I think we were all frightened of where this was leading, except for one or two trained divers among us. But the day came when several of us went to the top in turn. One took a look and sensibly climbed down. One sat for an hour, dangling his feet and staring at the water; twice he stood up as though ready to go and twice sat down again. And then, his face stiff with fear, he stood up and, holding his nose, jumped straight out, and landed safely. When my turn came I looked only once at the water, and my companions far below, and knew that if I hesitated I was lost. My whole body was dissolving in terror, but the touch of recklessness came to my rescue; I had seen others do this. I lifted on my toes, raised my arms, and launched out. The dive was long enough for one to have a sense of the water rushing upward at tremendous speed and of a blur of faces; there was time and just sufficient consciousness to brace the body as it hit the water with an impact that was like diving into wet cement. I went very deep, but by the time I came up I knew everything was all right, I hadn't broken or twisted anything.

It may be fanciful to think that this kind of experience helped me now. I was angry at John Linnell's news. Hugh Eayrs had offered me a job and I had accepted. What "other considerations" could have arisen between the time he had urged me to reconsider and his receipt of my letter? And what of our mutual commitment, was it only one way? At any rate I had no intention of sitting tamely until his return "about the middle of August". The Cornwall Public Library produced the address of Macmillans in London: St. Martin's Street. It was only a guess that Hugh Eayrs could be reached there but I fired off a cable reading, "Your letter not received awaiting instructions here." Within twenty-four hours I had my answer: "Awfully sorry completely forgot letter join us August 18th".

And so by chance encounters, by blind luck, and perhaps guided by some instinct, I stumbled into what was to be my career. It seems now probably to have been the right career for me; a career in which I was to be happy most of the time, and above all to be doing work that I always thought worth doing. But characteristically I was almost late for work the first day. Having awaited the day with almost breathless excitement I then dawdled that first morning, wakening too early, then slowing down too much. In the end I took a taxi, an indulgence that common-sense told me I was not going to be able to afford. A block from the office I dismissed the taxi and walked smartly down Bond Street with a feeling that everyone in the Macmillan building must be watching for my arrival.

7

OT ONLY WAS NO ONE LOOKING OUT FOR ME from Macmillans, no one knew what to do with me when I arrived. There was some awareness of "a new fella" due to start, but Hugh Eayrs had given no directions for my disposal and he was "not in yet" — just that. I was to hear the phrase many times in the years ahead, and to learn that it meant no action could be taken, no new plans made.

Meanwhile I was led into the main office, which appeared to be filled with typists and invoicing machines. Around its outer walls were little glass cubby-holes in which older people seemed to be doing serious things. This main office was boxed in between the library and the President's office on the Bond Street side of the building, and the shipping room which backed on a lane for delivery wagons and trucks. The cellar which lay under all this ran from the front to the back of the building. Low, dark, and crowded with shelves it was the main stockroom,where two men spent their days hunting out books to fill orders and, though there was a cumbersome freight elevator, carrying them up a steep flight of stairs.

I was ushered into a glass cubicle and presented to a tall, cadaverous, distracted man — Mr. Roberts — who looked at me as though I were all he needed to finish him off. "Let's see now," he said and seemed to be trembling on the brink of a great decision. He stroked his chin, and the phone which he had just abandoned began to ring, just as someone else arrived at his door looking harassed and on urgent business. Mr. Roberts took his decision. "Tell you what you do," he said. "You sit right there."

"Right there" was a small hard chair for which there was barely room between his desk and the glass outer wall of the cubicle. And there I sat for an hour and a half, a reluctant and unwelcome observer of what looked like the opening rehearsal of a bad play about the business side of publishing. Mr. Roberts' phone was never allowed to cool; when he was not calling he was being called, and whichever was happening there was invariably someone at his door with a problem and usually with a piece of paper. In the infrequent pauses his long, grave face would turn to me and he would try to carry on a conversation that had never really got started. Having ordered the binding of five thousand copies of Crawford's *Algebra* by telephone and called the shipping room to change instructions on the forwarding of some other book to Nova Scotia, he said to me, "I don't just know when to expect Mr. Eayrs." I nodded sympathetically. Ten minutes later, having dealt with two or three other problems, he added, "The fact is he didn't say."

I was never to lose that first impression of amiable but overpowering confusion. This was not, to be sure, a quite normal day. It was a Monday morning and it was just two weeks before school opening — a moment of crisis I was to know much more about — and it seemed that half the small bookshops, novelty shops, and drugstores of Ontario were inquiring about orders that had not been filled. The answers to some of the questions were assumed to be somewhere in the great piles of papers on Mr. Roberts' desk, and every few minutes he would almost disappear as he went rooting in one or other pile, like a dog going after a groundhog. There were little growling exclamations: "Where is that blessed thing, saw it just a minute ago"; and occasionally a yelp of pleasure as he emerged breathless but triumphant, a rare smile replacing the gravity and worry. "By gollies," he would say, waving his find, "here it is." Seeing me he added, "You pretty well have to expect Mr. Eayrs when you see him." I had already worked that point out by myself.

The unpredictability of Hugh Eayrs, of which I had already

had some experience, was to be a central factor of my life for the next ten years. The saga begun with the uncertainty over my appointment continued in the next few months. That morning there was suddenly a sense of tension throughout the office; people dug deeper into their work, chatter between desks stopped, and heads went down. Mr. Roberts' antennae, already over-extended, picked up the signal at once. "I guess Mr. Eayrs is in now," he said, and gathering up a few papers on which he wished to report or ask direction he added, "I'll just let him know you're here." I think I sensed then what I came to know well, that though he coveted the prestige of being one of the few members of staff who went frequently to the front office, the exercise of the right was hard-earned and always an ordeal.

A little later I was called in. I went keyed up — I was about to be shown a map of my future — but the predominant feeling was excitement, not fear. If I had known more I might have been appalled almost at once, for Hugh Eayrs, after a friendly greeting and the announcement that he had been married since last we met to Dora Whitefield, my friend Lee's sister, told me that he would leave for Western Canada on September 16, taking me with him as Macmillans' Western Educational man. "You won't learn all you need to know in a month," he said, "but you can learn a lot. So, get busy." I suppose I felt some apprehension as I went out, but all I remember is the excitement, the idea of seeing the West, and with Hugh Eayrs.

Three weeks later it was all changed; I had been bought an enormous second-hand Buick, and put to work calling on the schools of Ontario with a trunkful of books. Two weeks after that we had a new man to handle the West and my glamorous future had been indefinitely postponed; a more experienced man had come along. The whole confusing process was more interesting as an example of Hugh Eayrs' impulsive way of acting than for its effect on me. I was enjoying myself too much to worry greatly about the future.

A few days after my arrival one of the older salesmen, whom I shall call Bill Brant, had suggested that if I were given a chance to work closer to home I might be wise to take it. "It probably sounds pretty nice to make a trip west with the Chief," he had said, "but he'll drop you off out there after a week or so and expect you to produce results. And some of the people you call on won't mind taking a little of the starch out of a beginner from the East. If you can get some experience here, get to know the books, get to know the problems, you will enjoy it more in the long run, and do better."

I had been there just long enough to recognize the depth of my ignorance of a complex business, and when a few days later I was called in to Mr. Eayrs' office and asked how I would like to spend a few months calling on schools in Ontario I said I would like it very much. Bill Brant was in Hugh Eayrs' office at the time and it was clear enough where the idea had originated. "Let him cut his teeth here the way his Chief did, eh Bill," said Mr. Eayrs. "What do you think?" Bill turned back from gazing out the window and answered gravely, "I think it's a good idea, Mr. Eayrs." I felt a little as though we were playing charades.

I had known Bill's advice was good and never doubted that it was offered out of unselfish kindness, but it was a long time before I realized just how valuable a judgement his had been. In the years ahead I was often to find myself utterly despondent on a long trip and only the perspective of experience saved me from some act of utter folly; without that perspective my career might well have ended before it was properly begun. For Bill Brant the years were to be tragically different. He never lost the affection of those he dealt with nor their respect for his deep knowledge of the book trade, but some instability that flawed a brilliant personality, or some ultimate lack of confidence, drove him from job to job, always a little lower in the scale. In later years he was to be seen, still with a saucy grin on his ravaged face, making his way to the beer warehouse for opening time, in his bedroom slippers and carrying his empty bottles.

When Hugh Eayrs started for the West alone in September I was fumbling over answers to the simplest questions in the schools of Oshawa and Cobourg, of Lindsay and Peterborough. I don't think I had quite understood that I was giving up the leisurely country-gentleman life of a private-school master for a career as a travelling salesman, but little by little it became clear that that was the choice I had made. Probably it wouldn't have made any difference, for this was the way into publishing, and every day I became surer that this was where I wanted to be. On Friday afternoons or Saturday mornings I came in to the office to pick up samples of new books, and to give the perpetually desperate Mr. Roberts the few orders and the numerous complaints from the schools I had called on; by Sunday night or Monday morning I was on my way again, bracing myself for the first call. I had largely to make my own plans and my own rules, for no one then at Macmillans had ever done this work; but if the turnover in personnel prevented the accumulation of experience, it at least encouraged initiative, and after my first startled surprise I found this suited me. Hugh Eayrs had never worked on this side of the business, so, though he encouraged me to drop in and tell him the funny stories from my week's work, he never really knew at this stage whether I was doing well or badly. There was a check of sorts provided by Mr. Roberts' capacious memory, fed by his unending battle with the paper. He was quick to notice and generous in reporting results that seemed to come from my work.

It was mere chance that Hugh Eayrs had not started his career on the educational side of the business. He might not have had the patience for it but it might have taught him patience, and prepared him for the hard slugging-match of the depression that had now reached us but was not yet recognized. The educational books were the hard standing on which the business rested; they provided the volume, though at a narrow margin of profit, which until now had been predictable and sure. Now it was about to shrink, and the amount of speculative general book publishing that had been possible before should have shrunk with it. His lack of all-round experience impeded his diagnosis of the problem, and his interests and commitments prevented him from accepting and acting promptly when the evidence of something like crisis became indisputable.

Hugh Eayrs, who had come to Canada in 1912, joined

Macmillans four or five years later, after serving as advertising manager of *Bookseller and Stationer* at Maclean-Hunter. In that capacity he had caught the eye of the then President of Macmillan, Frank Wise, and had been hired as a promotional man and junior Trade traveller. In so small a staff the graduation from junior to senior traveller came about if only one or at most two people left or were fired. Within a year or two he had moved up and was clearly the coming young man in the firm. He was making the trip West with the General Books and calling on the bigger accounts in central Canada. He also found time to write in 1916 a short biography of General Sir Isaac Brock, which Macmillans published for school use, and to collaborate on a novel, *The Amateur Diplomat*, with a young editor at Maclean's called Thomas Costain. Costain later became editor of *Saturday Evening Post* and a best-selling novelist. The memory of those first five or six years remained vivid and exciting to Hugh Eayrs. On one of his western trips he had even become involved in the Winnipeg General Strike of 1919, and as a special constable had watched all night in the Winnipeg City Hall along with some of his customers, nervously holding a rifle, which he had never done before. Some of the customers in after years remembered him with affection, some with an almost blinding admiration, but by no means all. At any rate none forgot him.

I heard him say more than once that he left or was fired from five jobs in his first few years in Canada, and always quickly found another job at more money. Back of that was a period in England as a parliamentary reporter; how that began or why it ended in emigration to Canada for the bumptious boy from Yorkshire was never clear. Apart from that bit of background he used to refer to himself, at appropriate moments, as a son of the manse, and on his office wall was a photograph of a short, stout, bearded clergyman, his father. To him Hugh Eayrs gave credit for his real love of books and his wide, if superficial, reading. On his wall also hung pictures of the Macmillan partners in London and of Canada's Prime Minister, Mackenzie King, as well as one of Winston Churchill inscribed "for Mr. Eayrs, with the infinite respect due a publisher".

At the age of twenty-six Hugh Eayrs became President of the Macmillan Company of Canada in 1921. He had made a trip to England (I believe because of the illness of his father) and during it had visited the London offices of Macmillan, with Frank Wise's approval and blessing. What happened on that visit is not clear. There is no doubt that the management of the Canadian business had gone slack during the war. It was said that Frank Wise with one or two of his senior people had taken on *The Times History of the War* and run it as a private venture from the Macmillan offices with Macmillan facilities. For too long publishers had enjoyed a seller's market, and in the bad period that followed the war Macmillans suffered from the accumulated results of carelessness and neglect of customers. The signs had not been missed in London. Though Frank Wise had become the Company's first president in 1905, and prospered to the point of being able to put up a building on Bond Street in 1910, the decision to make a change had probably been taken, however reluctantly, long before young Hugh Eayrs arrived in London. But Frank Wise believed Eayrs had behaved treacherously.

When he did arrive the elderly partners were no more proof against his charm and wit, his cockiness and real capacity, than Frank Wise had been six years before. And yet for these conservative, solid men the appointment of this glittering youngster must have been a radical decision. They were already in their sixties, pillars of the British publishing trade and of its most conservative traditions. They were to live another fifteen years congratulating themselves on their decision, and all to die within a three-month period in 1936, just before they might have had some sign of its unhappy ending.

By the time Hugh Eayrs returned to Canada the change had been decided on and general arrangements agreed. The senior partner, Sir Frederick Macmillan, went with him to his boat-train. They walked up and down in the gloom of Euston Station going over last-minute things in the bedlam of blowing steam and warning whistles, of tears and waves and hasty good-byes. Sir Frederick said that with Hugh Eayrs' youth and limited experience it might be best if he didn't make any publishing decisions at first but referred them to London for approval. Hugh Eayrs liked to remember his reply: "If you have confidence in me to run the business . . . " Sir Frederick, uncharacteristically, withdrew his injunction, and the boy from Yorkshire was, in every sense, on his way. In the circumstances the Eayrs appointment gave rise to charges of treachery. There were those who cheered and those who muttered deeply; there was even talk of libel suits. But the decision stood, and Frank Wise, whom many remembered as impatient, even arrogant, but attractive and able, gave up his post to a man much like himself in character, and moved on to a life that was to bring him degradation and ultimately near-poverty.

One of the young manager's first decisions after taking over was to publish W. H. Blake's translation of Louis Hémon's *Maria Chapdelaine*. Neither his sales manager nor the formidable president of the Macmillan Company in New York liked the decision, or thought the book would sell; and at first it appeared they were right. Then, suddenly, the book took off, to become a brilliant success in Canada, Britain, and the United States, and young Hugh Eayrs took off with it.

To have started with so striking a success, to have been right where greater experience was wrong, conferred both prestige and immense confidence. At the core of his confidence was a belief in his luck; a belief all gamblers — and publishers — must have, but none should have too much; at once a great and dangerous gift. I was to see it make him by turns unbeatable and intolerable, and to see it contribute to his destruction long before his time.

With such a start, and with his own experience on the General Book side, it was natural, though mistaken, for the young publisher to direct most of his attention and effort that way; it was the glamorous area, the side that might produce a bestseller and a dramatic profit, and was more exciting because more of a gamble. Educational books might require greater investment, but their markets could be more accurately estimated and their successes were more lasting. Fortunately for him he had, quite early in his management career, found a remarkable young man, W. H. Clarke, to learn and ultimately to run the Educational side of the business — the school, university, and medical books. The two men had important things in common; both were bookmen and natural publishers, both had a bright intelligence, though of a different quality, both were forceful, fiercely competitive, and stubborn.

In time their differences were to be equally important and to prove irreconcilable. Hugh Eayrs' careless brilliance and flair contrasted with Bill Clarke's greater concern, superior scholarship, and dogged thoroughness. Eayrs worked spasmodically and played hard, Clarke seemed never to play. In a few years he had made himself a better-trained all-round bookman than Hugh Eayrs, with an impressive, if over-ambitious, list of books in plan and active preparation. The familiar story of the Industrious Apprentice was taking shape. Hugh Eayrs, who had once read every letter that went out of the Macmillan office and many that came in, now saw very few. His own letters became careless, wordy, and often pompous. He had an increasing number of outside interests, was away a good deal, played a lot of golf, and was a leader in a hard-drinking, reckless group in Toronto society.

Inevitably Bill Clarke and his brother-in-law, John C. W. Irwin, who had joined him at Macmillans, contrasted their growing share of work, of success and responsibility, with their limited authority and limited prospects. There were requests that became demands, there were probably promises that weren't or couldn't be fulfilled, and finally a parting in great bitterness. Bill Clarke and John Irwin left to found their own business, Clarke-Irwin, a few months before my arrival. And since Macmillans' Ontario Educational traveller, Colin Henderson, had also left to join Longmans Green a few months earlier still, the company's knowledge of past events and procedures in the educational field was mostly held in Mr. Roberts' over-taxed but remarkable memory.

Looked backed on, the work in Ontario was strenuous but simple. Since most of the books for use as texts went to the lowest bidder and were prescribed by the Department of Education on seven-year contracts, it was chiefly in the field of English literature that teachers had freedom to choose their books, and therefore welcomed a call. There were also books to be sold for the school library, usually run by the head of the English Department, who had very little money for books and was about to have less. Even this I had to find out for myself. But once learned, my work seemed largely to be a matter of exchanging enthusiasms about books with people of similar tastes. I soon learned to recognize those who were knowledgeable and those who were not, those who cared passionately that their pupils should learn and grow and enjoy, and those who were lazy or bored or even ignorant.

It was the informed and enthusiastic with whom it was a pleasure to talk, but in one way or another I learned from them all. My favourites were those who would if necessary come late to the hotel, looking for books to strengthen and freshen their work, and would stay to talk. They were the ones from whom only another appointment or miles to be travelled would drag me away; and on such days it was a joy to be up early and a pleasure to stay up late. But everyone I talked to taught me something, about publishing or selling or education, and I couldn't learn it all fast enough.

Of course, all the pleasure in work had not suddenly turned me into a model young man. In off hours I played hard, though I kept work and pleasure well separated most of the time. But in my first few weeks I ran into trouble that seemed in my inexperience to be serious. I was calling on schools in Hamilton and staying at a small, economical hotel called the Wentworth Arms. Every evening a few teachers came in to look at books, and I worked with them until ten o'clock. After that on two or three evenings, a friend from university days came in, and we sat up late talking and drinking beer. It wasn't a party and it wasn't noisy, but nothing passed unnoticed in that quiet little hotel. When I prepared to leave on Friday I suddenly realized

I was going to be short of cash. This was not the result of our mild dissipations, but merely of bad reckoning and a repair to the car; this was before the days of credit cards. Expense accounts were still strange and intimidating to me and I drew as little money as possible from the office; in those days it was considered that fifty dollars a week was enough expense for a careful man travelling in Ontario. I wasn't going to be short by much, but I was too late for the bank.

I had no experience in this sort of thing and probably approached the hotel manager with too much diffidence; though I tried for a casual air it would have fooled no one. "I'm afraid I'll have to pay you by cheque," I said. His eye-glasses glittered and I glimpsed a stored-up disapproval that had been building all week. "Oh no you don't," he said, "no siree. I know your type; there are too many of you around. You pay by cash here." He stood there glaring at me, and for the moment I could neither think of anything to say nor imagine what I was going to do. "Your type doesn't last long, young man. You'll not go far," said the hotel manager, and in spite of my feeling of wronged innocence, and rage at his pursy virtue, I was temporarily inclined to agree with him.

However, having squandered the cost of a telephone call from Hamilton to the office, I found that this was neither an unusual problem, nor hard to solve. The money was wired within an hour or two and I paid my bill with a flourish. The manager tried to recover his ground a little, but with all the chilly dignity I could manage I refused to notice his little flag of truce.

About this time John Linnell, manager of the Educational Department, and I had money troubles of a different sort; so unimportant and yet looming so large to our inexperienced eyes. Ontario was selecting books for prescription in Grade 13 English for the next three years. There were worthwhile prizes at stake, and it was suggested that Linnell and I should invite the most formidable person on the committee to dinner. This was Miss Evelyn Macdonald, head of English at Bloor Collegiate, and to our surprise — almost dismay — she accepted the invitation. We took her to the Royal York — newly built, the largest hotel in the British Empire, and very grand. The stated purpose of the occasion was talk, away from the interruptions of the classroom, to help us to understand the committee's needs, in the hope that we might be of service to them. Miss Macdonald, who always knew her own mind, and usually got what she wanted, said the Royal York had a very good planked steak. John and I looked uneasily at each other; "What a good idea," we said, and presently something approaching a side of beef was carried in on a plank and displayed with proper pride, to stimulate our taste buds, then taken away for carving. It was a splendid dinner, though at that time there were no wines or spirits served in any Ontario restaurant. Over good and helpful talk about the teaching of English and the objectives of the committee, John even ordered a big cigar. In due course, re-gretfully, he called for the bill, and turned a shade pale when it arrived. However, he did the necessary, which I hadn't the means of doing, and we saw Miss Macdonald to her car.

As I drove him home he said with a nervous little laugh, "By God, we've really done it tonight. Have you any idea what that dinner cost? Eleven dollars." It seemed a monstrous sum — in-deed in 1930, it was a lot. In the morning, nervously, John put in his claim and an hour later Bill Brant came up, caught be-tween anger and amusement at our uneasiness. "Something good had better come of this," he said. "What did you feed that woman, gold-bricks or goldfish?"

The committee for once broke away from the established tra-dition of a Victorian novel and prescribed Hugh Walpole's *Fortitude*, of which we handled the Modern Library edition. This was felt to be at least a move in the right direction, but within weeks there was a public uproar. A lazy teacher had or-dered one of the girls in his class to read aloud from the novel. Suddenly she stopped — "Do I have to go on and read that?" she asked. The teacher, who had apparently been dozing, said, "Yes, go on," either without looking or because he didn't know what else to say. The girl closed her book, gathered up her things, and marched in outraged virtue from the room, and home to report to her parents. She had balked at reading "God damn you, you would make your own daughter a whore." It was the end of the approach to the modern novel in Ontario for several years. *Henry Esmond, Jane Eyre, David Copperfield*, and the rest were restored to their sacred and comfortable niches.

By October I was almost an old hand; the necessity of learning the answers to a thousand questions began to give me a knowledge of our books and the business. Most of our titles were imported from London and New York, from the Macmillan lists or Cambridge University Press, the Modern Library or others we represented. We had far too many books to keep track of, or service properly, and in the opinion of most customers charged too much for them and too seldom had them in stock. As far as sales to schools were concerned, the number for which I could find openings in English classes or even school libraries was comparatively small and manageable. I recognized that my knowledge of them was superficial, and that what was merely a glib familiarity was often accepted as genuine bookishness. For the moment it had to serve, but whoever else my confident manner fooled, it didn't often fool me. For every day in publishing increased the recognition of my ignorance — the books I had not read, the great names I barely knew.

In so small a staff there was some general awareness of everything in the business, and though I was fully involved in my own work I was fascinated by the little trickles of news and gossip, by the appearance of new books carelessly lying about as though they were just an ordinary event; new books in that first season by Morley Callaghan, John Masefield, Bernard Shaw, D. H. Lawrence, H. G. Wells, and Maynard Keynes. I had always bought books, but to be able to buy them now at a substantial discount was enough to rock a judgement that these days was in almost continuous oscillation. I kept myself poor with my purchases, and warm with the illusion that to own books was almost as valuable as to have read them.

In the mood of euphoria which possessed me the news of what I can only call the Howard Ferguson caper seemed wholly splendid and exciting. The former premier of Ontario (the man from whom I still had an unused letter of introduction to Lord Beaverbrook), had just been appointed to London as Canadian High Commissioner. This prompted the suggestion of a short biography to be written and published quickly. That idea in turn had been developed into a publicity stunt: a book to be written in one month and published one month later. Wow! I was too dazzled to see what was apparently clear to everyone outside Macmillans, that such a book would not be worth reading, let alone publishing. To me it was all wonderful — what a business to be in, where such great things happened! If the newspapers didn't think it a good way to make books they found it good copy, in a dull period. There were pictures of Hugh Eayrs signing contracts, first with the author, then with the printer. His own rationalization of the project was that it would break the log-jam of a bad trade season, get the people into the bookstores.

The probability of disaster to come was confirmed when the author took his first payment and disappeared for about two weeks. At first there was a hope that he was in concealment, researching and writing, but somehow the position became clear — he was drinking beer steadily in seclusion. In the crisis a brace of newspapermen, and George McKanday from our own staff, went to work in a room in the Westminster Hotel on Jarvis Street. We got situation reports from George, whose attitude was one of cynical amusement added to a characteristic willingness to help out in a jam. Eventually the author turned up, took a cold, slashing talk from Hugh Eayrs to add to his hangover, and went to work. As chapters were finished they were rushed to the printers for typesetting (shades of Balzac, Dr. Johnson, and Sir Walter Scott!).

On publication day, as promised, finished books arrived in the warehouse. They had been printed and bound by Hunter-Rose in four and a half days. It was less than a splendid book but at least it was ready on time. Our two Trade men were out on selling trips, one in Western Canada and one somewhere in Ontario, and nothing much had been done about special sales arrangements. If there was to be any useful result from all the publicity the stores should have been filled with books on publication day, but there were few orders in hand. Eaton's, one of the biggest accounts, had said they would wait to see the book before ordering. Some time in the late morning I was called to Mr. Roberts' office. As I went in he handed me a copy of the Ferguson book. "The Chief wants you to take this over to Eaton's," he said. I was startled and flattered, then appalled. This might be, or ought to be, a big order if people were as interested as we had thought they should be. Now that I had seen the book, and the whole stunt had worn thin, I wasn't quite so sure.

Clutching a copy of the book I went slowly across to Eaton's, only three blocks from the office. I tried to frame up some winning remarks to open the subject, but nothing much occurred to me. With nothing ready I was introduced to the buyer for the book department. He was a short, wiry, bitter man, with a North of Ireland accent and a reputation for being tough and for bullying salesmen. It was the Eaton buyers' style at the time. I started by reminding him how many people were just waiting for the book; he barely listened. Then he took the book reluctantly, as though he were turning over a dead animal with a toe of his boot. "How much is it?" he asked, without interest, and I told him $1.25. "You've got one hell of a god-damned nerve charging $1.25 for a book like that," he said in a rasping voice. My nervousness vanished. "I didn't come over here for a mouthful of abuse," I said. "If you want the book I will be glad to sell it to you, if not I'll take it away." For a moment we glared at each other, then "Send us six" he said, and turned away. Going back to the office I knew this was a derisory order but couldn't believe my flash of temper was the cause. There were other signs that the book was doomed, and there would be many more.

Still, there were other things to try. That afternoon, with cartons of books in the old Buick, which looked like a battle-wagon, I went out to the end of Danforth Avenue and came in the miles of its length stopping every few hundred yards at any tobacconist or novelty shop, or indeed any shop that looked as though it might occasionally sell a book. Most were friendly and courteous, but totally uninterested; Howard Ferguson might have been dead a hundred years and of no importance in his lifetime. Just a few of the proprietors were hostile to Ferguson: "Why would anybody want to read about that man?" they asked. One man whose name was Macmillan, and who was good-natured, let me tease him into buying six copies on the ground that Macmillans had to stick together. By the time I had finished the cheerless job it was dark, I was exhausted, and I had sold perhaps two dozen copies of the wretched book.

I went back gloomily to the office and dumped in my cartons to join the great pile in the shipping room. It was a pile that was to diminish very little in the weeks ahead. Reviewers giggled over the book, or hardly mentioned it, and the public showed a total lack of interest — as did Mr. Ferguson's Conservative Party. One copy went to most libraries and a few to bookstores for those who had to appear to show an interest. In all we sold a few hundred copies and the caper was finished.

Fortunately there were more substantial ventures on the drawing-board or in the works, many of them legacies from Bill Clarke's administration. Among them was a new edition of Shakespeare's plays for schools and universities with newly prepared texts, and notes to be done by Canadian scholars. This was to be St. Martin's Shakespeare — after the street in London where the Macmillan building stood. Our own building on Bond Street was called St. Martin's House (a name we liked but many found pretentious). The Shakespeares were to be followed by an ambitious series of school literature texts to be called St. Martin's Classics. The Shakespeares were to prove a costly failure, partly due to the depression and what were thought to be their high prices (50¢), but even more to the reluctance of many English teachers to change from the edition they had used for years, in which they had noted all the likely questions and all the answers. That edition had two other solid advantages for many teachers; it had been prepared years before by O. J. Stevenson, who was believed to have a hand in setting the matriculation examinations in English, and the books, published by one of the older Canadian companies, Copp Clark, were priced at 25¢.

Other ventures to which we were at least partially committed rose to haunt us, some of them born of the euphoria of pre-1929, and now well beyond our means. Still others, lacking the guiding hand of Bill Clarke as sponsoring editor, were like little ships that had lost their rudders — some just sank without a trace, a few were brought successfully into port, and still others reached port only to sink at the dockside. No one person was actively aware of them all or equally concerned for them. John Linnell, nominally manager of the Educational Department, had not been in the position long. He was a scholar and a poet, newly arrived from England and employed on impulse by Hugh Eayrs on the recommendation of Professor E. J. (Ned) Pratt. Linnell found himself struggling to understand the Canadian educational system, to learn publishing and the whole craft of editing in between trips to Quebec and the Maritime Provinces as a traveller. I watched him with a mixture of sympathy and impatience, having little notion of his problems; watched him go home at night, his case bulging with proofs, and watched him in the morning red-eyed as he lugged them back corrected. By late spring 1931 he was gone, fired, a married man with one child, who had been pushed in at the deep end in publishing, and too hastily judged not a good enough swimmer. Though the depression had not yet bitten deep, employers were becoming very cautious and for some weeks John Linnell walked the streets in search of work, a picture of growing despair.

In spite of the difference in our backgrounds and interests, we had become friends, and he had done much to direct my reading and stimulate my thinking. He fastened on me the nickname of Bron after the appealing but bumbling boy in C. E. Montague's *Rough Justice*. Bron, as a little boy, finished each day with a gleeful call to his sister, "Fun tomorrow." Bron represented the amiable but underdeveloped heart and mind, the vague enthusiast, the typical English public-school prod-

147

uct. Was I these things? I suppose I wondered, but not for long. I was too busy enjoying it all.

The ill wind that blew John Linnell up and down Yonge Street job-hunting was to carry me to the Atlantic coast as his replacement. It was promotion by default but none the less exciting for that; not exciting as promotion, or as a sign that I was getting on — I don't remember thinking much about that — but as a passport to new worlds to conquer, new people to meet. Imagine getting paid to make a trip like this! so sang my youthful exuberance. And though I was to make the trip often, and there were to be disappointments, I was never to lose that sense of privilege and pleasure. It had been there all through the twenty-four-hour train trip aboard the Ocean Limited from Montreal, but it swept over me with a peculiar joy as I stepped off the train at last in Halifax, and walked along the still-panting train at the edge of the harbour, sniffing the sea and hearing a distant fog-horn. This was the life!

And so it was. Though I had been in publishing for just under a year and had learned little more than the preliminary passwords, my work had suddenly expanded. I was not here merely to talk literature with teachers of English but to be prepared to meet committees of the Department of Education, discussing revision of all parts of the school curriculum; and I had also to be able to talk to officials up to the rank of Deputy-Minister. I was expected to know what books we had in every field, their good points and their weaknesses. Though many of the people I had to call on were experienced teachers and some were learned men, all were facing curriculum revision — a real rethinking of the whole purpose and object of the schools — for the first time. Within the memory of most, change had amounted only to the occasional change of a textbook, and this much greater opportunity produced in all a common excitement which I shared.

In such company, breathing the heady atmosphere, it was easy, and intoxicating, to believe that we were about to see the world remade. A more perceptive and liberal curriculum would release new energies and capacities in children, lay the foundations of a new breed of people. The air was full of a new jargon from Teachers College, Columbia University — the song of a new legion marching under the banner of John Dewey, Bode, Thorndike, and Gates. Without recognizing the fallacy, I was ready to assume that the people I was observing and working with toward a common vision were about to find what society had been looking for since the days of Plato and Aristotle.

There were jarring notes, moments when men with imposing titles and qualifications seemed to be aiming a good deal short of the stars I was gazing at. On one such occasion I had travelled overnight to Sydney in Cape Breton to meet with the chairman of an English sub-committee and two or three of his associates. The chairman was an amiable but bumptious little man who quickly made his position clear. He wasn't looking to change anybody's life or hopes fundamentally; he thought kids had too many heavy books to carry to school these days and he wanted to change that. What he was looking for was an adequate English Composition text that didn't weigh too much. I listened, appalled, and watched one of his teachers roll up her eyes in horror and frustration. In a spirit of mischief I fished out a slim little book recently arrived from Macmillans in London and handed it to him, though I was quite certain it was not the sort of book most of his people were looking for or should have. His eyes lit up and without even looking inside the covers he hefted the book and pronounced it "a nice little book, the sort of thing we want". In a few minutes and after the most cursory examination, he had bullied his colleagues into agreeing that this would be a suitable recommendation.

I travelled back to Halifax knowing that a coveted recommendation for one of our books was about to be forwarded to the Central Curriculum Committee. If it slipped through, as it might, we would have an order for several thousand copies; but the final result must be bad for everyone. After a sleepless night I called the secretary of the main committee, Harding Moffatt, who in later years was to become Deputy-Minister, and told him the recommendation was coming through; if it stood up to a hard look I would be very happy, but I believed it should have that hard look. In the end the book was not accepted and I had perhaps forfeited a substantial piece of business, but I had at least demonstrated the genuine concern for education that I was developing.

Meanwhile the ill wind had blown me another substantial good. Since I was to replace John Linnell in Quebec and the Maritimes, someone had to replace me in Ontario. Hugh Eayrs asked me to see a "young man" and give him my opinion. The young man's name was Frank Upjohn, and my method of seeing him was to expose him to an evening of the fraternity house where I was living; I could see him there with a variety of people and later get to know him during a long talk over a few beers. As a method of personnel selection it was perhaps less than scientific, but it produced the right answer. Though we were very different types — he reserved, thorough in his work, neat in his dress, and well disciplined — we started with a common enthusiasm for books, and substantially the same values; and we laughed at the same things, indeed at almost everything. We had a fine evening, and when I told Hugh Eayrs that I thought the "young man" would do, we were embarked on a close association that was to last out our working days.

Gradually, encouraged in an absent-minded way by Hugh Eayrs, we expanded our travelling and promotional work — vaguely enough defined to begin with — to what in publishing is called field editing. This meant being alert, and always watchful, for needs in new books and, as time went on, knowing the people most able to meet them. If a committee was looking for a book that didn't appear to exist (or that at least we didn't have), could not something of ours be adapted to meet the need? Or why not do a new book? "That's a fine new idea. Why don't you, or you, work that out in a new book?" Sometimes the proposals amounted to little more than changing some terminology and spelling, and substituting Canadian illustrations for American or British — a process called Canadianizing. Sometimes the idea was a genuinely good solution. But too often we were assisting and tempting another man to reinvent the wheel because he couldn't or wouldn't see that his pet method, perfected over years of teaching, was not so different from those worked out in existing books.

More serious, these proceedings often trembled on the brink of corruption. It was not a conventional corruption by money — though a successful book might occasionally earn its author or editor a good deal of money by the standards of the wretchedly paid teaching profession. The corruption was at least equally the insidious appeal to vanity — accepted as a belated recognition of a valuable life's work and a hard-earned expertise; and it was doubly insidious because just occasionally it was exactly that. Either way, what the proposal often amounted to was the purchase of an influential name rather than an expert. A new book by Mr. So-and-so might be halfway to being approved before it was even written. And though Mr. So-and-so, recognizing a conflict of interest, would withdraw from any position of influence in a decision, the influence of his reputation would remain and the good-will of his friends.

Turning for home at the end of the five weeks of that first Maritime trip was at once exciting and sad. I was tired and eager to be back but I was aware of an experience not to be repeated. I had learned a lot about publishing, about education, about Canada and the roots of some of our discontents. And I had experienced much kindness often concealed by a near-surly abrasiveness. Two older men who later became friends and kindly advisers had met my first approach by saying bluntly that they didn't think they needed advice or help from young men from Upper Canada. When I turned their rudeness by saying I wasn't there to offer advice, but I couldn't believe some of our books would not be worth their looking at, both apologized readily and became generous with their time and experience.

I had worked hard and under strain. Just before I left Toronto it was decided, for economy's sake, that I would sell the Trade books as well as all the others. This meant adding calls on general bookstores and public libraries to all my other jobs. If this was more work than could be done properly, it was also more of a privilege than I knew. The last of the elderly and old-fashioned booksellers were about to disappear from the scene, their businesses swallowed by the depression, the radio, and the latest development in moving pictures known as the talkies. Those old men seemed to enjoy giving away their favourite books as much as selling them, and old E. J. Vickery, owner of the Book Room, made quite a ceremony of giving me Michael Fairless's *The Roadmender*, since he believed it full of wisdom and good counsel for young men. And I have a picture of old Mr. Allen of T. C. Allen, balanced precariously on a stepladder in his dark old store hunting through file boxes near the ceiling to get me a handful of the early books of James P. Gillis, author of *The Cape Breton Giant* — a priceless gift now — which he was determined I must have as a keepsake of T. C. Allen's publishing twenty-five years earlier.

But, as usual, I had played as hard as I had worked. In off-hours, and there weren't that many, I was welcomed into a select group through my friendship with Gavin Rainnie going back to Lakefield days. Gavin, least pretentious of men, with a dry, kindly wit, seemed to me always an amused spectator at the games of this hard-drinking élite in a Halifax that took its élitism very seriously, and meant to. For the sake of Gavin I was forgiven (or appeared to be) my Toronto origin, and my rather curious job. I was for the moment a privileged stranger and was included in parties that more than half of Halifax would have given its right arm (or in local terms its North West Arm) to attend. And they were fun, though the fun depended rather heavily on pink gin and rum.

Leaving Halifax I was to spend my last day in Nova Scotia at Truro seeing people at the Teachers' College there. My last call by arrangement was on Molly Beresford, who was doing some work for us on a series of school reading books. She was a Scot in charge of English teaching, an expert who loved her work. As we talked on in the empty, darkening classroom she probed my educational background and the depth of my interest in publishing. Inevitably she found out about my hopes of writing and asked whether I knew Charles Bruce, a young newspaperman from Halifax who had just gone to Toronto with Canadian Press. She spoke with respect of the quality of his work and his serious determination. "You should know Charlie Bruce," she said and launched into a story about him in her soft Scottish voice. He had paid something to have a collection of his poetry published by a good publisher, and she had asked Charlie why he would go to such an expense, which he could not afford. He had answered, holding up his book, that as long as he had *this* he would remember what it was he really wanted to do and be. The last line dropped between us in the growing darkness but it was not lost.

At the door she said, apropos my work in Nova Scotia, "Did you have a chance to get to know Mr. Morehouse?" I said we had barely met. "Get to know Mr. Morehouse," she said, "he is very experienced, fair-minded, and sensible," and then the canny Scottish afterthought, "and he's very influential." We walked back into the town, and I went on to the station. I was to take the train later in the evening, arriving that night at Sackville, New Brunswick. At Truro station I confirmed that my train would get to Amherst, where Mr. Morehouse was Superintendent of Schools, at ten-thirty that evening, with another train going on to Sackville early in the morning. On impulse, knowing it was a wild chance and an unreasonable request, I telephoned Mr. Morehouse asking whether, if I stopped over, he could see me briefly that evening. After a slightly startled pause he said he would come to the hotel soon after the train arrived. Carrying my bag across the cindery way to the unprepossessing building behind the station at Amherst I wondered what I could have to say to a stranger and an older man that was worth his precious evening. But I needn't have worried. No man ever had less sense of his own importance than Fred Morehouse. And sitting there in that grim little bedroom — one unshaded electric bulb, one small dressing table, one hard chair, one iron bedstead, one coil of rope attached to a ringbolt in case of fire — we had a fine talk.

As our energy ebbed about midnight, I spoke of going to Mount Allison University at Sackville in the morning. He re-

153

marked that he and Dr. Bigelow of Mount Allison had often talked of writing a chemistry book for schools which both felt was badly needed; Professor Bigelow was a senior chemist with an international reputation, and chemistry had been Morehouse's subject as a teacher. I asked whether he would mind my telling Mr. Bigelow of our talk, and expressing Macmillans' interest. He had no objection, but he reminded me that though they had talked and planned, they had put little on paper.

We said good-night, and though bone tired I went to bed with a sense of happiness — a kind of hunch that something good had happened. It was a feeling I was to know often in future years, and though it was not a sure guide, in this case it was right. I had just found my first book for Macmillans — stumbled over it, as publishers often do — and it was to prove one of our most successful. I did not sense the future, in which *Dominion High School Chemistry* would be used in at least four provinces for about twenty years and would sell many many thousands of copies. I had no real sense of these things as I fell asleep, but in that narrow iron bed I slept well.

8

I N MY FIRST FORMAL MEETING with Hugh Eayrs he had talked with airy confidence about opening branch offices all across Canada. This was in the spring of 1930, six months after the disastrous market crashes not yet recognized as either cause or symptom of the great depression already closing in on us. By the time I joined Macmillans conditions were said to be bad, but the idea of their becoming and continuing much worse was hardly contemplated.

Because so much school-book business was settled and ordered months in advance, the general prospects for 1930 were pretty well clear, committed, and promising before the crash in the autumn of 1929. In most provinces a provincial school-book depot ordered its year's requirements for the whole province in the late autumn, took delivery in the spring, distributed to local stores or school districts in the summer, and paid for the books after they received the money for them. We had to finance the transaction for about nine months, between the time we made our investment and the time we were paid. In November and December we had plenty of cash; during the rest of the year we were overdrawn at the bank and often in debt to printers and paper-makers as well. The company had never had more than the original capital of $20,000 with which it started in 1905. Out of its earnings it had put up a building on Bond Street in 1910 and in most years had paid a modest dividend to its shareholders. There was also a foolish provision that the president was paid, on top of his salary, a bonus equal to the amount of dividend paid. It is little wonder that although sales volume had increased steadily for twenty years the company had no cash reserves built up against bad business weather or extraordinary investment needs.

I had no knowledge or understanding of such things in 1930, but was about to acquire a certain amount of both, though largely by osmosis. Some time in 1930, with every indication signalling danger, the company embarked on the largest publishing venture it had ever undertaken. It would call for a total and effective orchestration of the Educational Department's presumed abilities, plus a good deal of capital, of boldness, and of common sense. But the Educational Department had few abilities and even less experience; our whole organization had gone and we were in process of rebuilding with new bricks that kept falling down. John Linnell had lasted only a few months and the "new" western man lasted only a little longer. He had had great qualities and was full of experience but his health, damaged by the war, was not helped by wild drinking bouts which resulted in his periodic disappearance and long silences when the office needed his news and his judgements. Then Bill Brant went for much the same reasons. No one could really quarrel with the decisions, but I had liked these hard-bitten men and been helped by them. Their faults were for many the occupational disease of publishing in Canada at the time, the result of brutally long periods away from home combined with a good deal of "entertaining", which traditionally was part of the job. Once again the ill wind for them blew good to Frank Upjohn and me. By default, on two years' experience, I became Manager of the Educational Department and Frank after one impressive year Assistant Manager. At twenty-five and twenty-four we were two young chiefs — without any Indians.

It is a habit, almost a tradition, among Trade publishers to say that Educational publishing is dull; the comment usually comes, and most emphatically, from those who have done little or no Educational publishing. I can only say that in the ten years during which it was my chief concern I never found it so. That it has less pizazz and gets less attention from the media is true. But it is infinitely more subtle than Trade publishing. A good Educational publisher must be at once diplomat, politician, educator, and salesman. Frank and I were about to be tested for all these qualities by the formidable venture on which Macmillans was now embarking and about which, up to now, we had known very little.

Some ten years before, the four western provinces had joined together to agree on a set of readers to be used throughout the elementary schools of all four provinces. That contract was coming to an end, and though it might be extended by a year or two, submission for the publishing of new books had been invited. Reading methods were changing and technology, especially in the matter of illustration, had made great but expensive strides in ten years. The leadership and the models which had formerly come from Britain were now coming from the United States. Many of those who would judge the submissions had done graduate work in the States and had become converts. When the submissions were first invited from Western Canada it was proposed that samples of bookmaking and illustration together with manuscripts would alone be required for approval. However, when one publisher — said to be Henry Button, head of J. M. Dent in Canada — announced that he would submit finished books, illustrated in full colour, the rules were changed for all competitors, and the expense and the gamble vastly increased. It was said that to produce our first submission — samples subject to required changes — would cost $250,000. Whether this was a careful estimate or a good round figure was not clear, but for companies with little capital it was a huge gamble.

The size of the investment had caused Macmillans to join the Ryerson Press in a co-publishing venture. For the same reasons W. J. Gage and Thomas Nelson had joined forces. J. M. Dent was going to go it alone. In our case it was supposed that the editorial skill of Dr. Lorne Pierce of the Ryerson Press and the drive and charm of Hugh Eayrs would be a winning combination. But we had also a secret weapon: Macmillan and Ryerson would contribute to our books — and deny to all others —

the work of the large number of distinguished authors which Macmillan, and other houses we represented, published in Canada, Britain, and the United States. Under no conditions and at no price would our competitors be allowed to include the work of these authors in their books. It was a bold and high-handed and so far as I know unheard-of application of copyright. My first naïve response was "hurrah for our side"; only later did doubts about the morality of such a position thrust themselves forward uncomfortably, and later still doubts about its legality.

The sheer effrontery of such a claim must, at first, have silenced all questions and objections. Macmillans in London and New York appear to have agreed that all applications for copyright material in their lists would be referred to us, but they can hardly have realized that all such requests would be automatically refused. Deputy-Ministers of Education looked unhappy but seemed to accept our claim and position as hard, but a fair business advantage. Our competitors raged and scolded but produced no effective counter-argument. Only in our books, we announced far and wide, would the work of Kipling, Hardy, Masefield, Yeats, and countless of the best-known writers on both sides of the Atlantic be available. The conclusion seemed to be inescapable that no one could make good books without material over which we claimed control.

To be fair, Lorne Pierce and Hugh Eayrs probably believed that their position was unassailable and correct. It was tough, but not more so than their competitors had been in the past and would be in the future. I have always thought Lorne Pierce too innocent to understand fully the enormity of this plan, and Hugh Eayrs had too good a sense of humour to sustain the role of villain for long. But for the moment they were carried away by the prospect of overwhelming success.

They decided to carry their collaboration a stage further. We would have *Canadian Treasury Readers* for the elementary school — prepared for the West, but perhaps to become national readers. This would be followed by the *Canada Books of Prose and Verse* for Grades 7, 8, and 9, which (from the States again) we were beginning to call the Junior High School. And then, what a good idea, we would carry the series through the Senior High School. The senior books would be edited by Professor Bennet of Dalhousie University. And right through the school we would apply our restrictions on copyright.

Theoretically the plan had merit. Given a directing editor with great knowledge and fine taste, a child might be wisely guided through the best prose and verse in our language and all at the appropriate moment. What could be better?

But there were flaws, too. The junior books were being prepared by a selected group of experts from all across the country under the general editorship of Lorne Pierce, and C. L. Bennet's name guaranteed the quality of the senior books.

Then it was announced that the intermediate books — for Grades 7, 8, and 9 — would be edited by Lorne Pierce and Dora Whitefield. Many at Macmillans and the Ryerson Press stirred uneasily. If the system broke in the middle the whole argument for continuity and an articulated course fell to pieces. Lorne Pierce was acknowledged to be brilliant and one of the best-read men in Canada, but he had not taught for more than a short time or been actively in the classroom for years. And Dora Whitefield was Mrs. Hugh Eayrs. That she was highly intelligent and widely read I knew, but that was only a partial qualification for school-book editing. What did either editor really know of the abilities and interests of children at these levels? That he had agreed to or imposed this arrangement suggests Hugh Eayrs' ignorance of or contempt for the inner values of good school-book publishing. Educators, prompted no doubt by our competitors, began to ask searching questions about the qualifications of our editors.

Slowly the three series of books began to take shape in spite of endless balking and biting within the complex team Lorne Pierce was trying to drive. My trips across the West seemed more often taken up with peace-making than selling. Our experts all proved to be prima donnas and all resigned at least once, and some several times, over minor disagreements — over content, or illustrations, or shares of royalty.

159

We were still clinging to our position on copyright, and it was Molly Beresford of Truro, Nova Scotia — a member of our editorial team — who put forward the unanswerable challenge to our assumption. It was wrong, she said in her soft, persuasive Scottish voice, to make any case for our books on the basis of copyrights we were withholding from our competitors. What teachers wanted for their children were good books, the best possible, and no publisher should seek to win — or be in a position to win — on such grounds. She was trying to make the best Grade 3 book in Canada, but if she could not, she wouldn't have her book chosen because it had a richer content that had been denied to others. Had the public no rights in a literary heritage? And in all this squabbling had anyone discussed the authors' rights?

I began at last to work things out for myself. We could refuse a competitor the right to use a story or a poem or an essay, though we might not intend to use it ourselves. In that case an author, perhaps in need of money, was done out of a fee. And suddenly it all seemed to me clear and hateful. As we were proceeding, the children in the schools might be denied the best books. That seemed far-fetched, but our competitor might have a better reading method, and better illustrations, and still have a content impoverished by our hold on literary material. Was it possible we could win with second-rate books? Could we really win with less than the demonstrably best series? I began to behave like the cannibal who decided that eating people was wrong. At first I simply stopped using the copyright argument with educators, and then I began to express my doubts to Hugh Eayrs.

To begin with he undertook to deal with my misgivings in a fatherly way — I didn't understand copyright. Copyright was a property right, it was what a successful publisher earned and accumulated; it was the reward of good publishing. I tried to remain polite and respectful; from my private-school training he was always "sir", no matter how warm the argument. But as the argument grew warmer I became mulish. Who could earn the right to give the children less than the best? They would have the best, he said, they would have our books. But why not demonstrate it doubly? Give our competitors access to the materials, rob them of any claim that they had been crippled. Let them pay, let them even pay premium prices for copyright permissions, but give them access.

The bright winning idea, too quickly taken up and made too much of, could not easily be abandoned. We were to return to the debate again and again, with Hugh Eayrs repeating his arguments like a creed and banging the desk with his fist: "Copyright is a property right. They have no more right to that material than they have to my house or my car." But that we could continue to argue suggests that he had begun to doubt the Company's policy, or that, justified or not, I was in a position of special privilege. For Hugh Eayrs had a low boiling-point and was not famous for reasonable argument. He fired and hired on impulse, or would cut off a bookseller's discount for criticism of our service or prices. Fortunately for me, a cheeky confidence was part of my make-up, and in any case I was not arguing for my advantage but for the Company's good name. And I was in a privileged position from all the circumstances of our meeting and, even more, because Hugh Eayrs and I laughed at the same things; sooner or later a joke would break the tension of our debate.

And something else had won me a special place. Quite unintentionally, chatting in a group around a friend's car I had fallen in love — for good; for better or worse, for richer or for poorer. Tony (for Antoinette) Lalonde seemed to me from that first moment to have more lovely, bubbling vitality and enjoyment of life than I had ever encountered, and that I wanted always to be near. She was at university still and I just starting at Macmillans. She wanted a career and I had yet to make a living. We were friends, great friends. We enjoyed being together, dancing together, and laughing together. But we mustn't get too serious. We agreed on that. Without discussing marriage directly we made it clear that it wasn't in our minds yet. But all the cool business of being sensible faded. We wanted to be married, and our parents' feelings that we were too young confirmed it. Macmillans raised my salary from $35 to $50 a week and we married in July 1932.

As at least a salute to independence we agreed we would have separate bedrooms — though with generous reciprocal visiting privileges. It was such a happy time that it seemed it could never change, and our days closed with Bron's nightly call in *Rough Justice*: "Fun tomorrow."

No doubt I accepted in theory the notion that as a young married man I had to be sensible and learn about managing our affairs, though up to now I had had little success in managing my own. What I didn't know was how much better my pretty young wife would learn to keep track of things, including me, and save us from a variety of disasters. But that was later. To begin with my airy confidence was at our disposal.

A year or two after we were married Hugh Eayrs encouraged me to take Tony on my trip to the Maritime Provinces; no doubt the impulse was both kindly and shrewd; it would be good for me and good for business. It would also be quite economical because of the pleasant custom at the time of being allowed to "deadhead" your wife. This had nothing to do with murder, but meant only that regular travellers bringing along a wife for the first time could have a double room for the price of a single. My Maritime friends saw to it that it was a happy time for us both. My only problem seemed to be getting my work done in the midst of so much fun.

In Halifax I remembered, or Tony reminded me, that a cheque for the rent of our duplex in Toronto was coming due. I had two bank accounts at the Bank of Commerce branch near Macmillans; one had enough money in it to pay the rent, $57.50, and one had not. Efficient as ever I sat down and wrote out the cheque, started to put down the wrong account number, crossed it out, and went to look up the right one. Something intervened and later, having forgotten what I had still to do, I mailed the cheque to the small mortgage company that was our landlord. On with the trip, the happy time.

Back in Toronto, a few weeks later, I was trying to settle back to work. My mother was visiting us and one afternoon

Tony, the young bride, was having one of my mother's oldest friends to tea. At the office I had a phone call. Tony was in tears; bailiffs had arrived in the middle of the tea party and wouldn't go away. They were tagging the furniture preparatory to removing it. I comforted as best I could and roared home, completely baffled as to why bailiffs should be there. At any rate I would start by throwing them out, bodily if necessary. One look at the bailiffs caused me to revise that part of the plan. They weren't discourteous but they were determined, and huge; they were going to remove the furniture. I stormed and threatened suit for trespass and stamped about still not understanding why they were there and finally phoned the landlord, whom I had never met. He was a dour Scot but not, I was to learn, unkind. My cheque had been bounced by the bank (against the wrong account); his attempts to reach me by phone had failed; clearly I had skipped, as many people were doing in those depression days; so, send in the bailiffs, see whether there's anything left to collect on. My dour Scot said it was my "own damned fault", called off his dogs, and we tried to put the ruined tea party together again. My mother, who had sat through all this, white to the lips, gradually came out of her state of near-shock, and finally someone laughed.

Since my airy confidence didn't include confronting the bank manager, my attempts at getting an apology or an explanation failed. What I did get was an insolent tongue-lashing from a young male teller who refused to concede the possibility that the bank had been even slightly at fault. He was learning banking manners as appropriate to the depression; the customer's always wrong; and probably in default.

I suppose being as transparently happy as we were was attractive. At any rate the Eayrses, themselves newly married and happy, took an affectionate and active interest in us from the first. We were often included in their parties and made much of, usually the only people from Macmillans to be invited. It was a tightrope; business and social relationships are a volatile mixture and to be petted as we were involved many risks.

163

And there were other bonds with Hugh Eayrs. I still had an office car — *the* office car — which was often convenient for ordinary chauffeuring, anything from getting the boss's liquor to driving him to a game of golf at Mississauga or Summit, and often making a fourth. His favourite golf partners were some of our notable scholar-authors: Ned Pratt, a joyous soul and a fine poet who loved golf as he loved life; Professor Pelham Edgar, a great teacher and fosterer of talent disguised under a rather pompous manner. Principal Malcolm Wallace of University College, a much-loved figure, was often a partner, and on one occasion we waited together on the fairway while someone beat the bushes for a lost ball. "Where did you go to university, Gray," he asked, with apparently real interest. Guardedly I said, "To University College." "Did you," he said. "I don't remember you there," and I could only answer with mock gaiety but picking my words, "I wasn't there very much." "Oh," he said, with a sad little smile, "it was like that, was it?"

Chauffeuring also included our distinguished Macmillan visitors and I was never sure whether my role was to entertain or merely to transport. The passenger usually established the tone, and in this capacity I met J. B. Priestley in a lonely and sour mood over adoring crowds who knew all about *The Good Companions* but had never heard of his other books. Frederick Philip Grove behaved like the gloomy Dane throughout our journey and I didn't try to change his mood. Grey Owl was one of my more interesting passengers, but our most exciting trip lay three or four years in the future at the peak of his fame. For the most part I enjoyed these chores, though the assumption that I was always available, or would drop what I was doing, suggested an irritating contempt for my work, and at times I regretted, a little stiffly, that I really could not stop what I was doing. But even just driving "the Chief" home was interesting to me, for we talked shop — of which I could never get enough — and the neglected work could usually be caught up in the evenings.

To be young was to have time and energy for everything. I hadn't altogether given up my writing hopes and for weeks at a time I would get up at six, make a pot of tea, and sit at my desk for an hour trying to use words. I wasn't working on a book but merely doing five-finger exercises — writing a book review, describing a scene or a person — and enjoying it all. In the process I even sold two stories and was greatly excited, but not fooled for long. Writing short stories for slick magazines was not after all what I meant by being a writer.

But all these things, in a young married man who was steadying down though slowly, were giving me confidence and standing, so that when Mr. and Mrs. Eayrs went to England in the summer of 1933 I was deputed to open his mail. I was surprised and pleased but not swept away by this access of responsibility. It was flattering and even a bit daunting, but there were no great problems in sight. Business, in spite of the depression (from which we had all taken a 10 per cent cut in pay), looked a little better. Part of the improvement was that we now seemed certain to win more than half of the elementary readers contract in the West, and the first of our *Canada Books* for Grade 7 had won out in Alberta and the initial order for ten thousand copies was already printed and shipped. It seemed probable that other provinces would follow Alberta's lead and we had visions of sweeping the country. None of us foresaw any special problems.

One morning's mail changed all that. Without warning came a letter for Hugh Eayrs from the Chief Superintendent of Education in Alberta, G. Fred McNally. He enclosed a formal letter from our rivals, Gage and Nelson, whose book we had beaten out for the Alberta decision. The enclosure made shocking reading. Our competitors claimed to have found some fifty examples of plagiarism in our book; the books plagiarized were all American texts for the same grade carried on an agency basis by Gage, and they were bound to act. The joint companies wrote that they were about to seek an injunction unless our book was withdrawn from circulation. McNally was chiefly concerned about the seriousness of the position from Alberta's point of view. Schools would be open in less than a month and distribution of the book should begin at once. Might he have our comments and proposals by return mail? Stunned, I could only rush off a note saying I neither understood the charge nor believed it well founded; I would write again as soon as possible.

Meanwhile, what was to be done? Trans-Atlantic calls were unheard of and the matter was too complicated for a cable. I knew that Lorne Pierce was away on vacation and the people at Ryerson, who stood guard over his health, said he had left in such a state of exhaustion that to call this frail man back was unthinkable. Yet Lorne Pierce and Dora Whitefield were officially the editors of the offending book.

No amount of argument or speculation could help. Hateful as it seemed, and alarming, we had to talk to Gage and Nelson. With as much bluff and confidence as I could manage I telephoned for an appointment. Backed by our lawyer, Billy McLaughlin — who kept insisting that he knew nothing about the case — I went over to the old Gage building at Bathurst and King streets, feeling as though I were approaching Castle Dangerous.

We were shown into a small conference room where we faced Harry Love, President of Gage, Sidney Watson, Manager of Nelsons in Canada, and John Saul, Gage's Editor-in-Chief. I had heard Hugh Eayrs in his reckless way refer to Harry Love as a tough, but though his manner was gruff he was courteous and seemed not unfriendly; I was to see him often in later years and never found him otherwise. Sidney Watson, whom I knew as one of Hugh Eayrs' golfing partners, was normally a stiffly polite man, though of a prickly and unforgiving temper; now he seemed so angry that he had trouble controlling his voice. Saul, behind a table in the corner, fussed impatiently with a pile of books in front of him, some of them bristling with bookmarks, others lying open with passages heavily underlined. One of the books was ours, and flipping over its pages while we went through greetings and introductions, Saul looked like a prosecuting counsel eager to open his case.

John C. Saul was one of the few men I have known who generated a substantial legend in his lifetime. He was tall with a

166

slight scholarly stoop, a shock of untidy hair, and an equally ample and untidy moustache. He usually wore a high stand-up stiff collar with a straight tie and smoked at a pipe whose intermittent jets of smoke suggested smouldering anger or impatience rather than relaxed comfort. He was said to have one of the finest libraries in Canada and to be equally effective at charming or browbeating a textbook selection committee. Many years before, he had given up the post of vice-principal of the Normal School in Winnipeg to become editor for George Morang when that American book traveller had started his own business in Canada. Saul had built a valuable list of school-books for Morang. When that list had been bought by Macmillan of Canada in 1912 he had come to the Macmillan staff as part of the transaction. Four or five years later he moved to Gage, where he had built the strongest elementary school-book list in the country.

It was hard to square John Saul's effectiveness with the more raffish parts of his legend but his career had been long and varied enough to encompass anything. Sooner or later one heard of the time he went to Edmonton when Alberta was in search of a geography book. It was said that each evening he entertained the members of the geography committee, listening to their views of what was needed or seeking their approval of what he had written during the day. At the end of two weeks or so the book was written and approved in manuscript by the Department of Education, and Saul left town with an order for several thousand copies and a contract for several years.

Legend also asserted that when away on business, living in hotels, he spent many if not most of his days in bed, a shrinking pile of detective magazines on one side of him and a growing pile of covers and torn-out pages on the other. Somewhere in the rumpled bed-clothes was a boot that he raked out absent-mindedly from time to time in order to strike matches for his pipe on its heel.

I had heard first about John Saul from Hugh Eayrs in connection with an interminable and embarrassing lawsuit in which the Company was involved. This was the Deeks *v.* Wells case, begun some years before and finally coming to an end after I joined Macmillans. A Miss Deeks of Toronto had written a general history of the world under the title of *The Web* and submitted it to Macmillan in Canada. For some months she had heard nothing and then it came back to her rejected. She was later to claim that at the time of the rejection John Saul, then Editor at Macmillans, had told her that he had sent the manuscript to Macmillans in New York (which he was later to deny).

The matter would probably have ended there if a year or two afterwards H. G. Wells had not published his *Outline of History* with Macmillan, New York. To Miss Deeks this was more than a coincidence. Examining Wells' book she became convinced that he had not only stolen her idea but had even, in places, copied her text. Two or three professors from the University of Toronto who had been asked to compare her manuscript and Wells' book were ready to agree with her and she brought suit against Wells and against Macmillan of New York and Canada. In due course other expert witnesses, including Professor Frank Underhill, disagreed and took the stand to testify that in their opinion similarities between the two works were the result of both authors necessarily drawing on the same sources — for some periods the only sources — Herodotus, Xenophon, Plutarch, and others. Twice Miss Deeks' case was thrown out of court in Canada, but convinced she had been cruelly victimized she carried it to the Privy Council in London, where for the last time she failed. When the heavy costs of the case were assessed against her she declared herself unable to pay, but is said to have called the Privy Council's attention to the fact that there was still a higher court (pointing upward) where she would finally have justice.

Saul had been famous for his untidy ways of working. Parcels of incoming manuscripts were tossed into a pile in the corner of his office until he could no longer ignore them. At that point he would go through them in a long evening session in shirtsleeves and puffing at his pipe, putting aside a few for further consideration and declining the rest — exactly the picture most unsuccessful authors have of publishers' hasty and cynical methods. But though Hugh Eayrs thought him a likable ruffian — a tough fighter — neither he nor anyone I ever talked to believed John Saul capable of stealing an author's work. Nor of course could they imagine H. G. Wells or the Macmillan Company of New York being party to the larceny with which they were charged.

I regret now that I didn't ask John Saul about the case when I came to know him in different circumstances. A few years later, when several publishers were working in Halifax to take advantage of curriculum revision, the old warrior, who travelled little now, suddenly appeared, and merely by doing so alarmed us all. We watched in fascination to see where he went and what he did, and were the more fascinated to find that he seemed seldom to leave the Nova Scotian Hotel. For ten days or so he was to be found sitting in the lobby reading detective stories or books about Russia as he smoked his pipe. Just occasionally a prominent teacher would join him for lunch or dinner.

During a chat in the lobby one day Saul asked me what I thought of communism, and I answered that I knew little or nothing about it and hadn't even thought much about it. The authority on nineteenth-century poets, waving his pipe, then delivered his judgement: it might be a kick in the ass upward for the Russians, but it would be a kick in the ass downward for us. It seemed to me this was economically and politically sensible if physically difficult. A few days later Saul's chair in the lobby was vacant. He had left, and it was only months later we learned that in his own mysterious fashion he had taken the authorization for new Junior High School science books with him.

But there was nothing amusing about facing the formidable old man across the room now. It was quickly shown that the marked and cross-referenced books added up to a stunning indictment. Someone who had prepared the notes and questions in our book had clearly borrowed wholesale from other books prepared, at an earlier date, for the same grade in the United States, scarcely changing a word. Granted that similar questions would be asked by any teacher on, say, Tennyson's "Lotus Eaters", the wording of note, question, and answer would not be precisely the same. When they were, again and again, there was only one conclusion to be drawn: much of the editorial material in our book had been hastily thrown together by cribbing from these others.

I tried such hasty defence as I could pull together. We were all dependent on junior editorial help. In the present contest we were all trying to do too much and too quickly. Somebody, I didn't know who, had let us down — and the same could happen to them, Gage and Nelson. Up to this point they had shown me some consideration as an embarrassed and presumably blameless junior, but now they closed in hard and cold. They had no time for rhetoric, said Saul; it was an open-and-shut case. We could withdraw the book or face a suit and perhaps heavy damages.

The arguments and pleas went on within and between our offices for a few hours more, but in only one place, Edmonton, could anything be improved — if improvement was possible. Filled with excitement and apprehension I caught the night train for the West, and was not surprised to find Sidney Watson of Nelsons on the same train. If we had some explaining to do, so had our competitors. For three nights and two days of sweltering heat and dust and cinders — sifted through the finest of screens to reappear as grit in food and bed-clothes — we travelled across Northern Ontario, Manitoba, and Saskatchewan talking of everything but business. I didn't know what kind of a plan of action Watson had for Edmonton, I only knew that I had none. My only hope was that McNally might persuade him to some softer attitude, on the ground that those most harmed by the controversy might be the boys and girls in Grade 7. But looking at Watson's short and stubborn face I found no comfort. Not only, I realized, did he find the plagiarism incomprehensible and outrageous, but all his bottled-up anger over the withheld copyrights was now flowing in the same channel. He intended a stiff reckoning.

On the morning of our arrival in Edmonton we saw Mr.

McNally in turn, then went away to think some more. McNally at this stage of his career was something of an enigma. Looking a little like Mr. Punch, he had a broad grin along with a quiff of reddish hair turning to grey. The most unlikely remark sent him into huge chortles as he slapped his leg and spun rather dangerously in his swivel chair. But a moment later he would be back upright and deadly serious with his lips pushed out and his finger pointing. So I had first the chortle, which was almost hysterics, over our predicament and then the dead-centre seriousness. "But now," he said, "whose-ever fault this was, what are we going to do? We must have our books." My secret and deepest concern had been that Gage and Nelson's book was ready and would be taken to replace ours. It came out in the talk that they were not ready. Alberta had to use our books, as they stood, or the year's work would be seriously set back. For us to correct and reprint the books would take two or three months and the cost would take any profit out of the contract for several years.

After a restless night I was back at McNally's office in the morning with a proposal that I thought might be acceptable — it seemed just possible. If Gage and Nelson would allow our books to be used for a year, without change, Alberta could take their book for Grade 8 the next year (there was after all very little to choose between the two series in quality). In consideration of this, we would relax our hold on copyrights for their book and they in turn would give us the full detail of the alleged plagiarisms. These would be completely eliminated in all future printings.

Fred McNally, listening closely to my proposal, pushed out his lips, then flung himself into a paroxysm of chortling and spinning as he slapped his legs. And then he was suddenly upright and staring seriously at me and pointing. His ruddy face lit up. "You're a statesman, sir," he said; "by George, I think this will work!" I felt bathed in the beginning of a flood of relief of relaxed tensions. On further thought he hinted that he would make it work — and later he did. Sidney Watson and I travelled back together, relaxed and chatting amiably. My for-

171

mula had to be accepted by all four companies, but ours at least had no choice — no ground to fight on — and Watson was certain that Gage would concur. Pleased with myself and enormously relieved, I inhaled equal quantities of gorgeous Prairie air and cinder dust, and caught up peacefully on the sleep that I had lost on the way out.

The solution was agreed by all parties and I was a hero for a day. In due course the plagiarisms were all overtaken and removed and the book, which was a good book in its own right, was, with periodic revision, to be popular in the classrooms of several provinces for the next twenty-five years. Discretion prevented one from asking who had done the offending editorial work and no explanation was ever offered. Lorne Pierce said, almost too often, that no one would ever hear the truth from him, and so far as I know no one did; but something in his manner — a foxy, almost libellous little smile, suggested the scandal he could unfold. He was after all Lorne Pierce and no one — not anyone — would dream of accusing him of such unprofessional and unethical short-cuts. Hugh Eayrs, except to congratulate me generously on my handling of the problem, never mentioned it again.

The great readers struggle didn't fill our lives, though at times it seemed to. By 1934 or '35 it was largely over, with the business more or less split between ourselves and Gage-Nelson. Dents, who entered the contest alone, and forced the pace, was the one firm to lose out so seriously as to be set back for several years. The educational authorities in the western provinces had become alarmed at the expenses we had all incurred under their rules and the disaster that most of us faced. This knowledge undoubtedly became a factor in selection, and since there was little enough to choose between Gage-Nelson's books and ours, adjustments of decision to do something to balance loss and gain could be managed without damage to conscience or curriculum. And though all of us complained, four out of the five companies were happy enough with the result. It provided a substantial increase in sales for a few years, though at such ruinous prices as to make it barely worth while. Still, in the depression, it was welcome; though Hugh Eayrs said grumpily each year after looking at the figures that the shareholders would do better to put their money in the bank. And the second cut of 10 per cent in salary throughout the staff was not restored. When mine was, quietly, I was almost as embarrassed as I was pleased and relieved.

These were such long working days, and frequently evenings as well, at home or "on the road", that it is hard to believe there was time for fun. But youth finds time and energy for all it wants to do and Frank and I not only had time for parties, to polish up wonderful anecdotes about our publishing experiences for the entertainment of our wives and friends, but also to form with others a group known as the Beer and Literature Club. The latter met once a month to demolish beer, poets, and the moral questions of our time in large quantities. Our numbers were small but we were all about the same age and had a lively if uninformed curiosity about the world that was changing around us and filled with increasingly ominous signs.

Some of our pet stories, embellished if not invented, came from Hugh Eayrs, and some of his favourites had to do with Mr. Roberts. He was a man we all liked and respected but the perpetual look of worry on his long, thin face, his sad nasal twang, and his almost clinical interest in funerals made him too tempting a target for young mimics. The Roberts stories reached a peak with the death of Sir Gilbert Parker in England. Though a Canadian who had made a reputation as a writer of romantic historical novels about Canada, *The Seats of the Mighty* and others, Parker had for many years lived in England and become a member of the British Parliament. It was surprising to learn that his body was being returned to Belleville, Ontario, for burial, and the news seemed to raise a special excitement in Mr. Roberts, who felt certain Macmillans would, or at any rate should, be represented at the funeral. Hugh Eayrs didn't like funerals, but Mr. Roberts regarded them almost as a perquisite of his office.

With the Parker remains being carried across the Atlantic, Mr. Roberts opened a small campaign. The first remarks to

Mr. Eayrs were casual: "Too bad about Sir Gilbert Parker" —
a name he managed to transform to Porker — "a very distinguished man, I always thought. Will you be going to the funeral, Mr. Eayrs?" Hugh Eayrs, busy with other things, agreed
that it was too bad — but, no, he wouldn't be going to the funeral. The papers kept Mr. Roberts informed; the casket had
been put on the train at Halifax and was moving westward towards Belleville. He had only two days. He began to hint that
it would be suitable if perhaps he went to represent Macmillans
and Mr. Eayrs. "Not at all necessary," said Hugh Eayrs. "Sir
Gilbert was not one of our authors." Mr. Roberts waited for a
more propitious moment but the Ocean Limited was approaching Montreal. When next day he tried again, Hugh
Eayrs waved the subject away impatiently.

There was only one more chance; the funeral was to be the
next day. The following morning he telephoned Hugh Eayrs
immediately on the latter's arrival in the office and after reporting on other matters came almost too casually to the point.
"I happen to have brought my car today," he said, "and I was
just thinking I could slip down to Belleville *very* easily (he had
his own way of indicating italics), "I mean it's *no* distance and
Sir Gilbert really was — I wouldn't mind at all." This was the
third or fourth time of asking and on a busy morning it was one
too many. "Roberts," Hugh Eayrs roared into the telephone,
"can you hear me?" "Yes, Mr. Eayrs," said Roberts, who undoubtedly knew the gist of what he was about to hear. "No one
is going to that God-damned funeral!" "I only thought — "
said Mr. Roberts but there was no one to hear what he thought.
"By gollies," Mr. Roberts said to me, "I mean, he's an *aw*fully
nice man, and he doesn't mean it, but he can get *very* angry." It
wasn't something any of us needed to be told, but Roberts at
any rate had earned the right to speak on the subject more often and more feelingly than any of us.

When, soon after, our elderly production man died, it was
appropriate for Mr. Roberts to attend his funeral. And since
the old man had lived in an upper flat with a narrow and twisting stair, and since his pall-bearer friends were old and tottery,

the funeral had a number of interesting features which Mr. Roberts was happy to discuss with any who were interested and with many who were not.

But that was not the only result of what was a genuinely sad event that we had all seen approaching. The production work had still to be done, even by people who knew almost nothing about it, like Frank Upjohn and me.

Nowadays a publisher of any size has a production man with an assistant or two, a designer with the same support, plus editors to find manuscripts and evaluate them — even to rewrite them; still others to secure illustrations and to copy-edit (to mark up the manuscript for the printer, to check facts and correct spelling, punctuation, and grammar, and finally to check proofs). All these things had been done in the 1930s for a surprisingly large list of new Macmillan books by the sick old man and two eccentric ladies of uncertain age, devoted to good causes, to their church, to Macmillans — and one, in later years, to gin. The only supplement to the work of this hard-pressed group had been provided by salesmen, secretaries, managers, and even the president. It was work done in odd moments of time in the office or more often in evenings or very short weekends — the extra work to be rewarded in the hereafter. It was strenuous and we sometimes complained, but for young people thirsty to learn the business and fascinated by its techniques and mysteries, most of it was satisfying work.

And it was only a short step from folding a sheet of paper into eight or sixteen or thirty-two pages, as a printer's machine would do, then crawling around the floor of my office, deciding on what page the illustrations of *Dominion High School Chemistry* must fall — doing a primitive layout — to editing at various levels, and developing book ideas from teachers' hints about classroom needs. Such hints and suggestions were common enough but they had to be tested and checked out before a real need — worth the risk — was identified. When a good idea was found, and the right person to carry it out, we were both triumphant and wholly engrossed in seeing it through to a successful conclusion.

Quite early in our travels Frank and I had both encountered the repeated wish for a good collection of narrative poetry for the first or second year of high school. It was in a way a strange request, for there were many such collections; but they were British or American and contained many selections that meant nothing to Canadian children, being rooted — especially the American — in an unfamiliar history. Our checking confirmed a solid demand. Our choice of editors to make the collection was happy — E. J. Pratt, himself an outstanding writer of narrative poetry, and Adrian Macdonald, a popular and experienced teacher of English. Their first table of contents was submitted to a number of teachers for evaluation, and we then ran a contest for a title among English teachers. The winning title — *A Pedlar's Pack* — came from an elderly scholar in Peterborough, Frank Morris, a notable teacher and an authority on orchids. Contents, title, editorial prestige, and publicity came together in a happy combination, and the book which perhaps did more than any other to make St. Martin's Classics known throughout Canada took off on publication day to a great and lasting success, selling 3,000 copies in its first year and continuing to enjoy even more dramatic sales before being declared out of print almost fifty years later. Its great merit was that it contained not only a well-chosen mixture of British and American poems but Canadian poems as well.

The response to Canadian material was striking and heartening, and makes me gape at the media announcers and journalists of today who talk as though Canadian nationalism began in 1967. Macmillan of Canada had published a book called *The Rise of Canadian National Feeling* before 1930. And when I came to travel across Western Canada in 1932 and '33 telling chemistry teachers that we had a new book preparing in their field by Bigelow and Morehouse — a Canadian book relating chemistry to Canadian research and industry with appropriate Canadian illustrations — the news was greeted wtih enthusiasm and the promise of a welcome. To many teachers in Western Canada Dr. Bigelow was "my old teacher at Mount A", and others had gone to school with or been taught by Fred

Morehouse. No doubt the lines were simpler and clearer forty years ago, but they provided evidence of the steel net that the Maritimes and Ontario had absent-mindedly flung across the continent to sink into the cement that binds Canada together. And in spite of great strains — of problems, of selfishness and stupidity on both sides — one cannot doubt it is still there, and still holding.

In the 1930s, travelling east or west, it was hard to believe it would hold. I came back gloomily from many trips feeling that the country would fly into five pieces. Perhaps if the United States had *looked* less troubled it would have done. But bank failures there and the rise of the gangsters made it clear that we were not alone in our troubles; indeed, others seemed worse off. But to travel across the West with meals in comfortable empty dining-cars, to stay in the great railway hotels and walk to calls past long lines at unemployment offices and soup kitchens, was to feel guilt-ridden and miserable much of the time. On every side were panhandlers, many of them big strong men who looked ashamed or desperate or beaten. But the people I called on were alive and struggling — as was the whole West — more eager to talk economics or politics than books.

With the deepening depression more companies cut back on travelling, while others lengthened the trips as an economy measure. There was no air travel and the long-distance telephone was a luxury; so we wrote long, sad letters and shepherded our iron sample trunks onto the trains, and bumped along catching up on our paper-work, writing up the few orders, and explanations at the lack of more.

Young men won't stay sad and the travellers compensated for their lonely and unnatural life with bursts of high spirits. We greeted each other in the hotels with glad cries: "Whenja get in?" "Whenya goin' out?" "Are you opened up yet?" (meaning have you unpacked and set up your samples) "Come on up to the room and have a drink." For many it was a short life and a merry one. We came to know the numbers and times of the trains, the best food at the lowest price, and the numbers of the best sample rooms in each hotel.

But not all the gentlemen of the road were reckless and light-hearted. I remember one grey, quiet bookman whose whole life seemed to be given over to the joys of administration in its unimportant details. In between trips he would devise cunning little refinements. He used to send his laundry home every week and his parcel would cross a fresh batch coming from his wife. At Calgary on his spring trip he would be overtaken by summer underwear and his raincoat just as he was leaving for the warmth and rain of Vancouver and Victoria, and he in turn would mail his woollies and winter overcoat back to Ontario. On the fall trip as he returned from the Pacific coast, the woollies and heavy coat smelling of moth-balls would meet him in Edmonton or Saskatoon, depending on the weather reports which he studied, and which were no less accurate then than now.

It followed that he had a very carefully worked out itinerary (in duplicate) and that no matter how important the business he was reluctant to stay over if his laundry was running low, and if he did stay he became as restless as Pavlov's dog after the dinner-bell had gone. His parcels from home also contained cookies and apples, and many a customer meeting him for the first time would be fascinated by what appeared a distinctly novel approach: "Would you care," our traveller would say, settling his glasses, "to come up to the room, and have a cookie?" And since no drink was ever offered, there they would sit munching dry cookies, an absolute conversation-stopper. His ways of working were always something of a mystery and he worked so slowly that I remember one of his employers complaining with a sour grin that they wondered if he was taking up a homestead.

But no doubt he came home at last, as we all did, steaming into Union Station in the early morning hardly able to contain our excitement and joy.

𝟗

B Y THE MID NINETEEN-THIRTIES much had changed in our lives and in the world around us. I was becoming an old hand at swinging on and off trains, at setting out two or three times a year for the West — torn between the excitement and challenge of each trip and the ache of leaving Tony standing on the platform and waving, smiling prettily and bravely but looking infinitely forlorn. The depression had lifted somewhat in central Canada, but conditions in the Prairie Provinces had been worsened by drought, soil erosion, and plagues of grasshoppers, and had reduced people to near desperation, ready for any radical change that held even wild promises of improvement. The casual traveller, especially in Saskatchewan, could hear enough heresy and mild treason to shock even a cynic.

Much of this had been heard in the East too — only a year or so before, when comfortable (the West said smug) Ontario had seemed ripe for the most mischievous experiment. One evening in 1931 or 1932 a group of us from the fraternity house had strolled along Hoskin Avenue to Queen's Park, where it was reported there was to be a Communist meeting which the police had given warning they would break up. It was said that Tim Buck, head of the Communist Party in Canada, would be there. None in our group regarded Communism as anything but a crackpot philosophy — amusing or interesting or evil, depending on the individual. But whatever we thought of it, we were strolling across simply out of curiosity — to see the show

— and to see what wild Communists looked like. It wouldn't, I think, have occurred to any of us that they might look like anyone else.

Toward the south end of the Park, between the bandstand and the Ontario Parliament Buildings, we saw an unimpressive little group of perhaps sixty people, some with children; they looked both ordinary and harmless, not remotely dangerous to the city or the country as a whole. We couldn't make out from a hundred yards away whether anyone was speaking or anything interesting was happening or was about to happen. There was no cheering, only a kind of irresolute shifting about in the little crowd. And then like an explosion came the police. On horseback and on motorcycles with sidecars they burst from the cover of bushes round the buildings and rode straight at the group. They had been only partially screened so that their eruption wasn't a complete surprise, but the size and force of it was overpowering and shocking.

For a short moment the group hung loosely together, as though they might try to face this out. But the brave and desperate impulse couldn't hold them; they hadn't a stick or a stone among them and moral force was meaningless here. They broke and fled in all directions and the police phalanx spread into little pursuit groups, better equipped and more determined. One man, at first unnoticed, came racing across the park toward us trying to reach and cross the road, but a motorcycle swung away in pursuit. The man was tiring quickly and the bike roared after him, cutting his head-start in seconds. He began desperately to dodge, darting this way and that in an attempt to gain a few yards, but the motorbike following every move among the trees pressed him hard. Inevitably he tripped and fell, and the policeman from the sidecar was out and standing over him, kicking him brutally as the man made feeble attempts to get up. At last he simply lay there trying to cover his head and crying out as his body recoiled under the heavy boot.

I suppose we all had some impulse to intervene, to try to stop this cruel nonsense, but we didn't. We weren't after all on the wretched man's side, except that each of us could feel the boot in his guts. Instead, we turned away sickened as the broken man was stood up and led away for questioning. For a while we were moody and thoughtful, ashamed perhaps that we had not even tried to help a fellow human, shocked at the picture of a hard world beyond our experience. But presently we were playing cards and singing around the piano, and in a day or two this glimpse of *real-politik* remained only as a trace that would surface less and less often as time passed.

But only the wilfully blind, the insensitive, or the stupid could remain unchanged by the events of these times. Not all the numberless griefs were as sharply pointed as the little drama of Queen's Park; most were out of sight and all levels of government worked at keeping them there. Remote work-camps had been set up for the unemployed and thousands of men were provided with a numbing existence in return for food and little more than tobacco money; the consciences of the more fortunate were spared much discomfort by the arrangement. But no matter what was swept under the rug, there were visible and uncomfortable reminders that things were seriously wrong, and that the country's leaders seemed unable to put them right.

In January of 1935 in a series of broadcasts the Conservative Prime Minister, R. B. Bennett, announced a program of radical reform that shocked and alienated many of his followers without convincing, or immediately helping, those for whom he intended both. The law's delays and the slow-grinding wheels of Mr. Bennett's mill left everything much as before, except that many people were that much more heartsick.

Crossing the Alberta–British Columbia border one night late that winter the train I was on slowed down as it ran between roaring fires alongside the track. Against the flames we could see from the windows of the warm and comfortable train men huddled around the fires in a desperate battle against the icy mountain air. As Vancouver was choked with unemployed and a growing stream from the Prairies was moving to its warmer climate, British Columbia had closed the border. The men we saw had been herded off the freight trains and left to find their way back to the cold and hungry Prairies or to perish in the Rocky Mountains.

But if the flood had been stemmed a little, the long lines at welfare and unemployment offices and soup kitchens remained on Vancouver streets. There seemed no menace in them; only bewilderment, helplessness, and humiliation. It was this bland and beaten docility that though reassuring was also shocking. Many of these big, powerful men had belonged only fifteen years before to a corps that we proudly hailed as made up of the finest fighting men in the world — the Canadians, "Our Boys".

They had a deep-seated tradition of respect for the law, but even that was not proof against hardship and frustration to which they could see no end and of which they could make no sense. Goading incidents multiplied, seeming both heartlesss and mindless: the foreclosures on mortgages, the repossessing of farm machinery, a drop in the sale price of meat that meant it cost more to ship cattle than could be earned by their sale, while wheat that a few years before had been over two dollars a bushel had dropped to thirty-two cents in 1932. Suddenly, people who had known a substantial if hard-earned prosperity had no money, and on many blown-out wheat farms there weren't even chickens and eggs and milk to sustain life. Wise old men were predicting with a bitter certainty that the West would never see dollar wheat again.

As a transient I was only brushed by these things but they left uncomfortable brush-burns. One day a quiet conversation at the Department of Education in the Legislative Building in Winnipeg was rudely broken into by a small, work-roughed man who was almost incoherent. He had burst into the wrong office in the wrong department, but in his half-demented state his story could not be contained. He had shipped his cattle ("fine fat beasts", he said) only to find that his net return was a debt to the railway company. The bright blue eyes in his brown face seemed to be imploring us to make some sense out of this as they flickered between tears and violence. Another man I met in Edmonton told me he had lost his land; walked off it after years of work. He could neither afford feed nor pay his taxes, and he had left his cattle to die.

One morning I was waiting in the outer office of the Superintendent of Schools for Winnipeg. When he came out it was in a rush and buttoning his coat. With an apologetic little wave of his hand he called out, "I've got to find out whether St. James Street will let us keep our schools open," and gave a savage little grimace. St. James Street, financial centre of Montreal, eastern big business, the banks, the mortgage companies, the makers of farm machinery, all shared with the government in Ottawa the role of villain — the faceless oppressor. These were the people who could — who must — find solutions to the problems of small people struggling in a net that relentlessly dragged them down.

There was concern in the East, if little real understanding, and there were attempts to help out with carloads of second-hand clothing, of apples and potatoes. These things were accepted with wry gratitude, out of necessity, by people who had always been proud and fiercely independent. But when Ontario's new Premier, Mitchell Hepburn, argued for political advantage against more substantial and practical help, he soured the taste of the little that had been done. His characteristic public statement that Ontario was not going to be a milch cow for the West was the kind of political gaffe that is never forgotten or forgiven, and seemed to embody everything that the West was suffering apparently at eastern hands. And it was not surprising that when, forty years later, Ontario was desperate for Alberta's oil and gas, at least one man in Alberta said aloud, "Let the bastards freeze in the dark."

If there were not many people in Ontario who could match, or wished to match, Hepburn's crudity, there were plenty who were equally insensitive. Coming home from a western trip disturbed and angry at a system that worked so badly, I found few enough of my friends who knew or cared much, and fewer still who were prepared to hear and talk about it. I was a bit of a bore, perhaps even a bit of a red. My old Uncle Frank and I had become friends as we had not always been — he seeming to have the same austere disapproval of me as a small boy that my grandmother had shown. He was a comfortable family solicitor and a kindly man, but on the subject of the unemployed, especially those in the West who had lost everything, there was no talking to him. To stories of hardship his response was a momentary sympathy, genuine enough — "too bad", he would say, or "what a pity". But talk of lowered interest rates, lowered freight rates, or interest-free loans shocked him.

He had the conventional eastern notion that western farmers in good times had left "by the trainload" for expensive winter holidays in Florida and California. "They had the money," he said, "and spent it. They didn't pay their debts and now they want to borrow more." "Are they to be allowed to starve?" I asked, and he looked as though I had been deliberately rude. "It is the way the system works," he said slowly and patiently. "When people ask you to trust them with your money you expect them, when they can, to make sensible arrangements for paying it back." The argument went on as it probably was going on in countless homes and restaurants across the country, ending always in futility.

But it was going beyond talk in the West. There, anger combined with the radical western spirit as it wrestled against the stranglehold which seemed to threaten survival. In 1933 in Regina a group of concerned intellectuals and humanitarians in a statement of economic and social principles for government laid the foundations of what was to become a formidable new party in Canada. The issuing of what became known as the Regina Manifesto was greeted with some respect and a good deal of derision, but probably no one, including those most active in its framing, could have guessed at the force of the seismic shock they had touched off. The shock wave was to launch the Co-operative Commonwealth Federation (CCF) on its way to winning several seats in the federal House almost at once, and the government of Saskatchewan within ten years, and soon after to scare the life out of thousands of people like my uncle at election time in solid Ontario. For many in our mild, unflappable country it seemed that Russia, 1917, rather than prosperity, was just around the corner.

Alberta had had its run at radicalism a few years before and now one began to hear talk of something that sounded wilder — Social Credit. Many of the province's soberer citizens began to express fears that the seeds of madness were working among them; they behaved a little like people who think they have a certifiable nut in the family; "Why does it always have to be Alberta?" I heard some of them wail. Whether there was any substance to their fear, it seemed certain that the discontented in Alberta were looking for stronger gods or stronger medicine. Both were supplied by a stout, bald, quiet-spoken high school principal in Calgary, William Aberhart. Whether political power was always an objective for him, or whether the opportunity merely grew out of a concern for the problems of unhappy people, may be uncertain, but when Major Douglas's ideas on Social Credit began to circulate, the way to power was ready to his hand. Weekly from his Prophetic Bible Institute in Calgary, Aberhart seemed to mesmerize an increasing number of people, and imperceptibly "Bible Bill" built his congregation into a formidable party. Initially his appeal seemed to be chiefly to the ignorant and the deprived. But when with a little local adaptation of Major Douglas's doctrine Aberhart seemed to promise free money on earth as well as glory in heaven, his appeal suddenly widened. His Sunday Bible Classes were packed houses and his growing radio audience spread throughout the province and beyond. Between two of my trips, perhaps six months apart, what was reported as a slightly comic possibility had become entirely probable. And Mr. Aberhart was openly saying, "Don't argue, don't discuss, just vote."

My friends among the teachers and at the University of Alberta, who among them represented the whole political spectrum, watched and reported, their reports moving from an amused detachment to a fascinated horror. It was going to happen — and it did. In the autumn of 1935 William Aberhart left the principalship of Crescent Heights High School in Calgary to spend the rest of his life in Edmonton as Premier of Alberta.

Not only had he vaulted to power on an apparent promise of "funny money", he had carried with him a group of seemingly fanatic members, unknown, inexperienced, and of very doubtful qualifications.

In a short time Aberhart's stunned critics had learned to take what satisfaction they could from stories about the ineptness of the rubes who were about to fall flat on their faces; but their hopes were not to be fulfilled. One such story was of the woman whose husband had become a member by defeating the Minister of Education, Perrin Baker. She couldn't think how her husband would get on because he would now have to be Minister of Education and his schooling had stopped at Grade 3. In fact, Mr. Aberhart himself took the portfolio of education and both publishers and educators waited apprehensively for the injection of Social Credit propaganda into the provincial school-books; but there was none of that. He left the Department's permanent officials to get on with their work exactly as before, and after an incredulous and wary pause that is what they did. I had called on the previous Minister of Education and on Mr. Aberhart as a high school principal, but when he became Minister there was no occasion to do so. The permanent officials said he was happy to do without such courtesies.

Where he did make his weight felt, and quickly, was in a suspension of interest payments on Alberta bonds, exactly the sort of thing the West wanted and the East feared. It made a good bracing start for all concerned; the pieces could be picked up later, and were. With a gun at their heads easterners were found to be quite reasonable people, and acceptable accommodations were reached — though the curses if not loud were deep.

In the next few months Mr. Aberhart, looking as though he had slept well, was to be seen every morning in the cafeteria of the Macdonald Hotel in Edmonton, his great bald head bent over a hearty breakfast. Close at hand, like a pilot fish, was Ernest Manning, his chief assistant and ultimate successor. We watched them at first with a nervous fascination as they discussed what we presumed was our fate, though it may well have been the weather.

After the Alberta election Hugh Eayrs, who had never seen him but enjoyed reckless statements, said cheerfully and daily that someone should shoot that man Aberhart. In the past Hugh Eayrs had been quite unlike the conventional business-man, but increasingly as the certainties of our world seemed to loosen and move under our feet, uneasiness made him sound like all the rest. In addition to business worries his health was giving him, and all of us, concern, and there were sad signs that the almost idyllically happy marriage of five or six years before was now less happy. It was the beginning of a worrisome time, and one indication of the change was that Hugh Eayrs settled into the pleasant custom of taking the trip across the West with me at least once a year.

He was stimulating and amusing company, and of course I was flattered; but the cost of it all was unjustified while busi-ness, though more promising, remained bad, and my job as courier or tour manager cut into precious business time. The Chief didn't concern himself with the detailed work I had to do — calling on members of curriculum revision or textbook selec-tion committees — and occasionally teased me about my ear-nestness. My seriousness about the work would sometimes merely stimulate Hugh Eayrs to light-heartedness. One day when I was to see someone on a curriculum committee he pro-duced an old English music-hall song for which we found a tune later — to be produced on all such occasions:

> One man on the committee
> Thinking to be witty
> Hit her on the titty
> With a hard-boiled egg.

If it suited him he would sweep aside some appointment I had, or should have, if he wanted me for golf or a bridge game, un-less I was prepared to insist on my obligations. He looked up old friends, called on the booksellers, made speeches at service clubs, and gave long and optimistic interviews to the local papers or radio stations on trends in Canadian writing and publishing, or on the depression.

The media, which found few travellers with so much colour, couldn't get enough of him, but the interviews were a two-edged sword. This lighted up the name of Macmillan and just occasionally put us in touch with a promising writer, but the unpromising who answered the call were far more numerous and demanding. Our phones rang until late at night and odd characters — some of them very odd — would lurk in hotel lobbies or in the corridors outside his room, clutching dog-eared manuscripts. In the evenings, if not seeing old friends, Hugh Eayrs would be charming and amusing to anyone it seemed well to charm and amuse. Some of the senior educational officials knew him of old and I realized that their views of him were very mixed. Those who were meeting him for the first time were almost uniformly bowled over, by his stories, by his wit, and by his air of casual sophistication. These easy conquests didn't impress him too much, but he enjoyed them and they helped to keep his own troubles momentarily out of mind. Unfortunately the trips seemed to be adding to his health problems. Entertaining usually meant some drinking; occasionally it meant a lot. I was convinced from what I thought were the effects that though drinking cheered him up, and helped him to sparkle, it worsened his condition. After a party he slept badly or not at all, would be short of breath, and then alarmingly, and sometimes embarrassingly, might fall asleep in the middle of an interview or standing waiting for a taxi. I dared to try gentle persuasion and even something like a lecture. He said bitterly but with a laugh that Mrs. Eayrs and I, and everyone except the doctors, knew what was wrong with him. But then he would suddenly be cheerful and seem well and once again everything would be a joke. "By God," he would say, after some evening that had been heavy work, "the things I do for you and Macmillans! What I suffer!"

One evening I persuaded him to go to a Schoolmasters' Club dance in Winnipeg and later saw him being wafted around the room in the arms of an enormous woman, wife of a school inspector. Clearly she was in charge and one had the impression that the Chief's feet hardly touched the floor as this masterful woman held his short, thick body firmly in her grasp. "Extraordinary experience," he said to me afterwards; "did you see that big woman who took charge of me?" I said I had. "Well," he said, "I've never had this happen before, but I was chatting away in my brightest fashion, gazing as I thought into her eyes, and by God it was her navel." With such nonsense we laughed our way across the country, invariably finishing an evening with drinks and shop-talk, of which I could never have enough; there was a shadow darkening the joy of all this, but the experience was still a privilege and I knew it.

On one trip in 1936 we were to travel from Calgary to Edmonton overnight, but the Chief, having no further appointments in Calgary, decided to go ahead on the fast afternoon train, the Chinook. I would catch up in the morning. The next day, just off the train, I joined him for breakfast at the Macdonald Hotel where, in great spirits, he told me how much he had enjoyed his trip and what an attractive and interesting man he had had as a seat companion. After breakfast as we waited at the elevator, it arrived and discharged Mr. Aberhart and Mr. Manning. There were general nods and good mornings all round and the great bulk of the Premier moved off towards the cafeteria.

"Do you know the name of that big man?" Hugh Eayrs asked. Suddenly I had an intimation of disaster, as I asked cautiously, "Is that the man you travelled with yesterday?" Happy at the pleasant recollection and smiling he said it was, "charming" he said once again, and "most interesting". "Did you by any chance tell him that somebody should shoot Mr. Aberhart?" I asked. "Yes," he said, "of course." I held my head. "That *is* Mr. Aberhart. Premier *and* Minister of Education." Our first appointment that morning was at the Department of Education.

After our first convulsion of horrified laughter we tried to take stock of the possible damage. Hugh Eayrs was sure he had told Mr. Aberhart his name because he could remember the Premier saying "That's very interesting, Mr. Eayrs" when the Chief had told him of his approaching assassination. He couldn't be sure whether he had spoken of his business or of what he would be doing in Edmonton, though it seemed to me he must have. If he had, presumably we could expect to be severely penalized, if not cut off, in our dealings with the Government of Alberta. But the morning at the Department passed quietly in talks with officials. There was no summons, no intimation of trouble, and none ever came. And though at first we dared not even tell the story, in time it was recklessly added to Hugh Eayrs' repertoire, along with his beloved Yorkshire jokes and his celebrated impersonation of Queen Victoria (for this he puffed out his fat cheeks, draped a napkin on his head topped with an inverted silver sugar bowl, and held a brass poker in his hand as a sceptre).

I suppose much of the laughter of that time — and there was a great deal of it, much more I think than now — was a defence, an alternative to desperation. My own seems now to have been a cover for the guilt I felt at what was happening in Canada — though I did little enough about it — mixed with quite irrepressible high spirits, though there were many young people who had been driven far past laughter. But in retrospect it seems that in those worsening days before the framework of society broke up — before the Hitler war, and the bomb, before the absolute triumph of the motor-car and the licensing of pollution and destruction of the environment, before the world became smaller and populations larger, before we began to live existentially, like spies in enemy country — hope was not destroyed but remained to warm most people's hearts, and we laughed like children before our tears were dry.

But faced with government impotence that looked like callous indifference, patience was running out and for many the sweet taste of hope was turning bitter. There was now a deposit of cynicism and distrust that would stay on the tongue of many for a lifetime, to be passed on as an inheritance to their children. One of the most threatening protests had taken place in the summer of 1935 with a decision by the unemployed to approach Ottawa directly. However the idea originated, the beginning of a wave came curling from the Pacific coast about mid-June. There was a first gathering in Vancouver and then a rolling out on east-bound freight trains; hungry and tired and dirty the ragged army moved through the mountains, gathering strength at every stop. That they were well behaved and sternly disciplined suggests by hindsight that both the inspiration and the management of the event were Communist in origin. In Calgary the men swung down off the freights in search of rest, food, a clean-up, and reinforcements; in orderly fashion they went to an arranged campsite.

Business had brought me to Calgary as the march arrived there. The men were to be seen everywhere, carrying tins to collect money for food for the group but not being intimidating; polite and grateful to those who helped, but not abrasive to those who refused — though not many seemed to refuse. And many people went out to the camp taking food and warm clothing, perhaps looking for news of sons or brothers or husbands who had gone in search of work, or adventure, a year or two before. The opinion was expressed on all sides that the marchers were "nice boys" and "well behaved".

During this visit a teacher friend of mine, John Laurie, from Mr. Aberhart's school, was coming to see me at the Palliser Hotel. He was serving on a Provincial English Committee and was coming to tell me what books they were looking for. He was a quiet, gentle man, who had been badly wounded in the 1914-18 war, and I thought in permanent shock since then. Only two things seemed to rouse him, his love of English and a concern for lame ducks (in later years he made the plight of the Indians his whole concern). Inevitably on this trip he arrived bringing with him one of the boys off the trains with whom he had struck up a conversation on the street. We ordered the boy some food and some sandwiches to take with him, but we couldn't persuade him to talk much. He was both shy and tired and perhaps over-awed by the shabby splendour of the old hotel, or the ease with which other men could command food and comfort beyond his means and perhaps his experience. We saw him to the hotel door and wished him luck, and he smiled shyly then for the first time, thanked us, and left almost like a sleep-walker.

As the On to Ottawa March gained momentum it grew in size. Moving slowly the wave grew bigger and more powerful as it rolled on. The original group looked more and more like an army in the making. On it went, gathering recruits from north and south, at Medicine Hat, Swift Current, and Moose Jaw, so that the rumble of the oncoming wave had become audible and alarming in Ottawa, more than a thousand miles away. The public attitude, which had ranged from mild interest to active sympathy, began to change; an appropriate protest, it appeared, might become a formidable danger. In the path of the March lay Regina, then Winnipeg, scene of the General Strike sixteen years before and dangerously unhappy once again. East of that the great transcontinental trains roared through Northern Ontario with its now stagnant mining towns full of the discontented; beyond that lay the larger cities of the East. It was not hard for the uneasy to imagine sleepy little Ottawa smashed under the impact of this rolling mass with uncontrollable anarchy to follow.

Whether there was any real basis for such fears, whether it was considered necessary policy or merely good politics to stop the March, will probably remain unanswerable questions. That orders were given to the Mounted Police there is little doubt; the marchers pulled up at Regina while some of the leaders were taken on to Ottawa for meetings with government leaders, then sent back with empty hands. The mood of the marchers camped at the edge of the city was becoming more menacing. Since Regina was the site of the RCMP's training barracks, there was a natural concentration of police personnel there, and more were brought in. Positions were hardening on both sides and a mass protest meeting made up of marchers and citizens in downtown Regina provided the setting for explosive incidents.

My travels had taken me on to the Pacific coast, and there in

Vancouver on July 2 I read the first news of what was to become known as the Regina Riots. The accounts were confused and included one story of a policeman being dragged over behind the railway sheds and beaten to death by the marchers. It was believed that there were a number of serious injuries and perhaps other deaths. Ringleaders had been arrested and the rest of the marchers were being dispersed. The March was over. The country which had appeared to want this to happen now behaved like a killer who didn't know the gun was loaded. In due course the police would be accused of brutality, and of having provoked the riot, but there is little doubt that most people, east of Regina at any rate, breathed more easily. They might dislike the means but they enjoyed the result of what they would not openly applaud.

Returning through Regina a week or two later I found my friends there in something of a state of shock. Those who had seen anything of the riot, without especially blaming either side, were suffering a delayed horror from their glimpse of violence: the spectacle of others' pain and the sight of underlying forces that could not perhaps be contained another time. Outwardly there was little else; some broken windows still unrepaired, a little splintered wood — reminders of men running and yelling in the streets, just short of killing and being killed.

All across the West I had discovered or made little oases around people I enjoyed talking to; wells whence I drew stimulus or wisdom or simply warmth to sustain the lonely life of "a travelling man". No one had heard of Willie Loman at that time, but when Arthur Miller presented him years later, there were lots of us to recognize and to suffer with him. With a happy marriage back of me and a bounding pleasure at being alive, I did not travel only on "a shoeshine and a smile", but there were moments that were just as black as any Willie knew.

One such oasis in Regina was provided by two men, Harold Fry and Dan Cameron, who were always to be found at noon sitting on stools at the counter of the Monico Café. Fry's lunch was invariably conversation, raisin pie, and a cup of coffee, and he could make it last comfortably for an hour. He was a big, powerful-looking man who ran an unsuccessful bookshop just across the street; there he moved about quietly, giving the impression he would just as soon not sell the books because he enjoyed having them round him. Dan Cameron, grey-haired, blue-eyed, and intense, was a music critic and teacher who always gave the impression he should hurry away but seldom did. Like Fry he preferred conversation as his main course, and like Fry he talked well. Both men were at once disturbed and stimulated by the events that were unfolding and threatening our world: the proven impotence of the League of Nations in the face of the Italian conquest of Ethiopia; the growing and sinister evidence of a reborn Germany under a man called Hitler — whom we knew only as a slightly comic figure on movie newsreels; the approach of troubles in Spain soon to become a wounding civil war for Spaniards and a chilling sand-table exercise for some of the great powers to try out their weaponry.

Unlike many of my friends, these two, from their quiet backwater, faced life and enjoyed doing so even when they didn't like what they saw. Being a spectator, as it were, of the depression in the West and elsewhere had shaken me out of my private-school and Conservative home view of the world, without providing any alternative I could accept. My stumbling approach to a mild radicalism — indeed to nothing more than a small-l liberalism — may have amused Fry and Cameron, but they listened and discussed without patronizing, though they had long since been over the course; they had been there and back.

Though some of Harold Fry's views would probably have been thought radical, even "pinko", by hard-shell conservatives, he could suddenly turn a light of steady common-sense on facile or recklessly expressed opinion on social or political questions.

More than once I felt caught out in this clear light. On one occasion that surprised me I had been expressing doubts about the value or even the propriety of private schools in our society. In England, though the preparatory and public schools reinforced class distinctions, they did at least have the justification of producing many men of remarkable attainments and the country's leaders. The private schools of Canada did not produce our leaders, except in business, where often it was a leadership they were born into through family connections, or in the armed services, in which the system tended to take care of its own. Leadership in the learned professions, in education, in religion, in the arts, and in politics — with a very few distinguished exceptions — came from men who had had their education in provincial schools. An élitist education seemed to serve no purpose in a society like ours; worse, it produced an artificial class structure and was a divisive force in Canada.

I don't know what Harold Fry knew about private schools or what he might have guessed about the sense of guilt from which I probably argued, but his defence of private schools was immediate, strong, and convincing. They might be less good than they pretended to be, but let us not wish them away. At their worst they were still almost the only guardians of standards of taste and manners and of certain codes of behaviour, the concept of a gentleman.

And so we went on, and were to go on for the next five years. My return visits, two or three times a year, always included a lunch or two at the Monico, where they would be perched on their stools, talking or sitting in thoughtful silence. I seldom saw them elsewhere except for an occasional chat with Harold Fry in the bookshop or a casual encounter on the street. The Monico was their club, and when I met them there it seemed a friendly and comfortable place. When, some years later, after both had gone, I went in for a cup of coffee and to recapture memories I saw it for what it had always been: little better than a greasy-spoon place transformed for short periods by companionship and good talk.

It was interludes such as these that made the lengthy absences from home tolerable. For a young married man the long trips, though they provided satisfactory challenges, had many moments of torment. Tony and I found time for letters back and forth almost every day, eager and tender boy and girl declarations. The ending "Fun tomorrow" seemed at times only to sharpen the aches of five or six, and in one case nine, weeks of separation.

I continued to enjoy the business and had reason to think it was going well, but even that in the face of hard times provided frustrations. Many of our books were finding favour, and the promise of business to come seemed greater than even my high expectations. But realization was delayed from year to year by still-curtailed government spending. Moreover, a favourable decision not implemented could be changed — though waiting for the decision had often involved an extra week or two from home while I stood by in case discussions of revision, price, or format might be needed to clinch matters. After all that a year or two's delay might throw the whole thing open again. It was as if we were holding large cheques that might bounce. So I lived on tenterhooks, pinning my hopes on promises I had won but that might in the end go unfulfilled.

After weeks of travelling I usually finished in a sprint to Winnipeg, followed by an exhausted but blissful thirty-six hours on the train, with no responsibilities but the writing up of a few notes, then total relaxation; to stare idly at the splendours of Lake Superior, to revel in reading, in good food and sleep. And it was the more precious because it had been earned in the finishing sprint, working every day and spending every night of the last week on the train — Vancouver to Edmonton to Saskatoon to Regina to Winnipeg. We knew nothing about jet lag but we knew about fatigue. But with homecoming at the end it was a delicious prospect, worth any effort.

On one such trip our passengers included a group of Buddhist monks and nuns on their way to England. I had seen them processing through the lobby of the old Hotel Vancouver and our paths had crossed again in Calgary or Regina. And now as I stood by the train in Winnipeg, with my bags on board and time for the first sweet breaths of relaxation, the solemn procession came down the platform led by no less a person than the train conductor walking beside their own leader. Even the customary tooting of whistles, the jets of steam, and the shouting of porters and trainmen seemed to fall silent as in their long dark robes they floated by on felt-shod feet and were led to their private car. The ceremony was both impressive and a little pompous.

The leader of the Buddhist party had a handsome, hard face, strong to the point of arrogance, and he appeared to rule his flock with great firmness. There was no shouting like a sergeant-major but by pointing and with little commanding waves of his hands he moved his people about with easy authority. I was to encounter him during our trip but it was not until later that I learned something of his extraordinary career; his name was Trebitsch Lincoln.

As the train ran east out of Winnipeg across the last and flattest patch of prairie I sat down to a relaxing drink, and the Buddhists were a natural topic of conversation. My companions were a young investment man from Toronto — Arnold Massey — and a bright girl from New York whom we had just drawn into our conversation — some would have said picked up, but it was more civilized than that. During our talk some memory of that little parade, moving soundlessly down the platform, suggested a practical joke; if their private Pullman car was accessible like any other, and if monks and nuns put their felt shoes on the floor under their berths like the rest of us, mightn't it be rather fun to move some of the shoes around during the night? Surprise the Buddhists with black or tan leather shoes from the other cars and some Toronto businessmen with felt slippers.

The idea took over. It delighted me, and once it had been incautiously mentioned I was halfway committed to its execution. The girl thought it the greatest idea she had ever heard of, but though Arnold for a moment seemed to flirt with it he firmly opted out. He reminded me that his sleeping car would be dropped off in the early morning at Fort William, but I thought he felt such games all very well for a young harum-scarum bookman, not for one of his more serious occupation.

During the evening we almost gave up the idea and then later, after a quick reconnaissance, I decided such an opportunity would never come again; it must be seized. It was a time of the evening when the train had settled down; most people had gone to bed. Outside, the train was jolting and thundering its way through the night; inside, the cars were merely narrow, dark corridors between the swinging green curtains of the sleeping berths. Many of the porters had gone to the dining car for their supper, so that the train looked unguarded, deserted. Still, there was an almost continuous trickle of trainmen and porters through the quiet cars; we would need a lucky few minutes.

Once the decision was made, I and the girl went quickly and boldly to work. I put on a topcoat to conceal my smuggling and on the way to the Buddhist car lifted two pairs of shoes where no light glimmered behind the curtains. It took only a moment to exchange them for felt shoes and return to the door where my accomplice had already arrived with more leather; then away she went to place the felts and I went back for more. A third time in for two more and it seemed impossible our luck could hold. Each time I stooped down beside a Buddhist bunk I thought I felt the porter's hand on my collar. But our luck held and with eight pair of shoes shifted and muddled with eight others in three cars we quit while we were winning. With a handshake, a wave, and a grin we slipped away to our respective berths confident that we had not been seen. In a moment we were part of the anonymous and innocent collective snore in the green tunnels of the cars.

I don't think I spent long wondering what would happen in the morning; it would be amusing to sit back and watch. My memory is that though I was chucklingly triumphant I was asleep almost at once. But the long morning sleep-in, always part of the bliss of the trip home, was not to be mine. I was awakened about six-thirty by the sound of high screaming laughter from the smoker-washroom where the black porters shone the shoes in the early morning. Then it seemed both doors of the car slammed and there were hurrying steps and angry voices, and then more laughter. I lay half asleep, grinning and wondering what would happen next. I didn't have long to wait and wonder.

Within a few minutes I heard someone moving outside my berth and the curtains were jagged violently; it was the equivalent of a loud knock on the door. "Lower 6," said the conductor's voice, "I want to talk to you." I tried protesting that it was early and I was sleepy, but he was busy undoing the buttons of my curtains; welcome or not he was coming in. He opened the curtains and sat down on the edge of my berth.

"What happened to the shoes on the train last night?" he asked. "Shoes," I said sleepily. "What is this? Look, Conny, I'm tired, I have had a hard week." For a few minutes we argued and fenced, I pretending not to understand. He asserted that he and the porters had fixed this on me because I was the last person up the previous night. "You know darn well what I'm talking about," said the conductor, and suddenly this big, aggressive, rough-talking man broke up in laughter. "Dang your skin," he said, giving me a dig in the ribs, then rocking back and laughing helplessly. I had pushed up onto one elbow to carry on the conversation, and as he leaned back I caught sight of my blue suit jacket swinging on its hanger just behind his shoulder. He hadn't seen it yet, but he would, and it provided all the evidence he needed. I had hugged the felt shoes to me in my hurry the night before and my jacket looked as though I had been walked over by an army at the end of a long, dusty march.

The conductor's problem was that though the porters had gathered up the felt shoes and returned them to the Buddhists, the latter would not give back the leather shoes; by appearing to offer them leather to walk on I had insulted their religion, and they were very angry. So he had eight business men in bed without shoes, three of them awake and wanting their breakfast (troubling deaf heaven with their bootless cries) and equally angry. The conductor and his train crew were in trouble, he said, and it was going to get worse. Things had gone far enough. I agreed to get up and dress and try to get the shoes back.

I was barely washed, dressed, and with my suit brushed almost to a high polish by a chuckling porter when the Buddhist company arrived at the washroom door on their way to breakfast. Silently as many as could filed into the room and formed a circle around me. Lincoln faced me in cold silence and then said, "What are we going to think of you on this train today, a man who does things like this, a silly, silly boy?" He spoke English with only a slight accent and his voice was as commanding as his presence.

I apologized and explained that my little joke was not meant to be upsetting to anyone, "apparently we don't laugh at the same things." After a little further exchange I assured him that no insult to his religion had been even thought of, and had it occurred to me I would not have disturbed the shoes. He turned away then, telling his porter he could go and return the impounded shoes, and led his flock to breakfast.

I thought that was the not very funny end of it, but during the afternoon the conductor was back. This man (Lincoln) was an important customer of the CPR. They had brought him across the Pacific and across Canada and would be carrying him to England. If "this man" complained to head office there would really be trouble; some of his men might lose their jobs. I couldn't believe this, but in the 1930s it was not a matter to take lightly. He thought I should ask for Lincoln's assurance that he would not make an official complaint. Though not convinced of the need, I was prepared, reluctantly, to do this further penance. So, in a different mood than on the last occasion, I went to the Buddhists' car to find the leader standing up, talking or reading to his followers. On my entry twenty-five heads lifted and twenty-five cold stares transfixed me. I felt like Saint Sebastian, in a poorer cause.

After apologizing for the interruption, I asked for a moment's talk and Lincoln waved me to a seat. I stated my concern and he lectured me sternly against doing "silly things", instead of things that would make people love me. He swept his arm around the car and said gently, "These are my monks and my nuns," and then suddenly with eyes blazing and in a dramatic hiss he said, "*and they are scandalized at what you have done.*"

I protested quietly; surely it was not as serious as all that.

200

And after a little more scolding he gave me the assurance I had come for: he would make no trouble (but he was glad that for a change I was thinking of someone else, etc.). We bowed gravely to each other and parted.

The conductor received my reassurance from Trebitsch Lincoln grumpily, with no apparent pleasure or gratitude. "This wasn't for me," he said. "You know that [which I didn't]. For me you could have shot the old bugger."

The conductor, having disposed of Lincoln, then turned on me. I could lose my Commercial Traveller's Certificate if this was reported (and then my hotel rooms would cost one dollar more per day). I could even lose my job. "My company will think this as much fun as I do," I said, "and anyway, I don't give a damn." This was really for his benefit and I could only hope both things were true. I salvaged what I might by prophesying that in the years to come as he made his boring, jolting trips through Northern Ontario he would think of this interesting day and tell people what it was like in the old days.

The Company's verdict meant only Hugh Eayrs' opinion, and at the first convenient moment I told him the story. A day or two later, after I had driven him home, he made me tell the story again to Mrs. Eayrs. We were all laughing heartily until I mentioned the name Trebitsch Lincoln and then her laughter turned to angry scorn at the man's lofty pretensions. She remembered a good deal about him and later I found out more. Having started life as a Jewish boy in Hungary he had begun his education toward becoming a rabbi in Germany. His early and over-eager pursuit of girls had ended that training and he then became a Lutheran. He next moved to England, where he became an Anglican; after a period in the church in Montreal he returned to England, where he was in turn ordained and elected to the British House of Commons. There was plenty of evidence of his striking personality and capacity. When war came in 1914 the record of his extensive and mysterious travels in Europe, together with his attempt to join the Secret Service, brought him under suspicion and he was ordered to leave Britain. This he did for a time, going to the United States, where he engaged in anti-British propaganda. When he incautiously returned to Britain he was jailed for three years. Then he had disappeared to the Far East, where he was watched uneasily by British Intelligence. Later still I learned from a friend that on his arrival in England after his modest shoe troubles in Canada he and his followers were taken off the ship and guided into a shed at the docks by the police. I never heard whether they came out.

To sit talking and laughing with the Eayrses on my way home at the end of the day had been a part of life for the past five or six years, but in retrospect it seems that this occasion was one of the last. The easy atmosphere in the house had changed, but there were other reasons as well. As Hugh Eayrs' health deteriorated a drink, though it momentarily cheered him, seemed to worsen his condition and I thought my refusal to come in might save him from a drink he probably shouldn't have. Besides, I was eager to be home to see Tony, and stopping on the way, if pleasant, seemed both a betrayal and a deprivation. There was no happiness to compare with the arrival home to my pretty wife bubbling with her account of the day, and the chance to pour out my story of triumphs and disasters.

Having gone along happily, and as we thought cleverly, for four years without children, we decided it was time to start a family. I had gained enough confidence to feel secure in my job — or if necessary to get another; my salary, which had stayed at $50 a week or slightly below for four years, had suddenly been lifted to $4,000 a year. If we were not settling down it was time we did. We still hadn't a car of our own — like many of our friends — or even a radio, so that for any great programs we sat on my desk beneath the radio in the apartment upstairs; if we kept still and if our neighbours did the same, it was quite a satisfactory arrangement; and sometimes in the darkness we danced to their music, doubly delicious because it was like an undiscovered theft. Sometimes this acoustical accessibility worked less attractively. When our neighbours gave one of their frequent parties we had trouble sleeping, and I would occasionally — playing man of the house — stamp upstairs in a rage and then, suddenly becoming mild, ask them gently if they would be a bit quieter; and for a few minutes they would try, and then forget.

This and the need for space for a baby decided us on a move. With a baby we took it for granted we would have to have help in the house — a maid–nurse–cook-general. All these qualifications might be expected or trained into one person, who for thirty dollars a month would be expected to start getting the baby's breakfast at about seven, and mine soon after, and might finish washing the dinner dishes at nine o'clock at night. The girls were for the most part good-natured, accustomed to hard work and long hours from their Ontario farm or small-town homes, and this at first disguised the iniquity of a system that was coming to an end — having dug its own grave.

In time I was to have long and fierce arguments with Tony and her mother about all this, both of them asserting that to pay more would only spoil the girls — they wouldn't appreciate it — and sometimes shifting their ground to the thesis that the girls were grateful for the chance to learn how to cook and run a house. In this there was some truth, and more than one of the girls that drifted in and out in the next five years came back later to thank Tony for what she had taught them. Indeed, the cruel irony of the situation was the bitter disappointment of those who didn't get the job; the quiet despair of one elderly woman who was quite deaf and otherwise inept and who after a trial had to be let go. This quiet, clean little house that was to have a lovely baby had seemed to her just the haven for her declining years. For us it was a hard decision, but though feeling we could live with or improve the ineptness, the deafness seemed to earnest young parents too much of a hazard in a baby-sitter. I dropped her at the YWCA and tried lamely to explain and apologize. Deafness isn't conducive to graceful partings, but she knew what I was trying to shout at her. "It's all right," she said gently, "it's all right, sir." She was being turned back, and not for the first time, I knew, to a world that couldn't use her and wouldn't help her. There was no welfare or unemployment insurance or health care for her; at best she might be an unhappy guest in the house of a relative, while she waited to die.

Having at last decided to have a baby, we moved forward into that great adventure with happy anticipation which was suddenly given a rude check. There was first the miracle that was happening and all seemed to be well, then the frightening setback. We had driven to New York for a College Sales Conference at Macmillan, a happy, carefree trip; then came the scare: something had gone wrong. Fortunately Jack Gundy, a doctor friend from university days, was near by in Rye, New York, to take charge and calm our pulses wonderfully. Tony was to stay in bed and travel home by train while Colin Henderson of our College Department and I raced the train home. Cars were not very fast in 1936, nor roads very wide, but at least the roads were not crowded. We almost won the race and panted in to find Tony's family and the doctor firmly in charge and reassuring; all seemed to be well.

I was due to go West shortly and when the time came the doctor thought no problem threatened, but he proved to be wrong. I left on my trip and he for a holiday. In Saskatoon, a thousand miles from home, I learned that Tony was in hospital and the baby probably lost; Tony was well, she wrote, was to stay in bed indefinitely after she went home, and we were both to keep our fingers crossed. I wished that I had retained my boyhood faith in prayer; without it there was only the hope of desperation. I knew in spite of the excitement of the dawning miracle that the baby as yet meant nothing. I was concerned only for Tony. I could picture her there alone, pale and weak in that big bed, and I too far away to help. It was a time of misery and guilt.

The trip that had begun so badly ended in disaster. Hugh Eayrs was with me, and on the way from Edmonton to Calgary he had some sort of seizure. In the crowded, stuffy coach, though he seemed to be sleeping heavily he looked very ill. I couldn't be sure he was conscious; his lips were blue and he was breathing with difficulty. In the cold fresh air on the platform between the cars his breathing was easier, and there he perched unsteadily, on a suitcase, while I held him; his colour slowly returned and we crouched swaying together for two hours until we reached Calgary. There a doctor ordered him home. Was this a heart attack? The doctor shrugged; too great an altitude for a patient with too much weight, perhaps too much drinking. We caught the night train east with Hugh Eayrs in a compartment which the porter and I kept humid with kettles of steam laced with balsam. I had the nearest berth at the end of the car and for two days and three nights the porter and I kept watch and watch about. There were no games with shoes, no drinks, not even any laughs. But by the time we reached Toronto the Chief, though weak, was perceptibly better and with relief I handed him over to Dora Eayrs, who met the train with an ambulance and took him straight to the handsome old house that had become Wellesley Hospital. I hurried home, not knowing what I might find.

It was still early morning but as I let myself in I heard the welcome voice call from the bedroom. And there was Tony just as I had pictured her, only prettier and looking more fragile. I was afraid that even holding her might do some terrible damage, but it seemed to have the opposite effect. Little by little I heard the story and understood — or misunderstood — our prospects. The doctor who had been handling the case in the absence of our own Dr. Cosbie had said that in his opinion, after so massive a haemorrhage, there could be no life left. The pregnancy was lost and it only remained to get the patient well. On his return Cosbie had said, "We'll wait. I've seen many things happen that aren't in the textbooks." And so we waited for some weeks, Tony in bed most of the time or just creeping around the bedroom, until the day Dr. Cosbie announced the baby alive and well.

I should have then asked the question that was hardly formed at first but was to grow into a nightmare: could the baby really be healthy or might it not be — was it not probably — maimed? I didn't ask it for another six months. Somehow we moved through the time with periods of happiness and intervals of terrible gloom. I seldom saw the doctor and never when

I could speak to him alone. The idea of a simple telephone call doesn't seem to have occurred to me. Meanwhile, Tony showed no sign of worry and seemed well, though the final weeks of waiting were an exhausting burden. Whatever might be wrong, the baby was showing signs of great vigour and enterprise. One evening, to amuse or distract Tony we went to a movie. It was Gary Cooper in *The Plainsman*, and the excitement stirred the baby to such galloping activity that it seemed certain he would become either a cowboy or an Indian.

A day or two later I had played golf with Hugh Eayrs in the afternoon and he dropped me at home and came in for a drink. As the three of us sat talking, he looking well and happy again, Tony asked him whether he minded my being late for work the next day. It took a moment for the meaning of the light-hearted question to sink in: "It" had started. She had talked to the doctor; she was to have dinner and then go to the hospital. Her bag was all packed. Hugh Eayrs responded in the ebullient fashion of his good days, "If it is a boy, call him Hugh and I'll be his godfather."

I don't remember whether we talked over dinner, or whether either of us could eat; all I know is that going to Toronto General Hospital in a taxi we held hands like children, between fright and wonder. We had arranged to be extravagant with a private room and there Tony was prepared for the great event. Afterwards I sat beside the bed, and we tried to talk between pains; when they came we held hands, harder and harder. During the evening Dr. Cosbie came in and I paced the hall like any young father-to-be while he examined the patient. I was right up against the terrible question I should have asked long ago, and had been unable to mention, especially to Tony. As the doctor left the room he stopped cheerfully to say that things seemed to be going well. And then, between fear and embarrassment, the question got itself out. With the near mis-carriage, was this likely to be a maimed baby? I added, stum-blingly, that neither my wife nor I wanted that.

The doctor took this fumbling layman's question and com-ment in slowly. And then, like a good doctor, he responded with understanding and kindness. He said gently, "I've no reason to think the baby will be otherwise than perfectly healthy. Don't worry," he said, "these things don't happen." I wasn't sure then, nor am I now, just what he meant, but it was a comfort.

The hours dragged by. I really could only watch and try somehow to share the increasing pain. Occasionally a nurse looked in and I would be sent away while she checked progress. I was exhausted and couldn't imagine how Tony, deceptively frail-looking — though I knew she had more inner strength than I — could bear this much longer. Finally, at four o'clock in the morning she was wheeled away to the labour room, giving me a triumphant little wave and a tired smile as she went.

I set out in search of coffee and something to eat, more to kill time and ease tension than from any appetite. It was a soft spring night and a gentle, steady rain was falling as with hat pulled down and collar turned up I tramped along College Street. Near Bay Street there was a greasy-spoon restaurant full of stale cooking smells and there I ate something and snatched at coffee, feeling that I mustn't be long. An exhausted-looking waiter moved around slapping tables with a wet cloth. The customers — the taxi-drivers and prostitutes and college kids — had all gone. I hurried back to the hospital fearing I would be wanted. I had only been away fifteen or twenty minutes but it seemed to me something — probably something dreadful — must have happened in my absence. I felt as though I had failed in my duty. Tony's room was tidy and empty and still a reminder of pain. I wasn't wanted there, nor did I want to be there. I tried to settle into the waiting room near by, pacing it and the corridor — almost to the nursing station. I couldn't settle to reading or think of sleeping. Up the hall nurses came and went, chatting and laughing, occasionally telephoning or being called. But nobody spoke to me and I couldn't bear to ask for news (though I knew it must be bad). I knew all about the jackass doctor who had "never lost a father yet". So I prowled and smoked and waited while my head filled with more and more horrifying visions of disaster. It was broad daylight now and outside on University Avenue the first cars and the milkmen's horses rattled and clopped by.

And then about half past six I saw Dr. Cosbie speaking to the people at the nursing station and turning away. He looked tired and my worst fears seemed on the point of confirmation. I started up the hall and halfway through a door he turned and saw me, apparently with surprise. He came back smiling and threw out a hand expressively as he called "A son for you. Looks like a short-stop." He didn't seem to be holding anything back, but for a moment longer I kept my happiness at arm's length. "How's my wife?" I asked. "Oh, she's fine," he said. "She's awake now and very proud of her flat tummy. She'll be down in a minute." And she was — smiling and happy and triumphant. Together we phoned her parents, then I left her to sleep and went up to have breakfast with them, trailing clouds of glory.

The rain had stopped and the sun was shining on a washed world. The new tulips in Queen's Park and the spring grass were startlingly bright. I had never seen such a splendid morning.

❧ 10 ❧

B Y EVENING, after some sleep, some work at the office,
and a visit to the hospital I had settled down a little.
Having seen Tony and the baby—whom I dared not
hold — I was heavy with the sense of new responsibilities. On the way home I stopped in to talk with a friend, Ross
Matthews — later to become President of the Canadian Medical Association — who was an intern at the Hospital for Sick
Children. Ross, though younger than I, was wiser, with a quieter, drier sense of fun and a clearer notion of what he hoped to
do and what was worth doing.

But if wise, he was not solemn, and our friendship had been
sealed by one of my last playful capers before Tony and I were
married. We had all been to a dance and having returned our
girls safely to their fraternity house Ross and I were walking
back to our own when we found ourselves confronted by a
milkman's horse and wagon. It didn't seem right to leave a deserted horse to die alone on Huron Street at four o'clock on a
summer's morning; so we didn't. It took only seconds to lift the
horse-weight aboard, to climb in, to slap the reins lightly on the
great rump, and to say "giddap". It was all we knew and all the
horse needed to know. He took off, tentatively at first, then
firmly; apparently we weren't planning on deliveries at any of
his accustomed stops, so he wakened up and headed enthusias-
tically for Bloor Street, the main cross-town traffic artery and
not far ahead. Perhaps both Ross and I had assumed a knowledge of horse-management in the other and both were disap-

pointed. For the first moment, in our tail coats and white ties, we were delighted with the adventure — Joe College out on a spree — but I began to see in Ross's laughing eyes what I knew was in my own: a question of whether we had started something we couldn't finish. Approaching Bloor Street, our milk bottles were making a merry jingle, the horse was moving strongly, and I wasn't ready for a confrontation. Without a pause he went straight across Bloor and fortunately no car disputed the crossing; not long before, a celebrating young blood had driven his car into a Toronto milk-wagon with tragic results, but it was a little late to be remembering things like that.

Ahead lay Dupont Street, where Huron ended. There the horse would have to be turned, so the problem of a turn might as well be faced nearer home. As a child I had occasionally been allowed to drive a wagon on one of the farms near our cottage, but only briefly and with the kindly farmer or hired man sitting ready to take over. All we could remember from playing around farms and stealing rides on bob-sleighs was needed now. I tried pulling gently but firmly on the reins — "Whoa, boy"; the horse slowed down and I felt as though I had just invented a new system of driving. I pulled gently on the right rein and the co-operative horse rounded the corner, to our delight and astonishment. Keeping a watchful eye open for policemen, we jogged over to Avenue Road and there, in front of the girls' fraternity house, the horse was agreeable to a stop. We anchored him and tied his reins to a tree. And as the sun rose we walked the mile home, our glee reinforced by relief.

But I had not come from the hospital to plan schoolboy games with young Dr. Matthews. We had not talked long before my new responsibilities began to show. I was not going to make the mistakes my parents had made, *no sir*. Now take sex education for example: how much better that could have been — should have been — handled. Ross was agreeable and quiet. I warmed to my thesis: "When I think of the mistakes my parents made — " Ross broke in gently, "There must be quite a margin of safety," he said. "When we think of the horrible mistakes your parents made and my parents made we ought to be gibbering idiots. But here we are, not apparently unhappy or seriously maladjusted. So you ought to be able to sleep tonight without worrying too much about bringing up your son, and sleep I suspect is what you need most." It was sensible and illuminating, reassuring and cooling — all the things I needed besides sleep. We learn slowly and educate each other. But sometimes I think I was slower than most and balkier than most — certainly more so than that affectionately remembered horse.

If all the extravagances of my cocky high spirits had been undergraduate pranks it might have been silly but it would have risked little. But high spirits and over-confidence lead where impulse directs them, and at least twice I came close to serious trouble. In 1936 we had published Margaret Mitchell's *Gone With The Wind*, which had taken off to a runaway success and a great boost in our sales, even to an expectation of considerable profit. Hugh Eayrs announced a bonus of two weeks' salary for all staff. It was less than a temporary restoration of the salary cuts but it was like a break in the clouds after a long darkness and the effect was intoxicating. It would have been well if we had settled for that, but after the ceremony in the Chief's office — the presentation of the little envelope and the handshake — a small group hung around. Someone produced a bottle and the flames of excitement mounted a little higher. Then we went on to lunch and a good deal of drink. With $150 in my pocket I felt like a king, leading the noisy story-telling and the laughter. As we broke up to go home someone suggested it might be better if I didn't drive the office car. I took the suggestion calmly, appreciatively — thanks, I'm fine; quite all right.

It was the Saturday before Christmas and as though the curtain of the depression had lifted for everyone, the town had been full of office parties. The result was a wild and dangerous traffic scene by late afternoon that produced a deep front-page headline in Monday morning's paper, BLACK SATURDAY. There had been so many and such serious accidents that my own contribution looked rather modest. Still, by College Street I had nicked two fenders and sped on. I thought, with some effort, that my timing might be a little off; I decided to be careful. Just above St. Clair Avenue, travelling north on Spadina, I decided to get some cigarettes — and proved the point about my timing. Pulling in to stop, but late with the brakes, I was stopped abruptly by a new Cadillac parked at the curb. There was a horrible sound of crunching metal and breaking glass. Confused, but with a realization that something rather serious had happened, I got out and had a look, then got in and backed up with more tearing of metal and falling of glass, and drove away. People had gathered, but there was no move to stop me. I reached home and navigated the narrow and difficult garage without mishap. In the house I gave Tony a brief and hardly coherent account of events and went to sleep.

I awoke to some of the horror — guilt and, even more, fear — that I had earned. Hugh Eayrs had telephoned. He had had a call from the Chief of Police of Forest Hill, since the car was registered in the Company's name. Where was the car, Hugh Eayrs asked. In the garage. He heaved a sigh of relief. The Chief of Police had told my Chief that the owner of the Cadillac had laid no charges — I seemed to be a nice young man — but the police wanted to be assured that my car was off the road.

The other episode was not only foolish and dangerous of itself, but threatened a serious collision with Hugh Eayrs. I had gone to New York for a sales conference at which traditionally the end of the day was the occasion for a drinking party that sometimes went on and on. It usually started mildly with three or four bookmen talking shop, then more would drop in, and the talk became tall tales and arguments. If someone sensible said, "We'd better eat," it might break off quietly, but if it was too late the talk and drinking went on.

One such occasion was my downfall. Very late, we had finally sauntered out in search of food and after that, as the only stranger, I wanted to see the town and wouldn't be talked out of it. People were concerned, but no one could persuade me to be sensible. They reminded me that we had to work in another three or four hours; that exploring alone at that hour was foolish, even dangerous. I could take care of myself. No one believed it, but they were too tired to pull at a deadweight. One by one they broke off and left me to my folly.

My last coherent memory, as I drove away in a taxi in search of a drink, was that I had cunningly dispersed my money in different pockets — overcoat, jacket, waistcoat — where no one could find it all. When I came to in broad daylight I was standing on the sidewalk high up on New York's west side — Hell's Kitchen — and fumbling through my pockets I couldn't find the price of a taxi. I remember gently, piteously, explaining my problem to a black boy lounging in a doorway who looked hostile and bored. Somehow then I found myself in a room where three or four black men were playing cards. Clearly my sad story was on the edge of accusation, and perhaps only my stumbling silliness and cloudy explanation saved me from serious trouble. They told me menacingly to shove off, none of them had even seen me before. A dawning glimmer of sober sense got me out again unhurt onto the street and I started to walk south in search of my hotel. When I reached it, about fifty blocks later, I was cold and clear-headed enough to be miserable. Through no fault of my own I had escaped one danger that would remain a chilling memory for a long time, but I was not out of trouble.

As I cleaned up, snatching black coffee and toast for which I had no appetite, I searched all my pockets once again. It was a bleak triumph to find one ten-dollar bill in a ticket pocket. There had been fifteen or sixteen of them when I set out. I slipped in to the conference late and looking ill, but those who knew of my expedition seemed both amused and relieved. The details, or the little I remembered, came out at coffee break and lunch time and there was no more amusement. My American colleagues rallied around warmly and generously with offers of loans — even a suggestion of passing the hat — and I borrowed enough to tide me over and wired Toronto.

Hugh Eayrs was due in New York two days later, New Year's morning, on his way to England with Mrs. Eayrs. Characteristically I compounded my folly by sending a jaunty wire asking him to bring $150 as an advance against my salary. Just that need not have surprised or troubled him or raised larger questions. But I fixed everything by adding as an explanation "Got in slight jam". Not only was my irresponsibility advertised to the whole office in Toronto, but it seemed probable that I had disgraced the Canadian company in New York by some clownish performance.

When I called Hugh Eayrs at the Gotham Hotel late New Year's morning I was met with a peremptory order to come over right away. Though, as an honoured guest, I had been to a rather grand party with the management group the night before, my own welcoming of the New Year had been very discreet. Nevertheless I approached the Gotham in a state of nerves and my greeting did nothing to relax me. We exchanged no Happy New Year wishes and conversation had hardly opened before Hugh Eayrs said savagely, "I wish to God you wouldn't get in jams." I answered fervently that I wished I didn't; periodically I seemed bound to make a fool of myself, but — I kept trying to do better. Well, anyway, he said, Mr. Harvey — the secretary of the Canadian company — was very angry and he just wouldn't agree to an advance on my salary. I knew this was eyewash — and he knew that I knew. Mr. Harvey had no firm opinions contrary to the Chief's, and the whole charade suddenly pulled me together. I said Mr. Harvey wouldn't understand me if he lived to be a hundred, but I expected Hugh Eayrs to understand me, even when he quite naturally didn't approve my conduct. So what was I to use for money? How was I to pay my hotel bill? I was not disgraced in the New York office; he would find quite the contrary; but if I were going to have to borrow and cadge I would be. "You can borrow from me," he said, "a personal loan." I answered hotly that I hadn't asked him or anyone for a loan, nor did I want one. I had asked for an advance on what was due me.

But I couldn't win that argument. In stinging humiliation I accepted the $150 which I had to have, but for which I couldn't even pretend thanks. My official punishment, of which there would be a lingering reminder for months as I repaid the debt, was over. Though I couldn't change gears quite so easily it was indicated that we could now relax and have fun. What followed was a continuous round of parties with various friends of the Eayrses until a champagne send-off on shipboard before they sailed the next day. Dora Eayrs, who had watched my glum participation of the day before, smiled and threw me a kindly aside at the cabin party, "Feeling better?" I was touched and grateful, realizing that I was more nearly healed than I had known or deserved.

One of the calls Hugh Eayrs and I had made New Year's morning, before Mrs. Eayrs joined us, was on Grey Owl, just back from a triumphant lecture tour in England. He had finished with some lectures in the eastern states which he had not enjoyed. And he hated New York, where he felt trapped and a figure of fun. Our conversation in his dreary little hotel room lightened a little when he produced a small skin drum and thumped out a rhythm that cheered him a good deal. He was sick of walking the streets of New York in Indian regalia and having playful people ask him what cigar store he was working for. In his unhappy mood they were lucky not to have suffered damage.

I had seen that smouldering side of Grey Owl some months before when he was in Toronto for a great Book Fair. I had chauffeured him from Eaton's Book Department, where he had autographed books for an admiring crowd, to the King Edward Hotel, where he was to lecture. There, while I parked the car, he stood on the pavement adjusting his buckskin jacket and re-settling the splendid eagle-feather bonnet that was too big to wear in any car. Conscious of my responsibility I led the way to the bank of elevators. Back of the elevators was a beer parlour called The Pickwick Room, out of which came a short, red-faced, rumpled, and slightly soggy little man. He was clearly headed for the lavatory when he suddenly found himself facing a real live Indian — or someone dressed up like one. With a little crowing noise he started toward Grey Owl and then stopped as though overcome by amazement. "Holy Jeez," he said, "where'd you get the Indian suit? Come on, I want to show you to the boys." Grey Owl, as taut as a bow string, said in a dangerously quiet voice, "I am here for another purpose." "Jeez, I just want to show you to the boys," pleaded the little man in an anguished voice. Fortunately, at that moment the elevator arrived and a wedge of people separated Grey Owl from his amiable tormentor. The doors closed and we had escaped.

Up in Macmillans' room while we waited for Grey Owl's lecture I tried to cover over the incident, but Grey Owl refused to be soothed. Astride a chair with his arms folded along the back he brooded angrily. "Just a God-damned Indian," he said, again and again. "Just a God-damned Indian." My little soothing words and gestures — "Oh, Chief, why would you care about that little squirt? He doesn't matter" — proved quite ineffectual. He seemed to be both nursing a resentment and enjoying it.

Suddenly he raised a hand and as though declaiming before a crowd said in a strong voice full of anger, "I am the custodian of the ancient dignities of the Indian people." I agreed — "and that little man can't change that fact. Forget about him." At last he quietened down a little and we waited until it was time to deliver him to the lecture hall. For the moment I was the complete chauffeur-bodyguard and was enjoying my role enormously. I had not heard Grey Owl lecture before and like his overflow audience I was captivated. He had fine commanding gestures and a simple clarity of expression that served every purpose. He talked, I suppose, about the stages by which he had moved from trapper to protector of wildlife and especially of his beloved beaver. His listeners sat as though under a spell.

Afterwards I led my charge down to the book display especially to show him the piles of his own books at Macmillans' booth. An admiring crowd followed him, competing to touch him — his buckskin clothes, his hair braids — and bringing books for him to autograph. The adulation had the soothing effect I had failed to produce and we left the Fair with Grey Owl in a glow of quiet triumph. I was to drive him to a dinner party, after which he would be brought back for an evening lecture. As we stepped into the elevator I wondered whether our little friend could still be around and comforted myself with the certainty that he must be long gone. But he wasn't. He was perceptibly closer to extinction but by a shocking coincidence his short, energetic body was lurching by the elevators as we came out. I tried to turn Grey Owl away but the little man was too quick. Confronting Grey Owl he gave something between a howl and a moan of incredulous joy. Rushing forward he grabbed Grey Owl's wrists. "C'mon," he begged, "c'mon and see the boys."

In Biscotasing or other places in Northern Ontario Grey Owl had often been Master of the Revels, and going to see the boys was just part of the fun; but not in the King Edward Hotel, where he was a painfully sober celebrity with a mission and with all the rage of two hours before boiling within him. With an upward and outward jerk of both arms he broke the grip on his wrists and sent the little man staggering backwards until he stumbled and sat down in a tall pillar ash-tray against the wall. There, dishevelled and frightened, he kept muttering, "I just wanted him to come and see the boys." Grey Owl, with feet planted apart and knees slightly bent, was leaning forward menacingly, one hand at his belt gripping the handle of his hunting knife. I pushed between them, which doubtless I couldn't have done had Grey Owl really been roused to the murder he appeared ready for. At this moment the hotel's house detective appeared and demanded to know what was going on. We had met more than once before, when I was a playful lad, and what he remembered of me he didn't like. But for once I appeared to be on the side of law and order. The little man was past pursuing his happy idea about seeing the boys and we left him facing the detective and sitting, a picture of misery, in his ash-tray.

On the way to the dinner Grey Owl shared the back seat with his eagle bonnet, but leaned forward brooding with his chin resting just behind my shoulder. "I wonder how that fella would have liked it if I had cut all the buttons off his waistcoat with my knife." I could see his hand flash up in the driving mirror. I laughed but said nothing. "I could do it," he said angrily, as though I were doubting his skill. I was reminded of Hugh Eayrs' statement that Grey Owl had left the north country some years before because he had killed a man. "If that fella's around tonight I'll fix him." I begged him not to get involved in a squabble whatever the provocation. At the moment he was the most publicized and popular figure in town, but this could backfire. Brooding and angry, he gave no promise and, unasked, I undertook to be there when he came back to lecture in the evening, and to fend off all such trouble.

Though my mission had been accomplished when I delivered Grey Owl to his dinner party, I clung to my role as bodyguard. Rushing home, full of amusement, excitement, and self-importance, I gobbled whatever food Tony could give me quickly and returned to the King Edward to prowl, long before I could possibly be needed. I circled the hotel lobby, watching all the doors, savouring my great mission. As the time for Grey Owl's lecture approached I became doubly wary, peering at groups as they came laughing and chattering through the doors on their way to the elevators, looking for a little beery man who must long since have been fast asleep at home or in jail. Lecture time went by and I had seen no sign of Grey Owl and his party. The hotel lobby had fallen quiet, empty except for me and a desk clerk who watched my circling patrol with open suspicion; clearly he wondered what I was up to, and I began to wonder myself. I took the elevator up to the Crystal Ballroom to see what had gone wrong, and how they were filling in for the absent Grey Owl.

As I approached the doors I could see that the room was crowded and still. On the platform Grey Owl, who it seemed to me now must have entered by the roof, was just beginning. Over at one side sat an Indian whose bare copper arms and shoulders gleamed beautifully above a purple blanket draped gracefully around him. Grey Owl introduced him as his friend Little Beaver from the St. Regis Reservation, and Little Beaver, standing up, unsmiling, raised his hand palm outward in the ancient and dignified greeting. For the moment he made me forget Grey Owl and my deflated sense of mission. St. Regis

218

village lay just across from our cottage on the St. Lawrence; it had been painted by Bartlett a hundred years before and its church contained a communion plate given the Indians by Queen Anne a hundred years before that. But more than these things, Little Beaver recalled in a vivid flash golden mornings on the river and sleepy little boys creeping down in wonder to the dock while out on the water an Indian fishing lifted a hand in greeting and then settled back to an immemorial stillness, the mood of the great river. I only saw Grey Owl once or twice after that. A year later he made another brilliantly successful lecture tour in England and on the way back he stopped in Toronto. At a small party for him he seemed desperately tired or ill, talking unconvincingly of the power he now had for helping the Indian people; his idea was that governments should set aside for them all the jobs as game wardens and fire-rangers, caretakers of their own lands. It sounded like a good but limited plan. At my request he signed a book for me and wrote "To one of the boys who is helping, very sincerely Grey Owl".

A few weeks later he was dead in his cabin at Ajawaan in Prince Albert National Park. Within a day or two there was a newspaper story claiming that he had been neither an Indian nor a half-breed, but an Englishman who, as a boy in Hastings, England, had been fascinated with stories of the Indians and the wilds. I was one of those who didn't, couldn't, believe the exposé. As for the conclusion drawn that he was a fake, a con artist, I could only weakly disagree; what about the Indians, like Little Beaver, who gathered around him wherever he went? Out of loneliness or admiration they had hunted him out in the cities where he was lecturing and together they would have long talks about their problems, and then try to forget them in dances up and down hotel corridors to the beat of skin drums, and the terror of the other guests. For a time I clung to a theory that if he wasn't an Indian he really believed he was, for I could still see the jabbing upright finger and hear the strong voice, "I am the custodian of the ancient dignities of the Indian people."

Many if not most of the literary stars in our small firmament of those days were attached to the Macmillan crown and I met many of them, either as their chauffeur or as a junior guest at one of the Eayrses' parties. I didn't care about the capacity in which I met them, just to be introduced or see and hear these legendary creatures was splendid. For them I seemed to be wearing a cloak of invisibility and since that required no conversation from me I was the happier for it.

At one such party I was introduced to Mazo de la Roche as head of Macmillans' Educational Department. She smiled very cordially and said, "That sounds very intimidating." And I? My memory is that I just grinned and grinned. I had been bowled over by *Jalna*; as winner of the *Atlantic Monthly* $10,000 prize it must be a great book and she a great writer — a great Canadian writer. Later, with successive books in the *Jalna* series most of this glow disappeared, but a real respect and affection for her was to take its place.

After the Eayrses' party I was not to see her again for several years. When she returned to Canada from a long residence in England I invited her to lunch at the York Club and we were put into a handsome little reception room, which has now become a serving pantry, and there while she drank sherry and I whisky we carried on a stiff little conversation: What was she writing? Wasn't I just back from the war? In the middle of this I realized I had lost my guest's attention; her eyes kept looking over my shoulder to the open door which was just behind me, from which came a strange mixture of whistles and hisses and a low, beseeching mutter: "Hey, Misther Gray. Misther Gray."

I turned around to find a young Scottish club steward, whom we all called Scotty, crouching in the doorway and pushing forward a handful of dollar bills. As a new and unconfident member I went into a state of pompous shock. Scotty was not to be deterred. "Can ye ge' me a ticket for the foobaw game on Sathurday?" I said stiffly that I didn't know; if I could I would, and turned away. "Take the money, take the money," he chanted. I answered firmly and a little angrily that I didn't want the money; if I could get the ticket we would see.

He withdrew then, reluctantly, and I turned back to see

Mazo smiling and a little puzzled; "Hardly a scene you would find in an English gentlemen's club," she said, and that broke the ice. I roared with laughter and then we both laughed. She said she had liked the scene, it was friendly and nice. But no sooner had we settled down to serious book talk than the hissing and whistling began again. I turned around; Scotty was back. "Will ye ge' thaat ticket in the covered staand," he said. "I don' wanna hafta si' oot in the rain." I didn't get the ticket but I was grateful to Scotty; he had relaxed us both and my meeting with Mazo was a success.

Not long after, Scotty disappeared from the York Club and I forgot about him. Weeks or months later I was at a reception at the Toronto Club and had a solemn conversation interrupted by a heavy elbow in my ribs. I looked around sharply to see Scotty sailing by with a tray of canapés held aloft, his voice drifting back: "How're ye doon, Misther Gray?" — friendly, innocent, and still in the wrong job. I saved up that story for Mazo.

Encounters like those with Grey Owl and Mazo de la Roche had two effects. They bound me more surely than ever to the publishing business, giving me a sense of being a hand in a creative process, and they were fun; I could be exhausted and angry and frustrated, but never bored. And they reminded me that I wanted to be a writer, so that intermittently I worked away at sketches and short stories. It is hard now to say why, because the more I read, and I was reading continuously with greedy excitement, the less I felt I had anything of value to say — or that there was anything new to be said. Still, using words — the very act of sitting down to write — remained a pleasure, though it was grinding work and there was little to show for it.

The editorial side of my job occasionally involved writing, and in one case involved Frank Upjohn and me in a bizarre if not disreputable venture. A prominent and popular teacher had come to Hugh Eayrs about 1937 and proposed that he should edit a group of the Shakespeare plays most used in schools. All over Canada, as we knew, most of the schools used the plays edited by O. J. Stevenson and published by Copp

Clark at 25¢ each. This was the series that had caused St. Martin's Shakespeare to fail and had been the death of other ventures. They were used so widely out of habit, because of their low price, and also out of a belief that Stevenson had a hand in setting the English examinations in Ontario, and Ontario was almost half the market in English-speaking Canada. Our teacher pointed out that he now set many of the English exams and that his editions could be as popular as Stevenson's if we could produce them at 25¢.

Neither Frank nor I liked the venture very much. It would take years for our editions to become as popular as Stevenson's, and unless the books sold in many thousands of copies a year almost from the first we could only price at 25¢ at a substantial loss. And if they never became popular we could go on taking a growing loss annually until we decided it was time to call quits. So, though the Shakespeare market was always substantial and tempting, we were not enthusiastic. But we discovered that even if we had been ready to veto the project absolutely it was already too late. Hugh Eayrs had accepted it and committed the Company. As his health deteriorated he was more inclined to bolster his confidence by taking rash decisions rather casually. He had taken to saying, half playfully but with an edge to it, "I'm still of some use to this business." No doubt he felt threatened, though none of us was waiting for or wanting his job. We wanted him there, and well.

So now we were to have Shakespeare, annotated cunningly for the under-educated or lazy teacher at a popular price. In due course the first two manuscripts came in, and if the finished books hadn't a brilliant sale they bolstered some hope of eventual popularity. A year later came a third play, but our editor was visibly tiring and losing interest; the books had not done what he expected and his other responsibilities had increased. Still, we had announced a program and made an investment which could only succeed if kept going. As the year went on with no sign of another manuscript we began to press for it, only to be fended off with promises that couldn't be, and weren't, fulfilled. Finally, when it was already almost too late, we recklessly proposed that the two of us might prepare the notes, to be approved by the editor. He agreed rather as though it was an idea we should have suggested before this, and with no apparent twinge of conscience.

And so we donned the mantle of Shakespearian scholarship. With a case of beer beside us, and all the best-known editions of Shakespeare spread out, we worked for several evenings on either side of a card table, arguing, comparing, agreeing. To begin with we also laughed a great deal, but the work went on late each night and by the time it was finished our chortling merriment had subsided. Our editor approved the manuscript, apparently without even looking at it very carefully. And the teachers? Some thought it well up to the quality of the earlier volumes in the series, some even thought it rather better — fresher, they said. The royalties, of course, went to the editor.

The next year the pattern of events was repeated. This time, like old hands, we went to work rather sooner but now without any sense of excitement or fun. With cynical distaste — entirely the wrong mood — we edited *A Midsummer Night's Dream* to follow our *As You Like It*. There the brave venture came to a final stop. Our editor was not well and though he seemed happy enough to have us go on editing books in his name, we felt we had filled a temporary gap, which was all we had undertaken or intended to do. If it was to be permanent we and the Company and the editor would be conniving in a major hoax. Our work had been close to cribbing from a long list of distinguished Shakespeare teachers and what had at first seemed to be a joke had lost any semblance of fun. The books were closed on an expensive and dispiriting project.

My writing involved me in a more innocent deception with a happier outcome. In 1937 or 1938 I had arranged to meet Hugh Eayrs in Vancouver, and since he had started ahead of me I flew at his suggestion from Chicago. Commercial flying was still not general, and there was no passenger flying in Canada except in the North. I had been up in a plane only once before, and the idea of flying out to the Pacific coast produced tingles of both excitement and apprehension. In those happy pioneer days passengers on night flights were put to bed in a berth much as on a train, except that at every fuelling stop we had to be wakened by the stewardess and made to yawn or open mouths wide to adjust to the change of pressure. There was something at once ludicrous and wonderful in being wakened by a pretty girl saying, "Would you open your mouth wide, please, we're coming down in Omaha."

The memory of it all was so pleasant and stimulating that on my return to Toronto I dashed off a familiar essay called "The Silver Whale". I was pleased with it and tried it on one or two magazines, who said nice things about it and sent it back. I gave up and put the essay in a drawer. A year or so later Professor J. F. Macdonald of the University of Toronto was preparing for St. Martin's Classics a collection of essays for use in schools. With his selection almost complete he said he would like to find something else of Canadian authorship that was a bit different, that was fresh. We undertook to canvass for suggestions, a normal procedure. When we had some candidates to show him they included "The Silver Whale" bearing a pseudonym. He took them away and came back a few days later, delighted. "The Silver Whale" was just what he wanted; where did it come from? Who was this author he had never heard of? It was time to confess, and we were both amused and pleased. When in later years it was chosen for use in other anthologies I was happy to have J. F.'s judgement sustained.

About this time I was revisiting Lakefield, which for the rest of my life would feel like home, and in the course of a general conversation the Headmaster said that he wished I would write a book about the School. I fumbled and thanked him and excused myself, saying I would like to, but I didn't write well enough, I found writing hard work, and I was fully occupied with my job. The idea had occurred to me already and been put away, but after his remark it remained as something to be thought more about. It was still in that position when I saw an announcement of a United States prize for a children's book. It was as though I needed just that announcement to impel me to reach for the paper. There were just two months before manuscripts were due and it was only my ignorance that prevented me from understanding the absurdity, the impossibility, of this venture. But ignorance was bliss and I plunged ahead, writing late every evening and through the week-ends. Tony endured my long silences, or listened with apparent approval as I read bits of my masterpiece aloud. An equally patient and kind secretary, Mrs. Fearnley, who was to work for another forty years at Macmillans (truly indispensable long after retirement age), took time from bringing up a family to type the manuscript in her off hours. For the first month the work went well and the deadline seemed attainable. I was tempted to write Dr. Mackenzie to say I was at work, then decided not to; I would surprise him. It was to be an affectionate gesture, but it was never made. The "Old Man", whom we all thought indestructible, died suddenly of a heart attack, following a game of hockey which he played as fiercely in his late sixties as in his youth. The book might have embarrassed him, for it contained under the thin disguise of fiction a recognizable picture of him as we saw him. And it contained the story of how, as a young Headmaster, he had lowered himself through a hole in the ice in a vain attempt to save a boy who had broken through, skating where he had been warned it was dangerous. It had been an act of the most desperate bravery, related incredulously across the years by the boys, but never otherwise referred to.

This setback to a pleasant plan, or something else, stopped my writing in full flight, and for two of my four remaining weeks I sat dried up and dismayed. I had plunged into the book without a plan, and it had moved along well, but the problem of shaping it to a conclusion seemed to paralyse me. It was out of hand. In the end I took hold roughly and finished the book, turning it into a boys' thriller; gaining something in excitement but losing quality. Still, it was finished and mailed just in time. I had called it *The Oriole's Nest* because of a tree house, built by the boys, and a focus of the action.

Then came weeks of waiting, and mixed emotions. I had no expectation of winning — part of the book I believed good of its kind, not the whole — but until I heard otherwise I was bound to hope. A friend who had entered the same contest phoned to say he supposed my manuscript had come back; he had received his some ten days before. A quite irrational hope, mixed with despair, spurted up. Did it mean I was in the finals, on a short list, or had my manuscript never arrived? Surely it must be the former and the postman might come along any day with great news and a big cheque. But was that possible? I knew it was not, so the manuscript must never have reached the contest. And then at last it did come back, with regrets and compliments, and excerpts from the judges' reports. Some comments were warming; the character-drawing was said to be good and some of the incidents were considered genuinely funny. I was happy enough with that. The contest officers kindly expressed their confidence that the book would find a publisher and congratulated me on it.

For several months I gave up a good deal of spare time to trying to find a publisher, and to the little continuous excitement of watching the mail. Since the contest judges had seemed so confident about the book's finding a publisher I at first was optimistic, but as time passed I sank into gloom. They had just been polite, the book wasn't publishable. I had hunted out the names of literary agents in London, Pearn Pollinger and Higham, and in New York, Marion Saunders, and sent off my manuscript like a mother sending off her child to his first school. I was to learn a good deal about the writing trade from those dealings, including one simple law: every publisher should write at least one book and try to find a publisher for it.

I never met Marion Saunders, but I shall always remember her with affection and gratitude for all the trouble she took over so small a venture, and above all for her kindly encouragement. The British agent, at first cheerful, reported sending the book to a number of publishers I was quite sure would not take it. I knew enough about their lists to be sure of that, which suggested that no one at the agency had looked at the manuscript, let alone read it, whereas Marion Saunders clearly had. When Pearn Pollinger and Higham wrote that, having tried the book without success, they would now have to retire it from offer, I wrote saying I would never have thought it suitable for the houses they had offered it to, but what about Blackie, and one or two others. They wrote unenthusiastically saying they would try. Clearly the houses I had suggested were not thought to be worth their time, and later I saw the point — their point. When the book was finally taken by Blackie's the return to the agent was four pounds, to me thirty-six pounds, outright payment for a sole licence to publish in the English language throughout the world (exclusive of the United States) for the life of the copyright. It was an iniquitous type of old-fashioned contract, but the war was on and there were more important things to worry about. I had also to allow the title to be changed, since British readers didn't see orioles and the idea of an oriole's nest — the safe little hanging basket on the end of a high limb — would just be a puzzle. So the book was published under the title of *The One-Eyed Trapper*, and when copies finally did reach me I couldn't greet them with any great joy. Still there was some satisfaction in having it published. Leaving for the war I inscribed a copy for my four-year-old son: "I hope to do better books — but, just in case".

Had the times and the circumstances of my life at the moment when the judges' opinions reached me been different, the excitement of these little triumphs might have sent my hat over the windmill — gone for a writer. But in my job and in the world around us tensions were mounting and events were crowding in. Only at home was there contentment. Though Tony and I had discovered a natural capacity for disappointing and wounding each other, though mutual joys didn't always prevent our eyes from wandering in a momentary excitement — and I could be both faithless and wickedly jealous — with every year our bonds were stronger and surer and more precious. And if they had not been, they were so tightly wound around the baby now growing into a delightful small boy as to be reinforced beyond any imaginable strain.

But outside the oasis of home lay a desert that grew more unpleasant and dangerous every day. To the immediate horizon lay the business, more challenging and with greater opportuni-

227

ties as conditions improved and I learned my trade, but less enjoyable as Hugh Eayrs' health deteriorated and he became more capricious; as his physical capabilities diminished, his reach and the demands on him from outside the business increased, and he was less available to us for consultation. Yet, though he had always claimed to want people who would take responsibility, to take responsibility now was to risk a slashing reprimand. Frank Upjohn, who had left our Educational partnership to become Manager of the Trade or General Books Department, said in a moment of desperation that he didn't know how long this could go on before someone ran out into the middle of Bond Street and began to scream. And yet we stayed on. A message reached me from Copp Clark, one of our most successful competitors in the school field, that they would pay me $2,000 a year more than whatever my salary was at Macmillans. It was a lot of money at the time — as the messenger, a senior educator from British Columbia remarked (it would, in fact, have been a fifty-per-cent increase in salary), but though pleased I never seriously considered it. To leave Hugh Eayrs at such a moment seemed unthinkable.

And beyond that near patch of uncomfortable desert lay the howling wilderness of the wide world and the certainty of an approaching war in which we would be involved. In a few years we had watched as the League of Nations died — with Canada as one of the assassins. On the news-reels we had watched a posturing Mussolini as his triumphant soldiers rode over the bodies of brave but unarmed natives of Abyssinia; we had seen a comic little man with a Charlie Chaplin moustache hurrying along the ranks of his Brown Shirt bullies, and then the German army marching unchallenged into the Rhineland, goose-stepping down the streets of Vienna, and finally Prague — at Munich we had handed over our principles, one of the best armies of Europe, and one of its greatest armament factories. It had become popular to say that Adolf Hitler was merely redressing the injustices of the Versailles Treaty of twenty years before. Moreover, he could always be held by France's Maginot Line. Everyone knew that the French Commander-in-

70 Bond Street, Toronto, the home of Macmillans when John Gray joined the company.

The Educationists Are Not All in the Schools!

HUGH EAYRS -- A BIOGRAPHICAL SKETCH

By Morton Dawson *Alias John Gray*

THE career of Hugh Eayrs, President of the Macmillan Company of Canada Limited, reads rather like a Horatio Alger novel, or a magazine "success" story—but with a difference. Perhaps the difference lies in his substitution of *flair*, or personality if you will, for the stump of candle by the flickering light of which Alger heroes usually swat up their Latin and Trigonometry through the long night. Had Mr. Alger been a modern educationist he might well have had his heroes developing right attitudes, instead of learning the Classics, and so eliminated our difference.

In 1912, at the age of eighteen, Hugh Eayrs landed in Canada, very English and very strange. At twenty-six he was made president of the Macmillan Company of Canada. The same year the company which he had taken over published as his first book a novel which was to move the English speaking world

Hugh Eayrs, President of The Macmillan Company of Canada Limited.

Canada was coming into being, a Canada matured suddenly by the

Throughout the files runs a string of poems published in a wide variety of papers and journals in those years. Most of them Mr. Eayrs assures us with a smile were written for the $2.00 to $5.00 they would bring in.

In addition to his free lance writing, Mr. Eayrs had, at the age of twenty-one, been an associate editor of *Maclean's Magazine*, a contributor to the *Financial Post* and, at the same time, editor of four of Maclean's trade papers. The year previously he was at once Financial, Literary and Dramatic editor of the *Canadian Courier*.

THIS then was the young man who faced his first problem of decision on editorial policy. The decision was a choice between two partial translations of Louis Hemon's Maria Chapdelaine; the one made by Sir Andrew Macphail— generally regarded as the dean of Canadian letters, and not a man

This excerpt from the magazine *School Progress* of December 1936 shows an article by John Gray (Morton Dawson) on Hugh Eayrs, who is pictured here.

John Gray and Frank Upjohn (right) strolling on Yonge Street about 1937.

The author's sister, Joan, was the flower girl when he married Antoinette (Tony) Lalonde in 1932. In 1937 the family was completed by the arrival of young John.

Mazo de la Roche, one of the authors whom John Gray encountered.

Grey Owl, one of Macmillans' more colourful authors, with
Jelly Roll.

The author leads his platoon of
the Toronto Scottish in a Victory
Bond Parade past City Hall,
Toronto, in 1940.

Brother Bob.

Captain John Morgan Gray, photographed in Antwerp in 1944, two days after the Germans withdrew from the city.

In Montreal on disembarkation leave, January 1946, at the Samovar Restaurant.

The "historic picture" described in the text. Tony and John Gray with Frank Upjohn and E. J. ("Ned") Pratt.

Chief, General Gamelin, had expressed a confidence and a readiness to roll through the German army "like butter" whenever he was instructed to do so. But I was reading the *Nation* and the *New Republic* and they presented a different and a less comforting view of events. Hitler was now talking about the Polish Corridor — another intolerable injustice — and the comic figure had long since become sinister.

It was no longer a question of whether there would be war, but only how soon, and the little/big question, what would I do? Ten years before, I knew I would have welcomed it, rushed toward it as the ultimate adventure, like a romantic, high-spirited boy. Now, though something of a romantic boy remained, and the prospect of war was exciting, I watched its approach with horror. I told myself that it was a bad war brought on by bad management; Britain and France could have averted it with a show of firmness five years before — or three, or two. Yet I stopped just short of a resolution not to serve under any circumstances — a resolution I knew I might be unable to keep, though I intended to try. A young man who lived across the street from us began to appear in officer's uniform and went to the armouries two or three nights a week looking important. He told me that when war came he intended to be well on his way up the ladder, in a not too dangerous job. It only increased my cynicism about the war.

This tension, this struggle between reason and emotion, was like a file along the nerves. My father had had a complete nervous breakdown in 1932, partly the result of a serious motor accident and the market crash, but largely, the doctors believed, stemming from his experience in the 1914-18 war. What that experience had been could only be a little understood from the snatches of stories across the years; funny stories for little boys and bits overheard of talk between old soldiers. "I remember one night we were moving up to the line. It was pitch dark until the Hun put up a star shell and then they began to shell the road. . . ." "A French soldier had been buried just in front of our trench, and his boots stuck out in the trench and the boys used to polish the boots." And there was an anecdote that seemed to tumble out in spite of him with a kind of insistence, of how he was standing with one of his men when a shell burst very close, leaving him unhurt but splitting his companion's head into two pieces, "like an orange" he would say earnestly, as though trying to make something important quite clear. This understandably seemed to be one of the horrors he could never bury, and he always used the same image, "like an orange". But apart from his snapshot memory of events it was the grief over his men and officers killed that remained a burden he could never lay down. In retrospect they were the finest men he had known.

It was the literature of disillusion that flooded over us in the 1920's and '30's — the books of Sassoon, Aldington, Graves, C. E. Montague, Remarque, and others — that had changed me, from the small boy in uniform standing at the salute as the battalion came by to the young man who believed that wars settled nothing except where the nations should bury their dead. I don't believe my father read any of those books and I would never have pressed them on him. He would have found them upsetting, and to have agreed with their collective thesis would have seemed to him a breaking of faith.

An anecdote, unconnected with action, played its part in the withdrawal I thought I was making — thought I was honestly trying to make — from involvement in the war that must come. Soon after the 21st Battalion had arrived in England in the spring of 1915 a group of the officers were invited to tea at some great house not far from Sandling Camp. Over tea one of the ladies of the house or the neighbourhood had said to my father, "It's frightfully good of you to come over and fight for us." At the time he presumably made some equally silly rejoinder, "Not at all", "Only too glad", "Any time", he couldn't remember. What he did remember was the delayed impact of the remark: Fight for you? Is that what I am doing? Is that what we are all here for? What are we here for? It was late to be asking the question. And I intended for my part to try to get both question and answer straight, in advance. But the excitements

230

of war seldom allow either straight questions or straight answers.

My father had grown up in a society in Toronto in which the solid goodness of things British was not open to question, and the virtues of the British Empire were considered as certain as its greatness. I loved many things about Britain and was grateful for the institutions and tradition which were our legacy, but for the rest I was less sure. The mystique of the Crown had been almost destroyed for me by the abdication crisis. The whole Macmillan staff had crowded into Hugh Eayrs' office to hear the abdication speech — dignified and moving, but it seemed to me unkingly and wrong. Some of the girls were crying almost uncontrollably and most eyes including mine were wet, but when the speech moved into a sort of hand-over statement in favour of the Duke of York I muttered furiously to Frank Upjohn, "Here comes the plug for brother George." It was no doubt a youthful and harsh judgement, but it seemed to me that happiness was not a perquisite of royal office, and England needed Edward VIII. The abdication was a crushing blow to my father, who like many veterans had seen the attractive and reckless young Prince of Wales tramping gaily through the mud of Flanders talking to the troops; they believed on little evidence that he would grow into the most popular of all the kings of England, and the best.

I had nothing against George VI, and admired the courage with which this apparently shy and nervous man steadied himself for the limelight and the responsibilities which must now be his. He had from the first earned respect, but when he came to Canada on a Royal Tour in the spring of 1939, presumably at the suggestion of the British government, I refused to turn out to see him and his charming queen pass by, though there were many opportunities for doing so, and dozens of my friends and relatives chased around the city to see the royal couple again and again. I don't think I talked about or explained this sulky rebellion, except to Tony. It was simply accepted that I "hadn't managed" to see the King and Queen. "Too bad," people said, "she's beautiful." Was I trying to shut out the sounds of a royal recruiting campaign that seemed to me demeaning to both parties, or hiding from myself? Everyman's duty is the king's, but everyman's soul is his own — if he can keep it.

I don't remember discussing this issue with Hugh Eayrs. Like most expatriate Englishmen — though he had lived in Canada for twenty-five years and was, with Lorne Pierce of the Ryerson Press, the most nationalistic of our publishers — he followed the Royal Tour with almost boyish pride and joy. For a few weeks he was almost his old self. But like all resurgences of his health in those days, usually following a spell in hospital, it was short-lived. The bright and laughing eyes grew dull, the slimmed-down body became fat, the hands and face puffy, and the process was speeding up. Everyone knew the reasons — except the doctors — it was kidney, it was heart, it was alcohol. The improvement that followed the sessions in hospital seemed to give weight to the alcohol theory, though in the gentlemen's-club atmosphere of the Wellesley Hospital of those days he could always provide a discreet drink for visitors.

But if his star was falling out of the sky it fell slowly and in its descent blazed brighter at times than it had ever done. His instinct for a good or important book by turns dimmed and flared up brilliantly, and his reputation still drew many of the most distinguished offerings to us. In 1938, '39, and '40 our list included Professor Wrong's *The Canadians*, Sir Robert Borden's *Memoirs*, E. J. Pratt's *Brébeuf and His Brethren*, Ringuet's *Thirty Acres*, Traquair's *The Old Silver of Quebec*, and a fine, ambitious series, partially subsidized by Carnegie, *The Canadian Frontiers of Settlement*.

Few of these made money but the rest of the business, which was regaining strength — the imported books and our domestic school-books — could have carried them and benefited from their prestige. Unfortunately the distinguished books were sometimes dragged down by bad guesses and bad books; we started a film department — a promising and expensive disaster. In the total balance the business, having survived the battering storm of the depression, still sailed an uncertain and lumbering course. It paid dividends that were not justified but it restored few salary cuts to staff and paid no more bonuses, except to the President. Sales increased but cash resources, and morale, did not.

One of the bad guesses brought on a scene with Hugh Eayrs that might have ended our association. An author and editor of no great distinction had brought in the manuscript of an anthology of contemporary Canadian poetry. When some weeks later she pressed for a publishing decision I happened to be in his office. Our department had been getting opinions on the manuscript and though our readings were not completed the advance indications were not favourable. I suspected he had not more than glanced at the book, but felt guilty at a verdict being overdue and at not having done his homework. Every publisher has such moments and they frequently lead to hasty and wrong moves. The blame or the explanation could have been thrown on our department; instead I was both amused and horrified to hear him say, "We're going to do your book; I like it; it is my kind of book. Mrs. Eayrs likes it too. As a matter of fact we were just talking about it last night; it's her kind of book." The author's mood of truculent and aggressive irritation was melted in a moment. She left, all smiles. "Don't like that woman much," Hugh Eayrs said and we went on with our talk.

But when our reports did come in they ranged from lukewarm to scathing. It was clear that we could not expect a welcome for the book in the schools. I was reluctant to tell Hugh Eayrs, but he had to know. When I told him opinions were unfavourable, he said casually that in that case we wouldn't do the book; silly to publish a book we knew to be bad. I said woodenly that I was afraid we were committed. "We're not committed," he said; "no one can make you publish a bad book." I pressed on, "I heard you promise to publish." The exchange only continued for a moment or two longer with the Chief denying the promise and then in a flash of rage he said slowly, "Don't be a bloody fool." For a moment I sat still, feeling as though I had been hit, then I stood up and walked blindly to the door; there I said unsteadily, "I've taken a lot but

I won't take that." He waved me back with a tired, unhappy gesture. "Oh, sit down," he said rather pathetically, "don't *you* turn against me. Mrs. Eayrs is against me, Miss Elliott [his secretary] is against me. I'm fonder of you than of anyone in this business and you can make me angrier. All right, we'll do the wretched book." I apologized for being mulish and pompous.

But the passing of that storm did not end his troubles or even help them much. A group of his friends, alarmed at his health, conspired to force him to take a long holiday away from the business. The movement seemed to have been led by Professor Pelham Edgar of the University of Toronto, a long-time friend, author, and golf partner. The outcome was a letter from a group of concerned friends to George Brett, the President of the Macmillan Company in New York. If Hugh Eayrs were required to go away for perhaps six months and to get well, Professor Edgar could supervise the business in his absence. The letter implied that Professor Edgar was well qualified for the task. George Brett, though a large shareholder, could not make such a decision on his own and passed the problem to the Macmillans in London, who in turn passed on the suggestion to Hugh Eayrs.

The response was predictable and sudden. He reassured the Macmillans at once — he hadn't been quite himself but was well on the mend. He then invited the concerned friends to his house one evening and confronted them with their well-intentioned plot which he believed had endangered his position as president. He insisted on going round the group asking each in turn whether he had signed the letter and still subscribed to the views expressed there as to his health. Some backed away a little in the face of his cold anger, but all stood convicted. The final and devastating invective was saved for Pelham Edgar, whose affectionate but patronizing attitude of many years toward Hugh Eayrs was paid in full that night. And then he ordered his oldest friends out of his house.

It was as characteristic as it was understandable, but one more blind had been pulled down to increase the darkness of his world. Though I think some of the old friends made their peace with him, he had narrowed his circle and deepened his loneliness. It was not a light in which he could work well or find any happiness. He flourished among friendly, bright people and they responded to him, or had in the past, like flowers to sunlight. Now with his marriage breaking up, or already broken, none of us knew which, with many of his friends backing away from a division of loyalties, he seemed to be on a continuing and hectic quest for new friends; in some he was fortunate, but others who came in and out of the office were free-loading light-weights for whom in better days he would have had no time. For those of us who were devoted to him but powerless to help it was sad and frustrating.

In spite of an air of increasingly forced gaiety, Hugh Eayrs was not unaware of what was happening — or might happen. On one of our last trips together in a late-night shop talk in the Empress Hotel he spoke of the future of the business, "if I blow up, as I sometimes think I shall," he said, and went on to imply — though he stopped short of saying — that I was the person to succeed him. "You've got nous, as we say in Yorkshire." I didn't know the term and he defined it as "common sense". Bob Harvey (Accountant and Secretary of the Company) he said could never run the business. Harvey was the man who was said to have refused me a loan against my salary and who when I was in my slight jam in New York I had told Hugh Eayrs would never understand me, so I had no trouble now in agreeing with this assessment, though outwardly I didn't comment. But a few months later Harvey was made a director of the Company and Miss Elliott, Hugh Eayrs' secretary, replaced Harvey as Secretary of the Company. It was perhaps paranoid of me to see this as a direct slap, a reminder to keep my place and mind my manners, but there seemed no good reason for the move. The Company had never had any working director except the President, but there may now have been pressure from London on account of the Chief's health to name someone else to the Board. Was it a kindly impulse or a form of teasing that made Hugh Eayrs attempt to explain some weeks later? Harvey, he said, had handled the Company's accounts for twenty years "without one penny ever going wrong." I nodded and nodded to show my agreement — sure a great thing, that. But it seemed absurd enough to reward a man so handsomely for not stealing from the Company, since that was largely what he was paid not to do. Whatever the cause of the appointment, it was to have far-reaching results, neither foreseen nor, I am sure, intended.

But there was not much time left in which to be either ruffled or wryly amused. The long-awaited war was suddenly upon us, and jostling for seats at the Board at Macmillans or elsewhere shrank to its proper measure. I was travelling in Central Ontario with a young man called Barney Sandwell, just graduated from the University of Toronto with a good degree. He was our newest recruit, part of the replacement of Frank Upjohn and destined later to become a leading Canadian publisher. War didn't seem far away but we didn't know it had arrived on the morning we came out of the dining-room at the old Quinte House in Belleville and stepped into the elevator. We had been comfortably and sleepily talking about the day ahead over breakfast and it was into that half-awake moment that the elevator man fired his shot. "Well, she's started, eh?" he said. Asked what he meant, he said, "The Germans have marched into Poland." He had heard it on the morning news, and it was as shocking as if he had dragged a dead body into the elevator with us and dropped it at our feet. There would be the usual protests and ultimatums but Germany would not now pull back because of a warning. She had been warned and had cynically protected her back by making a shocking deal with Russia. So this was it.

To go on as though this was a normal day was unthinkable. We turned for home, but first, as though to reassure and be reassured, I phoned Tony. What was happening? I think I expected flags and soldiers marching in the street. Not surprisingly she reported that nothing was changed. It was a beautiful day and people were just going about their affairs as on any other day. Out on the busy everyday streets of Belleville nothing was different, though everyone's life would in some way be changed. It was as though during the night we had moved from one train into another and were now sitting in that moment of expectant stillness waiting for the train to pull out on its trip through dangerous country.

On our way back to Toronto we stopped for Barney to make a call in Port Hope. The shoe-shine parlour where I went to kill time had the usual quota of wise guys. They were fairly cackling with merriment over the surprise "them Germans" were going to get when the Royal Air Force rolled out their Lysanders, and "all them secret weapons" — "Oh boys!" They almost ran out of breath with the excitement and glory of it all. Besides, it appeared that the Air Force had made and put in mothballs two planes for every one they had put in service — "Oh boys!" This all sounded like the nonsense it was and yet I half welcomed it, half believed it, though my information was that Britain was woefully short of everything it was going to need, except guts. But there was to be much more of this whistling in the dark before we all learned to live — and many to die — with the dangerous truth.

The next ten days prolonged the expectant hush almost beyond endurance; we were all edgy. Hugh Eayrs, braced by the crisis to his best form, called the Macmillan staff together and leaning forward on a desk in the general office made a fine little speech. He tried to create a mood of calm good sense. Whatever was going to happen would be protracted and testing, but there was no need for people to rush off and enlist. Don't let us get excited. However, if as things developed people felt they should go into the services, the Company would make up any difference in their pay and they would be sure of their jobs at the war's end. No doubt it was more than anyone was in a position to guarantee, but it was the appropriate intention.

Britain had declared war at once, but Canada had not and could not until Parliament met. Meanwhile the English-speaking part of Canada fretted at a delay imposed by public opinion after the first war and now found intolerable. Mackenzie King, the Prime Minister, had never had many friends among

237

the war veterans, on the not very sensible ground that he had "run away" to the United States in their war. Now they were clamorous. King, like a deaf man, moved on his determined course. I couldn't like him — indeed I had been brought up to despise him — but I had to admire his apparent calm in the mounting excitement. He had met Hitler not long before and had been persuaded with too many others that he was a reasonable man who could be persuaded to reasonable action. King now cabled Hitler asking him to reconsider the course he was embarked on. No doubt it was the ultimately futile gesture, but King intended to keep the record impeccable. It was a commentary on our state of nationhood at the time when one of my friends, edgy and over-excited like the rest of us, said, "Mackenzie King cabling Hitler, for God's sake, who the hell does he think he is? He ought to have his ass kicked." I was in no doubt my friend spoke for millions, and in a sense for me. Yet I heard myself say angrily, "He's the head of this country, does that mean nothing?" "Oh, I know," he said, in exasperation, "but when England is at war we're at war. Why doesn't he get on with it?"

My own attempts to remain calm and to keep a clear head were sunk with the Cunard liner *Athenia*, and the Germans' mindless drowning of scores of women and children, some of them our friends. It seemed to be a pointless brutality, an example of Germanic wrong-headedness — of a piece with the sinking of the *Lusitania* in the First World War. So — they had learned nothing. All the fine speeches, and the sad appeals from the harshness of the Treaty of Versailles, meant nothing. German history at that moment seemed to be a continuous and blood-stained tapestry running back to the Kaiser, to Bismarck, to Frederick the Great, and in distant mists to the Teutonic knights.

I telephoned the Colonel of the Glengarrys to ask what was happening. He said in a tired voice that they were mobilized, after a fashion, and doing what they had always done, guarding the river line and the canal above and below Cornwall. In 1812 they had turned out; in rebellion times, 1837-38, they had come trooping down all the roads from the farms in the back country between the Ottawa and the St. Lawrence rivers; they had stood guard in the Fenian raids of 1864; and in 1914 we had visited my father's post at Milles Roches, where the men did sentry duty in scarlet tunics and tartan trews and glengarry bonnets.

Though I was on the reserve of officers I had taken no part and felt no interest in regimental activity for almost ten years. When I asked whether I was needed the Colonel said, "Jack, I have almost more officers than men. What do you want to do?" I said that at thirty-two and with a wife and child I wasn't longing to join the colours, but I was available if needed. We left it at that, and having made my gesture I was, for the moment, a little more at peace. This relaxing of tension was helped by the illusory quiet of the phony war. Along their common frontier the French and German armies watched each other across the Maginot Line. I flung myself into work and found a renewed and deeper joy in my home and family. The baby had become an enchanting small boy who insisted on endless walks and songs, who on the walks could leave no dog or cat, no alleyway, no garage uninvestigated, until he collapsed — gorged with the wonders of this world — and came home asleep, hung over my shoulder like a sack. For months it almost seemed that the war might go away — had indeed gone away. There were comforting rumours that "we" were in touch with powerful anti-Nazi elements in Germany, that negotiations now in progress would bring peace. It was the same kind of thinking that had held us inert for six years while Germany re-armed and step by step enlarged her breathing space.

And then, in a few months, everything was changed. Late one afternoon in Calgary in the winter of 1940 I picked up some letters and a telegram on the way to my room in the Palliser Hotel. As the old elevator began its dignified climb I pried open the telegram. I had not asked urgently for any information but I opened the wire without any premonition of disaster; telegrams had become as matter of fact as the long-distance phone was to be. And then I was staring at news I couldn't ac-

239

cept; news that had seemed inevitable but with frequent re-
prieves and wishful thinking had been pushed away to some
unimaginable future. But the future had just gone by; Hugh
Eayrs had died that morning.

An era had passed at Macmillans, in Canadian publishing,
and certainly in my own life. I hadn't always been able to admire Hugh Eayrs, but he had been father, brother, playmate,
and boss by turns, and keeper of the key to a world I found endlessly fascinating, the world of books and writers. He had
opened the door absent-mindedly enough, but once I was in he
had enjoyed and shared my excitement, which no doubt reminded him of his own beginnings. I had not been blind to his
weaknesses — vanities and pomposities and a cheerful indifference to truth when it didn't serve — but in the end they seemed
endearing. I had once been accused of aping his mannerisms,
and though I didn't think it was true, it may well have been. In
an odd, painful sense I had to recognize that it was a relief to
have the hatefulness of much of the past two or three years
finished. He was at peace, and so were we at Macmillans, but
we were also in a sudden and chilly loneliness.

The next forty hours were like a long stumble through darkness. Somehow with help I made the necessary arrangements,
but there remains no memory of eating or drinking or sleeping,
only of slogging on, not thinking connectedly, moving blindly
toward home like an injured and lost animal. I had only minutes to pack and catch the train east out of Calgary. Then for a
night and a day I had time to sleep and think, but could do neither. Having crossed the Prairies I was still thirty-six hours
from home by the normal train journey, but I could fly south
from Winnipeg to Minneapolis and from there with luck to Detroit. Leaving Minneapolis I asked the stewardess for something to make me sleep but it might just as well have been a
sugar pill. This time there was no excited wonder at the miracle of flight. Like a drugged person I watched our descent into
Milwaukee and at last as the lights of Detroit appeared I fell
into a heavy sleep. Half awake, I took a taxi across the bridge
back to Canada and then from Windsor in the early morning I

caught a train for Toronto, where I had an hour's sleep before the funeral.

Back with my family and with my equally shocked colleagues at Macmillans the lights came on again, though they would remain dim for a long time. Over the funeral hung a cold and desolating sadness; in spite of all the warnings no one had been prepared. The idea of Hugh Eayrs being dead was a contradiction in terms. With all his impatience and arrogance he had for his friends personified vitality and the joy of living. Though the long illness and decline had dimmed his youthful appearance, though he had held centre stage for twenty years, he was still only forty-six when he died. Though friends, and enemies — which he didn't lack, would argue for years the cause of his death, I came in time to believe that the root cause was heart-breaking frustration; pulling at a dead weight in trying to publish imaginatively in the Canada of that day.

Frank Upjohn and I drove away from the funeral together in heavy silence. Outside the car cold rain turned the snow on the streets to a dirty muck, and a sodden, dark sky seemed the appropriate lighting for the scene. "Well, the poor old Chief," one of us said, "so that's it." "That's it" was the answer. And we drove on in a silence broken only by the splashing of the wheels. But the very finality of the comment forced us on. Life had not ended; Macmillans had not closed, though Hugh Eayrs was gone. "So what happens now?" one of us said at last. Neither had any eagerness for the discussion which came more from a brooding uneasiness than from any excited spurt of ambition. Each of us nominated the other for the post that must soon be filled, and with the nomination pledged support. Fatigue and gloom and distaste ended the discussion. Since something would be done we could only hope for the best, but we were not optimistic.

At the office we settled into an amiable but uneasy cabinet government which in due course was confirmed from London. The partners there with war on their doorstep could not give much attention to our affairs. Harvey, the newly named director, was to be General Manager, and would we just carry on.

241

Harvey seemed to have fixed his life on a few generalizations that had somehow been built into his system when he was young. These generalizations were like the pieces of a Meccano set; faced with a problem he identified it and fished out his piece of Meccano to be wedged into place. Thus, when France fell in 1940 he didn't have to think about it, he just reached for the piece that fitted and was ready with his pronouncement: "You can't trust the French," he said to me with great solemnity. "You can't trust the French. That's what I've always heard. They used to say that when I was a kid." That's what they had said in Lincolnshire forty years before and probably four hundred.

He was no less assured when it came to dealing with the poets we published. Since no one bought poetry it should not have been surprising that poets were always in need of money. But what that meant to Harvey was that they couldn't manage their affairs. "Funny fellows, poets," was his judgement, "always wantin' money." And then because Charles G. D. Roberts was one of the poets and had a reputation for pursuing the ladies, he linked all poets in this, too. "Wantin' money," and then with a roguish leer he added, "and kinda sexy," then almost choked himself with his chortles.

But for the moment our momentum and the limitations imposed by wartime regulations disguised the weakness of the structure. We had a manager without experience or confidence, with some interest in figures but none in publishing; he was at the mercy of his experts or of anyone who claimed expertise. With grim joylessness we got on with the work. The business philosophy of the new manager was quite simple: don't spend any money you don't have to; to all adventurous proposals say "no".

Some weeks after Hugh Eayrs' death I had a telephone call from Mrs. Eayrs, asking whether I would come to see her. She was then living alone in the St. George Apartments, comfortable, but in a good deal less elegant a setting than had seemed her proper milieu. I had not seen her since the rumours of the break-up of their marriage had begun to be heard.

We were old friends, and though she had always been the boss's wife, there had also been a big-sisterly kindness that sprang from my friendship with her young brother, Lee Whitefield, who had died rather suddenly four or five years after I joined Macmillans. Our talk was a little constrained by all that had happened since we last met. And then she came to the purpose of her call. Though it had nothing to do with her now, she said, she was interested in what would happen — who was to be the new head at Macmillans? I told her that as an interim arrangement Harvey was to be acting head; that produced a deep, sardonic laugh.

She said that anyone who knew anything about the business knew that Frank Upjohn and I had kept it on the rails "for years". She knew George Brett, Jr., the head of Macmillan, New York, pretty well, and would be glad to put in a word with him if I would welcome that. I thanked her and said I would probably be going into the army before long, so I wasn't a candidate.

This produced an immediate protest: at my age, married, and with a small child? I couldn't be serious. I explained as best I could and she listened, argued a little, and let it go. I was grateful, but remembering our meeting ten years before, when she was on the point of marrying Hugh Eayrs and I of joining Macmillans, I think we were both sad at parting. We had come a long way from the bright days of ten years before.

❧ 11 ❧

THROUGHOUT THE MONTHS that followed Hugh Eayrs' death, the war put Macmillan problems into perspective. We learned the word *blitzkrieg* and watched in paralysing disbelief as the German army swept to the North Sea and the English Channel, crushing Norway, Denmark, Holland, Belgium, and finally France. Every business appointment turned into a discussion of strategy. Was it a call of the blood, a surging to the assistance of a beleaguered England, or a real belief that we were now threatened? Suddenly the whole of English-speaking Canada was swept up in a great burst of energy and patriotic fervour and alarm. All militia battalions were mobilized and second battalions were formed to reinforce those that were already in England or en route.

The fever that had seized many in September 1939 and then relaxed its grip returned many times stronger than before. This was now everyone's urgent war. Churchill had taken over from Chamberlain and had begun the process of rallying his people and rousing the world.

In one of those moments of aberration when war seemed more important than its consequence I was brought back to earth by one of my old friends. I was having lunch in Vancouver with Professor Garnet Sedgwick, head of the Department of English at the University of British Columbia. Sedgwick was a great teacher — a product of Dalhousie and Harvard, and wise to boot — whose normal tone of wicked and profane glee could swing quickly to sombre reflection.

Partly because I was excited and partly to stir him to serious talk I asked whether in spite of the horror of it he was not stimulated by the prospect of war — a ringside seat at world history. The mask of joviality fell away at once and he said with a sadness he seldom showed, "Oh son, war will destroy our civilization, most of what I value in life. Don't ask me to enjoy the prospect." He talked on a little, and I listened. But he had said it all in the first moment, though it was to take me years to know how right he was.

That summer I became a part-time soldier with the 2nd Battalion of the Toronto Scottish, drilling one or two nights a week and going to camp at Niagara-on-the-Lake. Two or three boys from Macmillans had joined the Battalion and we had a whole platoon of one of the great Toronto Maple Leaf hockey teams, including Syl Apps, Gordon Drillon, and Turk Broda. The hockey players had as their platoon officer one of the brightest and best loved of all sports writers, Ted Reeve. Teddy, who had had many of his bones broken in football or lacrosse, never managed to look like a soldier, and never really wanted to; but he intended to be one, and in spite of the aches and limitations of his scarred body he was. Two weeks at Niagara didn't turn us into soldiers, but it did wonders for our smartness and morale. We hung over the sides of the little returning steamer as she edged in past Gibraltar Point to Toronto Harbour, the way by which travellers had come to Toronto since the days when great trees had crowded the waterfront a hundred and fifty years before. We came smartly down the gangways and formed up to crisp words of command, then marched along the waterfront through cheering crowds to Fort York Armouries, feeling as though we had won the war.

It was an immense relief to be doing something about the war, or getting ready to do something. Clearly I had not left far behind the small boy saluting at the roadside twenty-five years before, as the soldiers marched by singing "It's a Long Way to Tipperary". But as the months went by, our training came to very little. We were all doing something to get ourselves in physical shape but there was no ammunition to fire and hardly

245

any guns to handle. Once again there was a pause in the war. The Battle of Britain had been won and England had survived the Blitz, but the Desert War was just beginning. The pause could not last, but at the present rate of training the reserve battalions would be little more ready when their moment came.

Meanwhile there was a sort of mental preparation going on. Though many of us were too old or unfit for active service, we were all establishing in our own minds — and in our families' minds — the possibility, or probability, of separation. None of us could really know what was looming; we were like passengers waving from the ship's railing, and the posture created its own tensions. When we were alone, Tony and I would sometimes fall silent as though a dark shadow had crossed the sun. Much of the time we tried to screen the future by absorbing ourselves with our small boy, but sometimes with too much drinking and too many parties that weren't always fun. We were held together by strong fabric, but within us we were listening for a tearing sound.

Since we were not replacing staff at the office the business was demanding, and I was crossing the country from Halifax to Victoria on the Pacific coast once or twice a year. Educational authorities were hastening to make changes they had been planning before all change was frozen. It was a satisfaction to be reaping what I had sown years before, and to know that even if bad times were coming, Macmillans would be somewhat strengthened as a result.

On one of my trips to Halifax that spring two things made the war more personal and the need to be further involved more urgent. At the great staging camp at Debert, Nova Scotia, I spent a night with my brother and the officers of the Glengarrys who were expected to go overseas before long as part of the Highland Brigade of the 3rd Canadian Division. We spent the evening gaily, noisily, drinking and singing, followed by portentous talk. In the morning the Colonel undertook to apply for my transfer from the 2nd Battalion Toronto Scottish to the 1st Battalion Glengarrys. A day or two later in Halifax I

246

phoned Kay and Gavin Rainnie. Gavin, now a major of artillery, was on duty at McNabb's Island at the harbour mouth but was coming in that evening and they were going to a party; wouldn't I come along? It sounded quite like old times, but it wasn't. Gavin came in a little late, looking very soldierly, but grave. There was just time for a little romp and to say goodnight to his charming children. Then, as Kay tucked them in, he told me he had been warned that day for overseas service; he would be leaving almost at once. During the evening Kay sensed the news and got it out of him. Like Tony and me, they had both known the moment would come, but the knowledge had not sufficiently armed them. Gavin, though quiet, gave no other hint of what he was feeling, but Kay was inconsolable. To my too facile reassurance she answered only, "I'll never see him again, and you don't know how awful that is." She was right on both counts. They had never looked past each other since school days, and he was to die off the Normandy beaches on D-Day, doing artillery spotting from a small boat.

There was a quieter footnote to that last trip to the Atlantic coast that is still a pleasant memory. On my way back I stopped in Fredericton and there met a young traveller representing Copp Clark, one of our most formidable competitors. His name was Marsh Jeanneret, and though he had not long graduated from the University of Toronto to work in publishing, he had already shown signs of becoming a powerful figure in the business. His father, Professor F. C. A. Jeanneret, had edited several successful school texts for us, and during the years of our association had become a firm and kindly friend.

Once, soon after we were married, Tony had come with me to Quebec, and we had visited the summer school that Professor Jeanneret ran for Ontario teachers at Sillery. His dream, welcome in Quebec but not generally then in Ontario, was of a generation of teachers who would know and love Quebec as he did, and speak the language well. Given that, he believed the way would be open toward understanding and removing the things that kept the two peoples apart. No doubt it was visionary and impractical but I thought it splendid, and we visited the school and spent evenings with Professor and Mrs. Jean-neret at which I preached excitedly to the long-converted. They were kind and generous and obviously charmed by the happiness I am sure we radiated. Their own dream for the school was doomed; not enough interested Ontario teachers, no real enthusiasm in Ontario's Department of Education.

So I was glad to see Marsh, though we didn't know each other well. Lonely travellers marooned on that desert island, the Queen's Hotel, we had several long talks. Inevitably what loomed large in my mind tumbled out. I said a bit mournfully that this was probably my last trip until the war was over — if then. Marsh expressed regret and then, obviously wrestling with his conscience and his sense of discretion, told me that his father had been nursing the hope that he could raise the capital to start Marsh and me in our own publishing business. It was too late to do more than feel flattered and salute a kindly im-pulse. Whether it was also a shrewd impulse remains one of the questions filed under "might have beens". Marsh in a few years was to become head of the University of Toronto Press and to have a career that made him one of the most successful and re-spected academic publishers in the English-speaking world. His father, a controversial figure in his younger days, was to be-come Principal of University College and ultimately Chancel-lor of the University.

In the end I didn't join the Glengarrys, with whom I might have hit the Normandy beach on D-Day. Even as the papers were being made up for my transfer, the Toronto Scottish called for reinforcements and within two weeks four of us were on our way to the Machine Gun Training Centre at Three Rivers, Quebec. The activity of the last days continued to cloud the fact that there would be a final day; to hold it at arm's length while I gathered equipment, took care of last things at the office, and said good-bye endlessly at a series of parties.

Shortly before I was to leave for the army there was an appli-cation for a job as an Educational traveller from a lively little woman, Irene Welsh, who had been a teacher and had edited a magazine for teachers. She saw publishing and selling educational books as an extension of the teaching profession and was determined to try it. Though she was well qualified and seemed impressively keen and energetic, I couldn't believe she would find that selling satisfied her high sense of vocation as an educator, at least to begin with. So I parried her arguments and tried to explain my doubts. The tiny figure listened with great intensity, her eyes fixed on me like some homemade lie-detector. She wasn't persuaded.

Finally I said wearily, "If I am right this appointment would be a serious mistake for both of us. What would you do if you were sitting on my side of the desk?"

The answer came right back. "I'd hire Miss Welsh and make her work like Hell." So I took on the first part of the proposition and she the latter for the next thirty years and more, never losing her intensity or interest in the work. In time I realized that she saw herself as working "like H– – –"; "Hell" was only for special occasions.

And the final days produced a bizarre counterpoint. Some weeks before, Frank Upjohn and I had gone in confidence to Macmillans' lawyer, Bill McLaughlin, the only Director in Canada, apart from Harvey. In two meetings we had begged him to use his influence, with Harvey and in London, to persuade all concerned that it would be a mistake for Harvey to be made President; he had no capacity or experience for the job, and his appointment would ultimately be a disaster for the Company and for him. I think he believed that we were not just politicking in our own interests; in other circumstances we might have been, but the war was about to claim us both. Mr. McLaughlin undertook to try to hold the present interim arrangements, though we all recognized that it might be impossible; he said Harvey was already inclined to press for a permanent appointment. It was a gloomy prospect, for the new educational contracts were lifting the business, and without making a single major decision the new manager was going to look successful. But there were more important things to be upset about. I had already said good-bye to most of my friends in the East and the West, but to several I owed something more.

To a few people in education I wrote thanking them for kindness and for much they had taught me. What I wanted most to say, and said, was that it had always been a matter of regret to me, as I came to know them and we became friends, that I stood to gain by that friendship; it was good for business. If I came back I hoped we might meet in different circumstances.

Then there came a final meeting with Harvey. He had known all about my part-time soldiering, but the idea that it should come to this seemed to surprise him. Long ago John Linnell and I had agreed that he looked like Tenniel's illustration of the Carpenter in "The Walrus and the Carpenter". Now as we faced each other in shocked silence the shut mouth and squared jaw confirmed the impression. He fiddled with a pencil and then leaned forward and said with what was meant to be studied forcefulness and to give the appearance of long and careful reflection, "I don't think you should go. You have a wife and child."

I assured him I had been over that and much else a thousand times, as he must know. All I wanted now was to say good-bye and to have his confirmation that the office would make up the difference in my pay as Hugh Eayrs had promised. He said uneasily that these things were difficult; it was all very well to make promises in the heat of the moment, but not always easy to keep them. I listened in unhelpful silence and he went on fiddling with the pencil, alternately looking at me and then looking away.

He was obviously trying to think up at the last moment arguments that, if important, should have been prepared and put forward months before. Then suddenly and perhaps with more menace than he intended, he asked whether I expected to come back to Macmillans after the war. For a moment I sat stupefied, and then was surprised to hear myself answering quietly that I hoped to, and thought I might reasonably expect to be welcomed back by a company for which I had worked hard and pretty successfully for ten years. Suddenly the outrage and stupidity of the question destroyed my control. "But don't worry about me," I said; "I'm the best educational publisher in

Canada and if Macmillans don't want me there are others that do." I'm not sure that I believed either statement, but I felt better for saying it. Harvey retreated in confusion, flapping his hands and trying to explain — "I didn't mean — I only thought — these things make problems". We quickly made a kind of uneasy peace and I left with a promise that for the present the difference in pay would be made up until Harvey had a ruling from London.

The excitement of leaving deadened the pain of farewells. I had put publishing behind me, gladly enough in the circumstances, and for Tony and me the ultimate wrench was months away. She and "Cricket" (nicknamed for his happy chirping) were going to look for an apartment in Three Rivers; meanwhile there would be week-end leave in a month's time. So, whatever dread hung over our parting was held back and masked amid the chatter and the forced wit that seems inseparable from leave-taking. Four of us were leaving together, and our friends and families made a noisy and apparently gay group in Toronto's Union Station. For the moment it was only slightly more painful and much less lonely than the long separations of business trips which for ten years we had been learning to bear.

The Machine Gun Training Centre took us coolly, expertly, and moulded us, and on the whole we liked the process. It wasn't entirely easy or comfortable, but we wanted to be toughened, to be turned as quickly as possible from amateur soldiers into pros. For a month we were to be officer-cadets and it was assumed we knew nothing. The past year of evening drills, the years of school cadet corps, the Upper Canada Rifle Company, camps with the Glengarrys, and my peace-time commission meant nothing. We were an awkward squad to be remade, and in the mood of young novitiates we were strangely content. The army was at the work it knew best, a process it had refined for three hundred years and more, hardening men and preparing them for a single purpose. We stripped and cleaned and fired rifles and machine-guns and pistols endlessly; we marched, ran, and climbed, learned to maintain and drive jeeps and trucks and motor-cycles. At first when drills ended we stumbled away to our hut to flop down and sleep heavily, but after a month we were ready at the day's end to swim or box or practise unarmed combat, feeling a surge of a vitality we had almost forgotten.

The army apparently watched us with approval but seldom said so. Once in a while one of those models, the sergeant instructor, would hint that we weren't so bad, pretty good perhaps; but we looked to our own hardening bodies and our growing confidence for reassurance. If we didn't know that we were equal to what lay ahead, we knew at least that we were transformed from the office men we had been, and would never quite be again. Whether we were good enough — fit and tough and brave enough — to fight as soldiers remained an unanswerable question that hung over all we did.

Meanwhile we flung ourselves at the hardening process and at every military skill from map-reading to bayonet fighting, determined to be ready for the great test we must some day face. The motor-bikes, big Harley-Davidsons, frightened me. We were to have three days in which to learn to ride, finishing with some rough riding over rocky fields and hills and a long ride at night on narrow country roads above a steep river-bank. The brief course opened with a short explanation of the machine and a shorter demonstration ride by the sergeant-instructor. We stood in a group, our faces a series of question marks, as the sergeant roared back and pulled up easily among us. We were going to be asked to do that? "Now, sir, what about you having a try?"

I hoped he wasn't speaking to me, but he was. My companions grinned their sympathy and relief. What I wanted to say was "Who, me?" What I said was, as firmly as possible, "Right, sergeant." We were standing on the harness-racing track of the Exhibition Grounds that had become our training centre. The bike was pointed in the right direction; all I had to do was to start her up and remember to turn when I got to the corner. But either I didn't remember, or I remembered wrong. The start was all right, and I even tried a little speed and that was fine too, but the corner was coming up fast. I made some desperate moves but they weren't the appropriate ones and the big bike jumped a small ditch and flung me crucified against a stiff link fence while it lay roaring between my legs. The watching group came running down the track, the officer-cadets a bit white and breathless with their worst fears confirmed. "Is the bike all right?" asked the sergeant as he ran up. The officer in charge said, "You don't even ask about the officer." "Hell, sir," said the sergeant, "I can get lots of officers, but I'm short of bikes." In a watchful mood we went back to work, and by the end of the afternoon we had all circled the track several times with some near misses but no damage.

Our move out of cadet status was almost as unremarkable. The period of ignorance and apprehension shaded into knowledge and the ability to do what was needed. We hadn't learned much, but we had learned what the army required us to know at that point. It would take months more of training and of action to make us soldiers, but we had passed the first test. The white band, mark of the cadet, came off our caps; we were appointed to the command of training-platoons, served our turn as duty officer, and took command of a guard mounting, one of the army's dearest rituals. The first time was tense; the second the merest routine.

Against the great canvas of the war with its background of courage and suffering, our day-to-day fussing over Private Macdonald's boots or Private Smith's sloppy arms drill was so trivial as to be demeaning. How long was this to go on? Then came a day when we paraded to the railway station and watched Pte. Macdonald and Pte. Smith, crisp soldiers in full marching order, board the train and move out to our cheers, en route for England. More drafts went and new ones arrived as we moved up the lists, to take on a new platoon and start again the process of becoming proud of the group and then deeply attached, then tearing out the bonds with salutes and handshakes. In a few days there would be a new list of names, new faces, new problems, and new involvements.

Countless junior officers had written about their platoons after the First World War, always with a kind of love they could hardly understand or make clear. The platoon became for a time one's family (a warm little cell within the great faceless machine), challenging abilities, feeding the ego, strengthening — and sometimes destroying — confidence. The army tried to make it easy; there were manuals of hints and rules to cover everything, often outflanked by the complexities of personality, officers who didn't teach well, men who had trouble learning. There were officers who tried to dominate their men by an uneasy mixture of scolding and fawning; one moment a martinet, the next a clown. Others gave the impression of steadiness and experience, and a recognition of the humour in our common lot. The army watched and weeded out, occasionally staking up a weak officer with a strong sergeant; tinkering with a balky machine.

Most of the men in camp were drafts of volunteers from the Cameron Highlanders of Ottawa, the Toronto Scottish, the Royal Montreal Regiment, and the Saint John Fusiliers. But there were also batches of National Service men conscripted for home defence and not yet members of any regiment. They were organized into platoons and trained like the volunteers in the hope that as they learned to take pride in themselves as soldiers, they would volunteer for active service abroad. Some did, but most did not, and it was our hateful duty to try to persuade them to change their minds, to "go active".

Some officers went to the work as to any other duty, some with almost too much gusto, since the conscripts at Three Rivers at that time were largely French Canadians from the Lac St. Jean–Roberval — Maria Chapdelaine — country. I heard one Camerons officer, an Englishman, say to a group in the officers' mess with what he appeared to think unassailable logic, "The point is, is this a British country, or isn't it?" And I was a little surprised to hear myself snap back, "It isn't; it's Canada, and we do things our way." Fortunately that shut him up because I couldn't at that time have developed that statement very conclusively — or perhaps with much conviction. I didn't like the system, but I thought the government's compromise probably the best of the bad alternatives.

I was in no hurry to pop the question to my French-Canadian platoon. An immediate answer could only have been no, and I was not prepared to hector or bully or threaten as some were. So we drilled and marched and sang together in all weathers and at least one day for fifteen miles in the rain. Once again we were a good platoon in the making. The men for the most part were tough little fellows, endlessly cheerful and resourceful, equal to any test. The sergeant was intelligent and a natural leader, and I had to talk to him first about how to put the question to the men. He spoke some English, which many of the men did not, and my French, though limited and rusty, was usable. I felt a little sorry for myself but I felt even sorrier for those who spoke no French and were supposed to argue a difficult case persuasively to men who would know only the general drift of what was being said.

Everyone knew the question was coming, and the sergeant showed no surprise a week or two later when I suggested we have a talk. Together we climbed up into the bleachers above the race-track and sat in the sun while the men rested and covertly watched us. He nodded at once when after some fumbling I opened the question. The country needed them to be willing to serve outside Canada, in England and probably in France. This was France's war too. He shrugged over France as eloquently as if he had said "Je m'en fiche." Then courteously, rather gently, he explained in a mixture of French and English that he thought some of the boys would volunteer but most would not. I asked him why, and he said they were afraid that if they went away their jobs would be taken by people from England. At this I exploded, and my genuine amazement and disbelief must have been convincing. He grinned and shrugged and I reminded him that England was in a state of siege; all her people were in the forces or the factories. No English were looking for jobs in Canada and none could be spared even if they were. That reason, about jobs, was just nonsense; I could think of reasons why men might not want to volunteer, but that could not sensibly be one of them. Where did the men get such an idea? He seemed to hesitate and then said a priest had told them that. I went carefully past that point, saying that the priest must have been mistaken. We would know and be as angry as the French Canadians at the idea of English people coming to take our jobs. But it wasn't happening; it just wasn't true.

He then made me a graceful little speech, saying he and his men didn't know what to believe. He was sure I was telling the truth as I knew it, but who could know what was going on? He promised to talk to the men and he did, putting the case clearly and fairly. About half a dozen volunteered; the rest stood firm and looked vaguely puzzled and unhappy. It was about par for the course, and I couldn't believe that a hard sales talk would have accomplished more, if as much. They would be talked to again and again, but not by me. This wasn't a question of men's courage, as some of my fellow officers seemed to believe, but a question of understanding and motivation. Defending their own farms and villages I couldn't doubt they would be as brave as little lions, but remote wars they could hardly comprehend, let alone care deeply about. Life was a hard battle in their countryside and they were needed there.

Tony and Crick were sharing an apartment in Three Rivers for the summer and life was pleasant, if it could only last. And then, it appeared it could. Just as it seemed the next overseas draft might be ours, three of us were called into the Colonel's office and told we could forget about going overseas. We were too old to stand the physical stress on a junior officer in "the field" — I was thirty-four; we were good instructors and just what was needed at Three Rivers, so we were to settle down and do an important job — there was no appeal from that decision. The life went out of our work. It was not to teach people to shoot machine-guns, which I did poorly, that I joined the army. In a short time I had watched too many instructors already bored and disenchanted and becoming boozy; if I could do anything about it I was going to get away from the too comfortable, too soul-destroying future that loomed. When I learned further that the Colonel had me marked down to become his adjutant I knew I had to get out. Some people are born adjutants, but I was not one of them.

The first opportunity to break out I quickly abandoned. A group of Personnel Selection Officers under Brigadier Brock Chisholm visited the camp, and one of the group was an old publishing friend, Wilfred Wees, of W. J. Gage. During the visit he took me aside and suggested I join their branch of the service; it would mean becoming a captain at once. I said yes thank you, eagerly, and for a few days liked the idea, but when the papers came through I refused the appointment. And then with the connivance of the adjutant I was sent on a month's Field Security Course at the Royal Military College in Kingston. This was a quite different view of the army — interesting, important, and with just a whiff of cloak-and-dagger about it. And there was something satisfying about training in Kingston as my father had done in the Kaiser's war, and at RMC, where as a small boy I had dreamed of being a cadet. Old Kingston with its handsome limestone buildings and its memory of great events was full of echoes for me. At the end of the course as I packed for a return to Three Rivers it was suggested that I might become a member of the Directing Staff of the War Intelligence School. Back at Three Rivers I got on with training and held my breath.

And yet, eager as I was to be gone, it wasn't easy to leave all this; the officers with whom I had arrived and trained and shared a hard good time; my final platoon of Saint John Fusiliers who had come back to Three Rivers after two futile years of being "buggered about" on fortress duty in Cape Breton, tough and disenchanted old soldiers. After an unhappy start I was given two weeks to turn them into a precision squad, marching and executing intricate drill movements on whistle and arm signals. It was a job for an experienced platoon whose morale was high, prepared to drill long hours and any time, to get it right.

Our test came at the end of the two weeks before a packed Coliseum and against a crack American precision squad from Plattsburg, New York. There was no winner declared but we

257

were given a great ovation, and that night I wouldn't have traded my platoon for the whole Brigade of Guards. A few days later I was packing my gear, preparatory to leaving for Kingston, when there was a tentative knock on the door. It was one of the corporals from my platoon; confident and sharp on the parade ground, he was now awkward and embarrassed. After an uneasy exchange of greetings he dug into his pocket and produced an untidy little tissue-paper parcel. "The boys wanted you to have this," he said and thrust it at me. It was a silver cigarette lighter bought by men who during their first two weeks in camp had had no pay and couldn't even buy smokes because the army had lost their papers. It was also the kind of gift that officers are expressly forbidden to accept from their men; but I would have faced a court martial rather than say no to this. Two days later after the smiles and handshakes and salutes it was all over. With mixed feelings I left Three Rivers where I had arrived six months before, almost breathlessly eager to be made into a professional soldier. Whether that had happened or not would remain in doubt, but I was now committed to the role while the war and I lasted.

There remains a sheen over the memory of the months in Kingston. Though I arrived in January in piercing cold, my memories seem all to be of spring and a never-to-be-forgotten summer. Tony and Cricket moved once again and we managed a family life in a rather primitive apartment on Union Street, now demolished to make room for a new Queen's University building. We worked hard but there was time for picnics in the beautiful uncrowded countryside with ever-present sparkling water: Lake Ontario or my beloved St. Lawrence River, or the Cataraqui River and Rideau Canal draining from the height of land between Kingston and Ottawa. Cricket, who had had some nursery-school time in Toronto and Three Rivers, now perforce became a five-year-old drop-out, gathering such education as he could from us and the kids in the neighbourhood. With me one splendid Sunday afternoon he caught his first fish — a five-inch rock bass — with an excitement that he has probably never equalled, and that made

258

him a fisherman for life. The children on the street worked at enlarging his vocabulary with occasionally startling results. One night over dinner at the British American Hotel — once a drinking haunt of John A. Macdonald — I asked the waiter for horseradish for our roast beef. In the same second Crick's eyes were large and he was bursting with discovery. I knew what was coming, but I was powerless to stop it. "Do you know what I thought you said?" Choking with laughter I tried to wave him down. "Yes, I know what you thought I said." But he had to announce this funny thing in his high treble voice that carried to every corner of the old dining-room. "I thought you said horse shit," he crowed triumphantly, hugging himself with glee. I had already explained that the term was not generally used in polite society (which was true at that time).

Our joy in these arrested moments of happiness could not be spoiled, was perhaps even heightened, by the shadow of the unguessable future. The work was stimulating and a pleasure except for my continuing sense of inadequacy. Some of the gaps in my knowledge could be reduced by hard work, but others I could not fill. To teach the make-up of the German Armoured and Infantry Division on paper knowledge hardly prepared me for the questions of the experienced tank and infantry officers among our students. But I was backed up by congenial and able colleagues: Orville Edie, a former insurance executive with a clear, incisive mind, well trained and wise; Charles Krug, a former teacher of philosophy and psychology at Mount Allison University and a brilliant lecturer; Alan Macallum, a scientist with a love of teaching, and later Deputy-Minister of Education in Saskatchewan; Douglas Morris, a former Provincial Police officer from British Columbia, who added practical experience to his teaching. In time I was able to feel that we made a good as well as congenial team, and even to feel useful, if less than valuable.

Once again, as at Three Rivers, I realized that an army such as ours starts a war with few experts. Given the luck of time it finds and develops expertise of a high order. But I couldn't feel myself an expert until about two and a half years later when I was sent back from Nijmegen in Holland to lecture in Brussels to newly arrived drafts of British Intelligence personnel. It was the only moment in teaching when I felt in command of my subject. Having been in action for six months I had encountered all the normal problems and knew what our answers had been; what had worked and what probably would not.

But in spite of my continuing uneasiness — the sense of being a fake — I enjoyed Kingston enormously. The atmosphere of the handsome college area was at once relaxed and serious, like that of a hard-working holiday. The object of our course was to spread Intelligence and Security consciousness through the army and to provide trained personnel as reinforcements overseas or to fill vacancies in the Divisions and establishments still being formed in Canada. We were beginning to know our enemy: the Abwehr (the German Secret Service of countless books) and that Nazi refinement, the Sicherheitsdienst, with its many tentacles, including the Geheime Staats-Polizei — the Secret State Police, the infamous Gestapo. We had to know all we could about the enemy, and prevent him from knowing about us. This was the twin thrust of Intelligence: to gather information about our enemy, evaluate it, and pass it on to those who could use it, and to prevent the enemy from learning our capacities and plans.

Five courses with a few days in between to catch our breath and revise our notes came and went. The students divided into the very bright and the almost hopeless, reflecting the attitude of colonels to Intelligence. Some thought it important enough to send excellent officers to the course; others thought it the place for misfits in a war to be won by chaps with rifles and bayonets. It was believed by many that some colonels, if they found an officer reading a book in the mess, would either make him the Unit Intelligence Officer, or get rid of him.

At some point in that happy six months Wilfred Wees, the tempter, arrived again. I was now a captain; would I like to be a major? I could be, in personnel work. This time I didn't even flirt with the idea. Having learned two jobs in the army I would stay with one or the other. Besides, I had joined the army to get to the war. He said I could forget that, I would be stuck in Kingston for the duration; but within a few weeks he proved to be wrong. There was a call for reinforcements for overseas and for appointments to a new division and various headquarters on the Pacific coast, to be made on the recommendation of the Commandant of the Royal Military College on reports from the War Intelligence Wing. My name was down already for overseas service, and after a series of interviews I was warned for draft. Some of my colleagues thought I was making a mistake. They could be right, but I had taken my decision in Toronto two years before, and I had not intended merely to change desks.

At this point I wrote Harvey to ask whether the pay differential to my wife was to be continued. He replied that he had written London but had had no answer; it was probably due to the submarines in the North Atlantic. He would write again. In my bones I felt certain he had never written, and answering him I enclosed a memorandum reviewing my service with the Company which I suggested he send to London. I had extra copies of the memo which I told him I would forward to London if he would not. The answer which came almost at once was a complete capitulation; rather than bother London, *he* had decided my army pay would be supplemented until the end of the war if necessary.

I was relieved at this outcome, though the sly bargaining (including my own) had been distasteful. But I felt better about that when I learned later that one of Harvey's first moves after my departure was to try to lure Cecil Eustace, Educational Manager at Dents, to come to Macmillans to replace me.

The last few weeks in Kingston provided a splendid finale. With the last graduating class the Royal Military College closed to cadets; it was the end of the old RMC and it was done with style. There was a fine Marching Out ceremony and the laying up of the College Colours in St. George's Cathedral in Kingston, to which RMC cadets had marched every Sunday for seventy-five years. There was a final June Ball, once the most glamorous event in the lives of the most glamorous girls in the

261

cities of Canada. Was it my age, or the fact that these eager boys were going straight to the army, that made this less than glamorous, merely "sounds of revelry by night"?

This time there was to be no joking away the parting; it would be long and it might be final. As I sorted and packed gear the weeks rushed by like speeded-up film. Every day of the lovely rich summer seemed precious, to be caught at and held only for an instant as it slipped through our fingers. I wished there were things I could say to my son, things that might help as he grew up. But he was only five and full of the joy of living, and I wasn't sure what things I would say even if he could understand.

There came the last twenty-four hours and a savage reminder that the real war was my destination. A barber who was giving me a last hair-cut remarked that we had opened the Second Front — it was as casual and portentous as the elevator man in Belleville announcing the start of the war. "They're fightin' in France, heard it on the news a while back." I said it must be a raid but he was quite certain it was the Second Front, the invasion. I felt both excitement and chill. We knew later in the day that it was the Dieppe Raid, but it was to be another ten days before the full shock of its failure and its cost became clear. The war drew closer. Even as the barber chatted away, a dozen of my friends from school days were lying dead on the beach or being rolled about in the waves, and a dozen more were being herded into long lines on their way to prison camps. For a large part of the crack Second Division it was the first battle, and the last — the end of almost three years of hard training.

The final morning, still almost too painful to think about; a desperate good-bye with Tony who wasn't coming to the train. She was packing up and driving to a cottage on the St. Lawrence below Cornwall that afternoon, where with Bob's wife, Margie, each with a small boy, she would spend the next four summers. I don't know on what impulse I took John to the train. He was a little quiet, puzzled by my going away but settled in his mind that I would be home for Christmas. The troops had all the windows open and were leaning out and shouting excitedly to each other or to anyone they could see. I walked up with Cricket on my shoulder. A soldier called out, "You can't take him with you, sir." I suppose I managed a hard grin, but I didn't need the reminder which every step nearer the parting-time drove home. In a minute, in a second now, I reached the steps of the train. RMC Corporal Entwistle, who had been driving with me for six months, said gently, "I'll take good care of him." I could only say "Thanks" and "Don't wait". They left then, and the men standing around the steps of my car fell into a compassionate silence while I went aboard, chucked my stuff onto a rack, and somehow found a seat.

I have very little memory of the trip to Halifax except that it was interminable, with long waits on sidings. But pleasant memories of other trips down the line took some of the harsh edge off my feeling of desolation. We ran past the station at Cornwall, which since childhood had been the first joyous moment of homecoming for holidays. We ran through Montreal as it was getting dark, and in the early morning saw across the river the splendid ramparts of Quebec. Then a long day through the beautiful Matapedia Valley and across the scarred shoulder of New Brunswick, past Sackville and through the mysterious marsh of Tantramar to Amherst and Truro, and at last late at night to the dockside in Halifax. Though still panting the engine looked fresher than we did as we filed on board and stumbled about, lugging kit-bags and haversacks, finding our quarters. I was sharing a normally two-bed cabin with eight others — four in double bunks, one cheerful youngster on the floor.

In the morning we were still at dockside, but the harbour was crowded and back of us in Bedford Basin lay still more ships, the skeleton of a great convoy. Our ship was suddenly alive with the little hurrying noises of impending cast-off and almost at once we began to move out into the stream. I assumed we would anchor and wait but it appeared that the convoy "being in all respects ready for sea" had only been waiting for us. We went straight out through the boom and in the next few hours were surrounded by big and small ships, busy with the naval version of musical chairs as they took station in a great phalanx advancing slowly across waters that grew more menacing with every mile, as Nova Scotia slipped below the horizon.

It was to be a comparatively uneventful cruise, but it never felt like that. Shortly after we all settled down on our first night at sea, there was an explosion we could both hear and feel. The duty officer, in the bunk next to mine, pulled on his boots and went out; I was longing to follow but the army didn't encourage us in chasing fire-reels. When at last he came back he muttered, "They fished one of the ships." I asked whether that meant there was a submarine within the convoy; he didn't know. I lay in the darkness tingling a little with excitement. Most of the young men around us hadn't even stirred.

In the morning there was a noticeable gap in the formation. A large troopship just back of us had disappeared and I could only assume she had been sunk. But in the next few days the story was put together. Apparently there had not been a submarine, but an American destroyer, thinking there was, had dashed into the convoy in pursuit and had sliced the bow off the troopship to our rear, blowing itself up in the collision. The troopship, carrying elements of 4th Armoured Division, including Divisional Headquarters, had closed its bulkheads behind the torn bow and limped back into Halifax. The rest of the division steamed on with us to a dawn when we rounded the north of Ireland and, as Duty Officer, standing on the flying bridge, I watched a coastal aircraft come flying out of the rising sun to greet us. That afternoon we steamed into the Clyde past the great shipyards where thousands of men downed tools and swarmed onto the platform at the water's edge to cheer us all the way to Greenock.

That first afternoon everyone's feeling seemed to be that the war could start any time now, but the feeling wasn't to last. After a few days of being shuffled around I found myself in barracks at Aldershot doing what I had fled from at RMC, teaching what I didn't really know. It was only slightly less frustrating;

264

there was at least a feeling of being closer to the action, of dealing with some people who did know, and of everything mattering a good deal more. Among my first classes were the Intelligence Sections of some of the regiments that had been on the Dieppe Raid, beginning with the Fusiliers Mont-Royal and the Queen's Own Camerons of Winnipeg. They were smart, confident soldiers but their experience had marked them and set them apart. They had had their baptism of fire and survived it, but scores of their friends had not, and they moved like people in shock.

Slipping into the cheerful fatalistic mood of those who were by now old soldiers (especially the young ones) wasn't easy and was sometimes bruising. On our first day the new arrivals were called on parade and given a talk by an officer who had been in England for some time and was obviously enjoying it. He asked whether any of us had been in England before; mine was the only hand that went up. He asked when and why and I said I had been there as a child in the first war. How could that be? "My father brought my mother and us over." He stared, incredulous. "Your father brought your mother over?" I nodded. "My God," he appealed to the squad, "isn't that a hell of a way to ruin a perfectly good war?" It was a measure of my low spirits that I could only manage a wry smile as the rest roared.

My brother Bob and other friends were in Aldershot, which helped to make it tolerable. But I found few enough to admit it was even that. Bob, who had been in the army from the first, had been overtaken by an old football injury to his knee and seemed to be stranded indefinitely with an administrative job that he discharged with grumpy good humour; there was no appeal from damaged cartilege. Aldershot was a catchment area for the unplaced, the misplaced, and the discontented. Those who had just arrived, those who were about to be sent home — for bad cheques, bad health, or bad behaviour — nearly all passed through Aldershot and it became a focus of unhappiness. It had lived off soldiers for a century and did so with cynical relish which the soldiers repaid with anger and an occasional riot.

One such riot had occurred not long before I arrived. A pub-keeper who found Canadians rough — though he liked their drinking and spending — used to close his pub at night by calling: "Time, gentlemen, and Canadians, please." His joke was such a success that he kept it up night after night until it became an irritation. If he had been a little more clever he might have realized that one evening his pub was unusually full at closing time of the cheerful roughnecks he had been teasing so recklessly. The call of "Time, gentlemen, and Canadians" touched off an explosion that reduced the Public Bar to a shambles in minutes — mirrors, bottles, windows, lights went in a cheerful reminder of the Blitz, and the rioters waded and crunched through broken glass and furniture to slip away in the blackout.

The British soldiers in the area who had endured Aldershot longer than we had were cheered by this spirited response to insult. They didn't like Canadians much, but they liked Aldershot people even less, said they were a shower of bastards. But none of this provided much of a lift to the spirits. I realized that I was deeply homesick; not that I would have wished myself home while the war lasted. I was on the way to where I had wanted to be, but I wanted it finished, and found this a dreary staging-point. It was in this mood that I found myself Duty Officer one night at No. 1 Canadian Reinforcement Unit (where Intelligence personnel among other odds and ends were gathered and trained, and held). Being Duty Officer meant spending the night in the Camp Headquarters Office, making a round of the camp from time to time, and in between times reading or snatching sleep. The Commandant, Lieutenant-Colonel Frost from Montreal, dropped in to see that all was quiet and remained to chat. Colonel Frost was an older man wearing ribbons for gallantry from the First World War. He was interested in whatever I was reading and for a while we forgot the war and talked books and plays. Knowing I was recently arrived and guessing at my loneliness he said that this was a bad stage. The first few weeks. "You'll settle down," he said, and added almost with a sigh, "the years go by." The

Years! my God, THE YEARS!! And then I realized that he and others like him had been here, and waiting patiently, for almost three years already; I, less than three weeks.

I couldn't imagine that it would still be years from that moment, but it was to be. Having served my time at Aldershot I had a happy few months with my own command, a Field Security Section stationed at West Humble, near Dorking. I didn't like the work but I liked the men and we worked and trained hard together, including frequent games of rough touch football in off hours. This seemed to astonish, but also to please, the English people among whom we lived, who assured me that British officers would not play like that with their men. I couldn't believe it, but it didn't seem very important. Our job of teaching units about security, of checking on bad security, was both boring and distasteful. But it was important — no one could doubt that — and once in action our role would change; units would become responsible for their own security and our duty would become active Counter-Intelligence, searching out enemy agents. Meanwhile we lived and worked in one of the softest and most beautiful of countrysides, Surrey, under the shadow of Boxhill. If I wasn't happy I was at least working with a purpose and more contentment.

There followed periods of work in Intelligence at Army Headquarters, an attachment to the planning staff at Norfolk House in beautiful though battered St. James's Square in London, where every morning brought bundles of slips of paper across our desks to be sorted, appraised, and recorded; information from occupied Europe, much of it gathered at great risk. I had had a short Intelligence course at Matlock in Derbyshire, pretty much what we had been teaching at RMC in Kingston. And then for four months came one of the greatest training experiences I was ever to have — the Administrative Staff Course at the Royal Military College at Sandhurst. Though I liked some of my fellow students, who came from almost every regiment in the British Army and three from the Canadian Army, and admired many of my teachers — survivors of Dunkirk and the Desert War — it wasn't a pleasant experience, but it was valuable. We worked very hard and seemed to be judged wholly on how our responses compared with the "Official Solution" to every problem; sometimes I found the official solution mindless and said so; that didn't help me and I passed out with only a limited approval. But I passed out, as the army intended, with something else, an ability to check my normally intuitive or emotional response to problems. Long drills on "the appreciation" — what is the object? — what are we trying to do? — nailed down some of my impulse to run at things without measuring them. It was not a lesson proof against every circumstance, but it was to slow me down and serve me well for the rest of my days.

We were to finish the war with an experienced and effective Intelligence Corps, but in the early days it was more like a squirrel's nest with a variety of odd pieces jammed together, and just barely holding; a few veterans, a few ex-policemen, a few German-speakers, a few bright misfits. But gradually, from the British I think, a plan of what was needed emerged on paper — an establishment — and slowly, with the help of Personnel Selection, the gaps began to fill.

Wherever it started, the visible starting-point to many of us was the arrival at Army Headquarters in 1943 of Lieutenant-Colonel Peter Wright to be Senior Intelligence Officer. In the months that followed other changes took place; Major Graham (Bud) Macdougall became Senior Counter-Intelligence Officer in the field, and at Canadian Military Headquarters in London Felix Walter took charge of the Intelligence Office. None of them were professional soldiers. Peter Wright and Bud Macdougall had been lawyers and Felix Walter a teacher of French and German at Trinity College, Toronto; he had been a student of mine at RMC and Macmillans had published two of his books before the war. All had clear, well-trained minds and all worked to only one purpose, to identify our needs against the big day and to fill them in time. An element of meanness, of scrambling for appointments, that had been there, and was all around us, was washed out. It seemed to me we worked in a healthy atmosphere. There might be honest mistakes but not

268

the mistakes of politics and ambition. Gradually an able and devoted group of men gathered round them.

A year and a half of "the years" had gone by when I returned to Army Headquarters from Sandhurst to await posting. There were new faces and a sense of something important about to happen. People were more professional. The Second Front, which had been a distant prospect, was now imminent; and then in March I was told how near. On June 5, landings would take place all along the north coast of Normandy. I fell within the category of those who needed to know, but it seemed an unnecessary responsibility. By now hundreds, if not thousands, knew, and to my security-trained mind it appeared impossible that so great a weight could be held in so loose a net. Fortunately there were several layers to the net and the secret was well kept. The one or two who did while drinking boast and hint in public about what they knew were quickly and quietly sent home.

But if I felt sometimes that I was walking on eggs, at other times I was walking on air. Whatever the outcome, this was ringside at making world history and there was no missing the tension in the air, the excitement we were all sharing. It now mattered very much that we should be good at our jobs when the time came. My posting came through, to be G3 Ib at the newly forming headquarters of 2 Canadian Corps (translated into a captain on the general staff responsible for Counter-Intelligence). Commanding the new corps was to be General Guy Simonds, already marked out as our most impressive soldier by his command of First Canadian Division during a successful campaign in Sicily and of 1 Canadian Corps in Italy. His arrival was awaited with some apprehension, for though he was known as a brilliant commander there were also rumours of his unsmiling toughness, which had earned him the nickname of "Giggling Guy". But the apprehension included the confidence that if we were the makings of a good fighting formation, under Guy Simonds the corps would be formidable.

The General arrived, and almost at once we moved out of buildings and under canvas and then "into the field"; that meant learning to pack up and move quickly, to unpack and be organized for operations. At first the great machine — one armoured and one infantry division, corps artillery, corps engineers, along with stores, maintenance personnel, and supply and service components — creaked slowly into motion. We had learned the term SNAFU almost from our first moment in the army but now we learned both the comic and the dangerous meaning of it. Forty-odd thousand men with their machines and supplies had to be moved at predictable speeds to designated points. A mistake could be disaster, and though there was the danger of mistakes at every level — division, brigade, and unit — a mistake at corps could be carried right down the line. General Montgomery, fresh from the triumphs of Alamein and North Africa, had rubbed in that lesson in one of the last lectures at Staff College. "You are about to become Staff Officers," he said, "and I dare say you think you're the cat's whiskers. You may be," — a long pause — "All I know for certain about you is that you are the only people in a position to make a complete balls of the whole thing."

It was neither new nor news, but it was an arresting reminder. With my father and his veteran friends blaming their problems on "the staff" after the first war, I had never wanted to be a staff officer. Since that was the role in which I was cast I was — like most of my colleagues — determined to be a good one. Monty's warning struck on especially responsive ears because during a training attachment before Staff Course I had once lost a whole brigade-headquarters transport through insufficiently close map-reading with a pencil flashlight; only the alertness of a sergeant had saved the mistake from being worse than it was. We arrived at our rendezvous to find the brigade vehicles rolling by and the brigadier in the middle of the dark crossroads swearing and directing traffic. We were fed into the stream twenty minutes late.

But if we all had a sharpened sense of our responsibilities the tone of Headquarters was not solemn; we were on tiptoe. As our force moved like a leviathan eastward across Kent and toward the sea we were conscious of movement skilfully controlled on all the roads around us; it was as though a great colony of sea-turtles having hatched and buried its eggs was now crawling back to its element. Nightfall found us all off the roads and cunningly camouflaged, sunk into the landscape and all but invisible. Around us the trees were in blossom and by day we moved through a gentle green country of hop-fields and old farmhouses with only an occasional German plane overhead to remind us that we were moving to the war.

Toward the end of May we came to a stop behind Dover and pushed our vehicles into a wood of young trees on the edge of meadows that rolled down to the white cliffs. In a great arc for miles around us in hop-fields and woods the trucks and tanks and guns crawled under camouflage nets threaded with branches and settled down to wait. Across from us the big German guns near Calais slammed their great shells daily into a battered Dover. At night in the young trees all around and above us came a beautiful counterpoint from the nightingales. Almost within arm's length, straining as though they intended to drown the guns, they drove up pillars of joyous sound that tumbled around us in a lovely melody that challenged the importance of war.

But however enchanted, we could only listen briefly. June had come and we were listening for the guns and the deadly mines along the Normandy beaches. The news came, our forces were ashore and driving inland fast. To begin with it looked too easy; then came counter-attacks and hard fighting. At any spare moment we listened outside the wireless truck but the news was sparse and filtered. We didn't really know how it was going or how heavy the casualties. There was nothing to do but wait, meanwhile contributing by our position to the pretence of a main thrust still to come across the channel to the Pas de Calais and thus keep large German formations pinned down and unable to reinforce the Normandy battle.

Then it was up in the dark of an early July morning and long convoys of trucks moving toward London; through the Blackwall Tunnel and into smashed East London and the dock area. A few hours' wait and we slept where we could, I on a bare tent

271

floor without even loosening boots; it seems now the most delicious and refreshing sleep of my life. Then we formed up and marched on board an American liberty ship, where we waited again while people called back the crew, exhausted, dirty, and grumbling; after weeks at sea they had expected shore time at least for beer and maybe for girls, and they had barely managed the first. As the afternoon faded we moved out of the ship canal and then into the Thames Estuary. With luck we would be off the Normandy beaches in the early morning, but first we had to go down the Channel under the guns of Calais.

With three other officers each in charge of a quarter I was responsible for the troops in one quarter of the ship; in command of all troops was Brigadier King Black from Montreal, an engineer officer and an impressive-looking soldier. In the event of submarine attack or shelling, troops would gather in our four areas and we would act as needed. It was heady stuff standing on a foredeck explaining the plan to two or three hundred eager, smiling faces, eager to be told, eager to get going. We crowded in below decks on wide shelves, three or four to a shelf. Most of us slept almost at once, but two or three times in the night I went up and prowled the deck. Once at sea the American sailors had steadied down, tidied themselves, and were quite unrecognizable from the rabble that had poured off the ship as we came aboard. In the darkness now, one sailor keeping a sharp watch told me in a low voice that we were just between Calais and Dover. The ship was moving slowly and the Channel was unusually calm; we were almost through. I went back to my shelf and fell into a heavy sleep. We wakened to a glorious summer morning. We were at anchor a few hundred yards off Arromanches in the midst of hundreds of vessels: liberty ships like our own, carrying troops, destroyers, corvettes, landing craft. We had seen it all in pictures in the paper that looked just like this; only this was real, and the reminder was the occasional aerial combat or the boom of the big gun from Le Havre on our left or the fortress which still held out on our front.

That day off the beaches seemed the longest of the war, the

272

supreme demonstration of the army doctrine "hurry up and wait". Just out of sight, though not of sound, the war was raging, and we were leaning on the ship's rail chatting and still trying to guess what it would be like and how we would measure up; miraculously, food was served and we ate as on any ordinary day. But by late afternoon things began to happen. Under orders we gathered our gear and went to our waterproofed vehicles in the bowels of the ship; we drove them onto landing craft — great scows with high steel sides — and were run in to the beach. With the sunken hulks around us and the slam of guns from Le Havre there were reminders of how dangerous this journey had been. It wasn't often now, but mine was the lead jeep and there was a little surge of excitement as the ramp went down and I drove off into shallow water along the beach and up a steep road, waved forward urgently by a series of guides. We reached a staging camp as darkness came down, and slept in a crawl space below stretched tarpaulins. There was a reminder of the need for absolute blackout when a German plane cruised over us just to see how we were making out, or where we were. It was to such hit-and-run tactics that the mighty Luftwaffe had been reduced.

A day or two later came another demonstration. As I drove down a narrow village street on a recce trip a Messerschmitt came flying low and splattered the street with machine-gun fire. The unreality of it all kept me watching an old woman who had been making her way slowly across the road carrying a pail of water; in clumsy terror she began to run, spilling the water, then dropped her pail and flung herself into a doorway. The plane roared just above our heads and was gone with only a little brick dust sifting down as a reminder of its passage.

The still-shallow bridgehead was becoming crowded and we were developing both the strength and the necessity to deepen it. For the first week after landing many of us were camped in the medium-gun lines, but though the blast was enough to lift safari beds and sleeping-bags off the ground, it was soon not enough to waken us. In that first week the objectives of D-Day — the taking of Caen as far as the River Orne and Carpiquet

Airfield — were achieved, a month behind schedule and after bitter fighting. Before the final attack was pressed on Caen we watched waves of bombers come in from England, pouring out of the setting sun like a gigantic swarm of bees about to take over the world; passing overhead with a beat of thunder that shook the ground, they flew over the target, unloaded their bombs, and turned unmolested for home. A few days later 3rd Canadian Division stormed across the Orne and four miles down the road to Falaise.

In spite of the devastation of the heavy bombing, artillery bombardment, and street fighting, Caen was very much alive. The destruction was horrifying; whole streets were so choked with rubble and great blocks of masonry that it was not only difficult to make one's way but sometimes impossible to recognize the original course of the street. But as we moved in, and through, the French people were suddenly everywhere, and beginning stubbornly to put their lives together. Driving with difficulty down a smashed street, I saw an old woman sweeping the dust of bombardment from the doorstep of a house of which little more than the doorstep remained. One could either cheer at that blind courage, or weep at its apparent futility.

But everywhere life was surging up and asserting itself. A day or two before, back of Caen, a little group of elderly people and children had gathered because there was to be an issue of rations. They waited patiently in a light rain, the old women in their black shawls muttering together like characters in an O'Casey play. Over all there was a smell of burnt wood and the stink of dead bodies: cattle that had been caught in a cross-fire, and the unburied bodies of soldiers of both sides lying undiscovered in the wheat and the hedges. As people waited for food to arrive a broadcasting van from the Psychological Warfare Section drew up. Some genius put on a record — "Sur le Pont d'Avignon" — and after a little pause of disbelief the children began to dance. One of the old women stood up, tapping her foot and clapping her hands, as she directed the children into a figure. Surrounded by every reminder of war's horrors, within sound of the battle and under a dark and weeping sky, the children danced until they were breathless with their effort and laughter, as though it were a country fair.

᭦12 ᭦

OW, with civilians in and around the battle area,
there was both the room and the need for Counter-
Intelligence to be busy. The Germans certainly
needed news from behind our lines and we knew
they would try to send agents through in refugee streams or
simply leave them in place, to be overrun as we advanced, and
then to wireless such information as our vehicle markings and
uniform patches, heavy traffic on particular roads, notice of
special equipment, locations of headquarters, and so on. It was
on just such information as this, furnished often by Resistance
groups or by fighting patrols bringing in prisoners, that we
built our knowledge of the German Order of Battle on our
Front and became aware of the arrival of fresh divisions and
the withdrawal of others — to refit or to reinforce the Front
against the Americans. Our Counter-Intelligence sections had
already made contact with the leaders of the Resistance in
their areas and with the police, and this was to become the routine for much of our work as the battle opened and speeded up.

With Canadian 2nd and 3rd Divisions attacking astride the
road towards Falaise, it was difficult to keep in touch with their
Counter-Intelligence Sections from 2 Corps Headquarters
back of Caen. Roads, and especially the Orne bridges, were
crowded, so that movement was in a continuous traffic jam and
we had no ready means of communication. My supervisors at
Army Headquarters, Major Graham Macdougall, Senior
Counter-Intelligence Officer, and Lieutenant-Colonel Peter

Wright, Director of Army Intelligence in the field, agreed to my moving forward of Corps Headquarters. I would have trouble keeping in touch with Corps and Army but would be in a position to react directly to events.

We found a big house on the forward edge of Faubourg de Vaucelles, a southern suburb of Caen, and with the Corps Counter-Intelligence Section and a few others we moved in. The house was said to belong to a member of one of the French Fascist groups and to have been recently occupied by a German unit. Almost at once we had three women working in the kitchen and doing miracles with our rations.

At first our plan for a screen to filter those who might move between the armies had seemed more desirable than feasible. But as the battle moved away from the houses of Caen and Vaucelles the ground behind it became easier to control, or so it seemed. Men from our Corps and Divisional Sections patrolled day and night between the forward units — lonely and dangerous work, which in time we came to feel had been overeager, and perhaps a bit amateurish. Incredibly, a few young Frenchmen did crawl through the German forward positions and were picked up by the infantry or our patrols and brought in for questioning. For the most part they were high-spirited boys, eager only to join the Free French of General de Gaulle. All had to be checked carefully, but once it was clear they had neither weapons nor suspect materials, their final disposition was left to French authorities. Two cheerful fellows on being cleared begged only to be allowed to return to the battle zone to pick up a small keg of Calvados (the Normandy apple brandy) which they had carried through the German lines and left in a ditch and would now like to share with us. This seemed to be *entente cordiale* in fact and spirit, so they were driven back to the keg which miraculously had escaped the eyes of the forward troops. They then spent their first afternoon of liberty happily decanting the keg into all the empty wine bottles we could produce, and ceremoniously presenting bottles to many of us. I suppose it was Calvados, but on my only taste it seemed more like high-octane fuel imperfectly refined. We remembered them as perhaps the most engaging boys with the least engaging Calvados in Normandy.

For these encounters with the French I had been immensely strengthened by the arrival of a liaison officer from the French Service de Sécurité Militaire. Captain Antzemberger, an Alsatian from Colmar, was an experienced and dedicated soldier. A veteran of the First World War who had afterwards served in the Occupation Forces in Germany for some years, he was equally devoted to serving General de Gaulle and to hating Germans.

Our little forward organization was fully operational by the time the advance of 2nd Canadian Division exposed a whole new set of problems. The Divisional area included an escarpment above the Orne Valley. From the rim there was a fine view across good farmlands and beyond to Carpiquet Airfield, all blackened and torn up by the fierce fighting of the previous month.

Just below the rim a narrow, rough road ran along the face of the escarpment in front of a series of old caves and scooped-out shelters. Whatever their origin, the deep caves in recent times had been used for growing mushrooms, but the battle had driven people from the farms and nearby villages to seek shelter here, and what we found was a whole village of refugees. Many had been wounded by shell and bomb fragments and one large cave had been converted into a hospital where old people and children lay packed together on straw palliasses, nursed by a group of nuns with little food and few medical supplies. With a horse stalled at the entrance to the cave it looked like a picture of Florence Nightingale's hospital at Scutari. The other caves reflected the people who waited there for sanity to return to their world; some were like teeming gypsy encampments, others were neat and orderly. In one shallow cave an elderly couple sat quietly on upturned boxes, their few cooking pots hanging shining against the rockface, plates on a ledge, their blankets neatly folded and their clothes looking brushed; they might have been waiting at a bus station. The mood of a few was joyous, but the majority, though friendly, lived in the quiet of shock and exhaustion and unmanageable misery, waiting for the soldiers to finish their terrible war games and go away.

It wasn't easy to see how they were to be handled and, except from the one point of view, it was not our concern. The fighting army wanted them not to move, to stay off the roads. Military Government wanted to take them to places where they could have cleanliness and proper food. The move, when it came a week or so later, was hurried and untidy. A convoy of trucks scooped up the whole colony and moved them to an old stone building — a convent or hospital — with huge rooms, where they were to settle themselves as best they could on piles of straw and await disposal. Watching them climb down awkwardly from the trucks and submit to being squirted over with delousing spray — a final humiliation — I couldn't fix my attention on the potential we had foreseen in them for acting as a cover for stay-behind agents. For the most part they were simple people — many of them country people with lined and leathery faces — clinging to a few poor possessions, physically and emotionally exhausted. In the group there was one couple that didn't fit easily into that general impression. Their flashy clothes and his rather swaggering manner made them look like a cheap gambler and his tart — but it didn't strike me that they looked suspicious, merely unpleasant.

It was Tex Noble, Counter-Intelligence Officer for 2nd Canadian Division, already nicknamed "le Capitain Electrique" by the Resistance, who checked my philosophic and sympathetic ramble among the refugees. Tex had at one time been my sergeant-major; knowing his energy and capacity I had recommended him for a commission and pressed my recommendation in the face of some opposition — opposition based on the simple view that it was a pity, even madness, to make an officer of so good a sergeant-major. Now I found all his energy and determination turned uncomfortably on me. Though I was inclined to let the people settle down in such comfort as they could manage, Tex was insistent that whatever discomfort it involved, they must all be checked now. There could be no close control hereafter and agents could easily slip away unnoticed to do their work. However hateful it seemed to drag out those who had settled in and line them up once again for questioning and inspection of their papers, I knew he was right.

In a few minutes tables were set up and a queue formed. People began to file patiently by, clutching crumpled papers and cautiously answering questions. It was a crisp and orderly procedure and I left them to it. Early that evening there was a hammering on the door of the house in Vaucelles. It was Tex Noble, triumphant. "I want these people locked up for the night," he said. In his jeep under guard sat the tinhorn gambler type and his sleazy wife. Their papers showed that they had come from Paris to the Caen area very recently — since our landings — and in the queue they had been pointed out as proprietors of a sort of shabby restaurant–night-club chiefly frequented by German officers. Our house was not a lock-up, but there was an empty room on the third floor where they could be kept under guard until morning. In the morning Antz interrogated the man sharply for half an hour while his wife sat on a bench in the garden crying. "J'ai peur," she kept saying, "Oh, que j'ai peur, pour mon mari." I tried the formula I was to use again many times: "If he has done nothing wrong you have nothing to worry about." At that she cried even harder.

The rule was that suspects were not to be questioned in depth in the forward areas. If preliminary questioning established a suspicion, suspects should be sent back at once to the Interrogation Centre. This was based on the knowledge that when an agent broke he might go on talking for hours or days, and at the Centre there was more time and expertise for making the best use of information he would yield.

The couple left for the Interrogation Centre sadly reduced from the brassy couple we had seen in their cave a few days before. Apart from their apprehensions they had had a bad night, as we all had. Soon after dark, German planes had come over, looking for the Orne bridges but dropping their bombs indiscriminately around us. We had brought our prisoners down to the basement and from an open cellar window had watched nearby houses burst into flame, listened to the mad drumfire of our anti-aircraft guns, and seen one German plane race back down the Falaise Road almost at roof level, turned into a blazing torch. The only calmness in the scene had been a Canadian provost corporal, outlined by the flames from the burning houses, who stood steadily in the middle of a crossroads fifty yards away directing traffic. When traffic was finally held back by the raid he answered our shouted invitation by sprinting across and diving in through our open window. After a quick cigarette and an exchange of nervous jokes he climbed out and took up his dangerous station again in the middle of the road.

After the raid there was quiet except for the roar of the fires and desultory gunfire down the road. I slept soundly but probably our suspects did not. That they were quickly losing their nerve became even more apparent on the drive back to the Interrogation Centre. The interrogation didn't last long. The man at first affected an arrogant confidence but quickly became entangled in his explanation of their reasons for moving from Paris to Normandy after the invasion and his association with German officers. Then came a confession that he had been trained as an agent and the unearthing of two wireless sets buried in his garden ready to be put to use. Tex had caught our first agent. There were to be many more but perhaps none that gave us the same satisfaction, or that did so much to convince us and the staff at various levels that there was a genuine role for Counter-Intelligence. That our prisoner was a low-grade agent, and that that was what we would chiefly deal in, was not the important thing. Our job was to deny information to the Germans, and our war was against anyone who might furnish it.

We heard now of perhaps several hundred refugees living in an old mine which was about to be overrun by the shifting battle. From the offices of the city engineer in Caen we obtained maps of the mine and prepared a detachment to move in as soon as the battle passed over the area in the drive for Falaise. Two Counter-Intelligence men and two 2nd Divisional engineers were put under the wing of a forward regiment ready to move to the exits of the mine when they were freed. At a final meeting, the Caen engineer burst out to our sapper corporal — a fine young man — "You don't know what you are doing. You are amateurs, you are children. You can't beat the Germans. You will be killed, killed." His voice rose to a shout and I watched the young corporal against whom the attack had been launched. His face was a shade paler and his jawline tight, but after standing quite still for a moment he went quietly on with his questions about the mine workings.

I was neither to see him again, nor to forget him. For three or four days there was no news from the detachment while the regiment they were with had been held up. And then news came: all four were dead. Apparently, impatient at the delay, they had set out for the mine area as soon as the battle moved forward, had driven recklessly down a sideroad, and had run over a landmine. They were discovered from a slab of metal bearing the serial number of their jeep that had been blown onto a low roof near by. A few of us went down to bury them and were issued with several grenades, since it was thought there were no troops between us and the enemy, who might counter-attack at any time. The remains had been sewn into grey army blankets and over the scene hung swarms of large, loathsome green flies fattened on the dead. The tall padre looked tortured, as with his hair and surplice blowing in the hot wind he read the burial service before hurrying off to read the service again — and again. *Man that is born of woman hath but a short time to live, and is full of misery. . . . In the midst of life we are in death. . . .*

At times it seemed that the Normandy battle would never end; that years hence the guns would still be slamming in the ruined fields with trucks and tanks and Red Cross jeeps moving up and down the dusty roads. Counter-Intelligence work had become static and routine again; much of it the vexatious chasing down of rumours and nervous complaints from civilians or from irritable colonels pestered by curious farm people who merely by hanging around and asking questions came under the suspicion of being spies. We had had much the same sort of thing in England, only this had to be taken more seriously. At least it was worth while calming choleric colonels.

On the night of the 7th of August, as we were settling down at the house in Vaucelles, there came a frantic knocking and a report of lights flashing towards the German lines from a small apartment building on the edge of the town. Flashing lights! The things we had chased all over the south of England, beloved of everyone suffering from spymania. Flashing lights, for God's sake! Operation Totalizer was just beginning down the road, with great searchlights bounced off cloud to produce artificial moonlight, a massive world-ending artillery barrage moving ahead of the armoured troop carriers, and streams of red tracer directing the advance on both flanks. Flashing lights indeed! What could a flashing light do in this mad hatter's fireworks display? Still, grumbling, we tumbled out and drove to the twin-columned building to find it surrounded by hundreds of civilians, most of them certain there had been lights flashing, but all confused as to when and from which part of the building. There was at any rate some reason for concern; even as we arrived, the advance elements of 4th Canadian Armoured Division were moving along the road in front of the apartment building and turning south just there to join the battle that was now screaming and raging like the Inferno, under a pall of pink smoke laced with darting fiery insects.

We soon found that the building, though undamaged, had been evacuated and all apartments locked. From somewhere we acquired a young man with a Sten gun who seemed to be off duty and who obviously enjoyed spending his leisure time blowing locks off doors. Slowly, noisily, we worked our way up through the dark building, finding no one and almost nothing. It was unpleasant work tramping through other people's apartments, looking into cupboards; rather mean apartments, not well furnished, but not enemy country. And then we did find, before an opened window facing the German lines, a chair placed on a table, and behind the chair there hung a big rattan screen — a kind of reflector — and in a cupboard a flash-lamp. It was no one's idea of Secret Service equipment, but perhaps enough to call down artillery fire or bombs on the area at the right moment. And with the armour clanking past in the darkness below this was a good moment. But so far there had been no bombardment, and if there had been flashing lights, whoever had flashed them was gone.

There was still the twin apartment building; but as the two sides of the building didn't appear to connect, our flasher was either on the roof or gone. I had never learned in training, even in battle drill, how to push up a trapdoor and draw a pistol while climbing a vertical ladder — let alone doing it with a soldierly dignity. Besides, wrestling on a high roof with a powerful stranger had long been one of my pet nightmares. So my scrambled arrival on the roof was neither dignified nor menacing, but fortunately there was no one to judge it — or to throw me over the side — only an empty flat roof, and the terror and splendour of the battle rolling away from us, and the grumbling of the tanks going by in the road below. For a moment or two I watched, noticing a point man directing the armoured column where it turned south toward 4th Armoured Division's first battle. I wondered what the tank commanders sitting up in their turrets in the dark were thinking — and what I would have been thinking in their place.

The search of the other half of the building went faster but was no more productive. We were moving up quickly and perhaps carelessly, shining our lights around, when in split seconds there was a flash, the smack of a bullet into plaster, and the report of a rifle near by. We were all on the floor at once and I was running a finger over a line above my left ear that felt as though it had been touched with a hot iron. In the darkness someone said, "Jeez, some bastard is shooting at us." I said, "and he has nicked me;" but I was feeling in vain for just a little blood. There was none, and later on just a thin red mark like a scrape.

After the search one of our sergeants produced the man who had fired the shot. It wasn't our flasher or his friends from a nearby building as we had assumed. It was the 4th Armoured's point man, who had become worried lest the lights bring down fire on his vehicles. He had consulted a provost sergeant, who had suggested that he "fire above the light". They had both been a little trigger-happy, but we had been careless in showing lights and in not ensuring that — as we had thought — everyone knew what we were doing and why. We parted with the sort of pleasantries that I suppose are normal on such occasions: "Jeez, I'm sure glad I didn't shoot you, sir;" "Well, as a matter of fact, so am I!" But when I finally turned in wearily, thinking of the men down the road moving forward in the smoke, watching for the taped paths through minefields or tossing grenades into slit trenches, I found I was just a little glad that I had been shot at — even if it was by the wrong side and for the wrong reason.

That night was really the beginning of the end for the German armies in France and Belgium. The remnants would fight some fierce rearguard actions but they were already in the jaws of a trap at Falaise in which thousands would die and about 200,000 would be taken prisoner. Still, we had scotched the snake, not killed it. There was no longer a danger that we might be thrown back into the sea; nor a doubt that we would win the war. But the cost still to pay was uncertain.

The swing in our fortunes after the long slogging-match produced a lift in spirits that was at once joyful and dangerous. In spite of stiff, short battles everyone seemed to be off and running. For a few days the roads were filled with long convoys of trucks filled with German prisoners; at front and rear rode one Canadian soldier pointing a Bren gun. And across the fields and out of the woods along the roads came long lines of disarmed Germans escorted by two or three Canadians with Sten guns. It was unbelievable, but it was sweet. Everyone produced stories of a colonel or a cook stumbling into a detachment of Germans and taking them prisoner. Inevitably people became over-confident and careless; the most unlikely people — not from the regiments but from headquarters or auxiliary units — set out to get them a prisoner and sometimes got more than they bargained for; some were killed.

For the moment Counter-Intelligence hardly seemed to have a role. There was no question of exercising control. We might be missing agents, but if we did could it matter? At the speed at which our armies were moving, what could they report and who was in a position to make use of the information they might furnish? On one of the roads north-west across France streamed 4th Canadian Armoured Division, led by a man driving an armoured bulldozer, not to fight Germans but to push their smashed vehicles and dead horses into the ditches and keep the tanks and trucks rolling.

It was heady stuff and some of our people were to fall victim to the dangerous optimism that was everywhere. First Canadian Army was to move up the coast clearing the Channel ports: Le Havre, Dieppe, Dunkirk, Boulogne, Calais, and Ostend, a list full of bitter and tragic memories. If the pattern of recent weeks was followed they would tumble like a pack of cards. But we needed the ports and as it turned out, the Germans meant to deny us the more important ones. A British Corps turned aside to take Le Havre. Dieppe was not defended. Second Canadian Corps swept on. It was like a newsreel reversed as the towns we had seen overrun by the Germans in 1940 were now, in 1944, set free again: Rouen, Abbeville, Dunkirk.

As our convoy crawled through Rouen, with long halts, I could recognize nothing of the old city I had seen in 1928. It had not been fought through but it had been heavily bombed as we denied its roads and bridges to the Germans. The whole face of the town close to the river had been blown off and turned into rubble.

But the terrible damage seemed not to have quenched the spirits of the people, who had already crowded the pavements to throw flowers or give precious wine to thousands of the first troops to go through, and now were out again, cheering and chatting joyously with us at every stop. While I talked with one middle-aged couple during a long halt, they pointed out an elderly woman standing back and quite alone. Her lined face was heavy with sadness, and they told me that all her family had been killed when their house was destroyed by our bombs; she had no one left. When they moved on she looked across at me and, making the only gesture I could, I saluted her. After a little hesitation she came forward and stood beside the jeep, stroking my arm while I patted her hand. With her head covered by a black shawl she was the personification of a sorrowing world; and yet in her lined face there was both indestructible courage and peace. We had not spoken, when suddenly she burst out, "Contente, monsieur, je suis contente." I could not respond except to nod and to go on with the patting of the old brown hand. The convoy began to move and she stood back. I threw her a kiss and, just before we moved out of sight, a wave. She raised her arm. For a precious moment we had shut out the war.

The loosely strung-out pursuit battle meant everyone moving fast and often on too little information. In Montreuil one rainy morning in early September I encountered Tex Noble. His Section was on its way into Boulogne, he said, and he was waiting for news. We hadn't heard that the Germans had given up the city yet, but it was assumed they would. The Section was going to follow the leading troops in and had arranged a meeting in the town square with the Resistance leaders and the Chief of Police; they should be there now.

We sat out the long and anxious wait until, towards dark, the missing Section appeared, without their vehicles, and in something of a state of shock. Confident that Canadian troops were already in the city, they had taken a short cut and driven down, without realizing it, through our own forward position and along the valley below. They had moved too quickly for the troops they were passing through to have put out the customary signs: "Enemy past this point". On the high ground and amid the buildings to their left there were no waving civilians, no sign of life, only a menacing quiet.

Sergeant-Major Bert Sutcliffe in the lead vehicle, deciding something was wrong, signalled and started to turn his little convoy around. The quiet was suddenly destroyed and the menace made real. Machine-guns, anti-tank guns, and mortars opened up as the quiet hillside flamed along its crest and slopes. The Section was into the ditch on the far side of the road and crawling away at the first shots. Bullets cut the grass over their heads when they moved, but gradually in the merciful rain and poor light, and covered now by fire from our side of the valley, they slid away and came out unhurt, leaving their vehicles between the lines.

The real concern here was that the vehicles contained documents — our so-called Black List — that must not fall into enemy hands. The Canadian regiment overlooking the position was reassuring. They would see that the Germans didn't have access to the vehicles, which would lie there safely until our attack overran them.

Two mornings later the vehicles were gone — vanished — sneaked out from under the Regiment's guns, unheard. The vehicles and the stores were of no consequence; they could be replaced. But the Black List of suspects if put to good use might endanger hundreds of Resistance people, as well as our agents in the Pas de Calais and the Low Countries. If the Germans had time to study it and were able to distribute the information, our sources would be compromised, and wanted people might be warned in any areas still in German hands.

But we needn't have worried. When, a few days of hard fighting later, the city had been captured — except for a fortress area on the coast — the cabinet with the Black List was found, pitched carelessly into a corner outside General Heim's bunker. It was upside down and there was no evidence, then or later, that it had ever been looked at.

There were to be similar dangerous mix-ups on the fringes of the pursuit battle. On a sunny afternoon Mike Dubois, attached to 4th Armoured Division's Counter-Intelligence Section, drove into the courtyard of a convent on the edge of Ostend to keep a rendezvous with the rest of the Section. Mike, a cheerful and relaxed character, was driving a captured German car and as there was no one in sight he settled back to snooze in the sun while awaiting the others. He wakened to hear the tramp of a squad marching smartly by him into the courtyard, whereas he had been expecting his friends in jeeps and on motor-bikes. Even in his half-awake state it seemed to him that there was something odd about this, and when the squad halted on the far side of the courtyard to a command in German he knew what it was. By the time the squad had broken off he had his car part-way out the gate and the hail of bullets that followed was just too late.

A week or two later another divisional Section stormed into a Dutch town with the leading troops just at dark, commandeered a house, parked their vehicles, and settled in. Too late they realized that our infantry had withdrawn and they spent a tense night crouched at windows watching a German gun crew which had returned to fight, its gun just in front of the house. In the morning the Germans were gone and our troops back in firm possession.

But if our Counter-Intelligence move-up was disorganized, it was remarkably successful. The Section Commanders were bright and enterprising men and the stunning outcome of the Normandy battle had both encouraged our friends and quenched any enthusiasm in the agents the Germans had left behind. Many of them tried to buy forgiveness by turning themselves in and telling us what they knew. Others tried simply to slink away — keeping a low profile we would say now — hoping to be forgiven or forgotten. But forgiveness did not come easily from those who had suffered during the German Occupation, and suffering sharpens the memory. No doubt some escaped, but what is certain from later interrogations is that the Germans got little information — and quite possibly none at all — from the many scores of agents they had trained and spread across our path.

Agents were recruited from those who wanted the prestige or needed the favours the Germans could confer, or from those who had engaged in resistance work or in some way got into trouble with the Germans and saved their lives by taking training as agents. It was such an unpromising and cynical method of recruiting that it suggested recruiters were paid on quantity

— a sort of capitation grant — or worked from desperation. Neither group was good material. Those whose support was for sale could not be counted on to perform dangerous missions once their paymasters had fled — and seemed unlikely to return. With indecent haste they buried or handed over their wireless sets and the explosives they were to have used for sabotage. Those who had been forced to appear to serve the Germans were obviously not to be relied on once the Germans had gone. There was still another group made up of those who had accepted the Fascist doctrine and served the Germans gladly, lording it over their countrymen with contempt. They at least might have remained faithful to the Nazi cause, but their arrogant behaviour during the Occupation had marked them out, and those who did not simply disappear into hiding or retreat with the Germans were quickly rounded up by their angry countrymen and jailed to await trial.

One of the apocryphal stories that came out of this collapse of the agent network was an account of a stay-behind agent who tried to turn himself in to the British after the fall of Brussels. Shown into a large office carrying his wireless set in a little satchel, he asked in a conspiratorial whisper to speak to the officer in charge; he had something of great importance to reveal. He was told briskly to wait in line. After waiting impatiently for a time while the queue seemed hardly to move, he made his way to the front again and whispered to the sergeant, "I must see your officer. *I am a German agent.*" "I can't help that," said the sergeant, "you'll just have to wait your turn." He indicated the long line of men also carrying satchels — "These are all German agents." Apocryphal or not, something of the sort was happening all over France and Belgium.

One night in mid-September, near Cassel in the north of France, a guard brought a man to my tent accompanied by a message from the Intelligence Officer at 3rd Canadian Division. I thought at first the young man was a German. He wore a German officer's long grey leather coat and the message said he had come out of German-occupied Calais. With his Nordic features and blond hair he did not look French. He gave his name as, let us say, Volendam, claimed to be a native of Amsterdam, and produced an extraordinary proposal. In excellent English he announced his ability and willingness to rouse the Resistance in Calais to attack German posts within the city to coincide with our assault, and to prevent sabotaging of the port. Such part of his story as I heard seemed as extraordinary as his plan — and as extraordinary as his assumption that we would discuss our plans with a suspect stranger. He claimed to be Assistant Port Engineer. He had a wireless set that he had been given and trained to use by the Germans, by which we could communicate. Why would the Germans give him a wireless set? "They trust me," he said. How was he going to get back into Calais? He smiled mysteriously, "I have a way."

Overnight I put him with a Counter-Intelligence Section near by with instructions that he be treated as a friend but watched very closely. In the morning I sent him back to the Interrogation Centre with an interim report saying I had not questioned him in any depth because his story clearly needed considerable investigation and meanwhile I believed he should be treated like an enemy agent. Just as he was leaving to be driven back to St. Omer I asked Volendam if he was armed — it was a bit late to be asking. He hesitated and then produced a loaded Browning from his breast pocket. He argued hard to be allowed to keep it; was he not an ally; when could he have it back? I told him we would never knowingly send an armed stranger to another headquarters and he could have it when we sent him back into Calais. On their return his escort told me that on the drive Volendam had become increasingly nervous, and driving through St. Omer had tried to keep his face hidden.

A few hours later came a message from the Interrogation Centre: Volendam had confessed to having taken training as an agent of Abteilung VI of the Sicherheitsdienst; he claimed to have taken it under duress, having been suspected of spying for the Dutch Resistance. His connections and the level to which he had been trained made him perhaps the most interesting agent we had encountered so far. If not dangerous, he was valuable. Within a few days he was flown to England for continuing interrogation in depth. If he had ever expected to return to Calais, that hope was now doomed, and indeed long before he was cleared by British and Dutch, Calais had capitulated and the great cross-channel guns had been silenced.

The valuable Port of Antwerp had been taken undamaged on a brilliant dash by the British 11th Armoured Division a day or two after the Guards Armoured had taken Brussels, but there were to be exhausting and bloody weeks of fighting for the approaches to Antwerp before it could be used, and until supplies could begin to pour into Antwerp advances had to be limited and concentrated. It was a period when, more than ever, the real war seemed to be different from the one I was engaged in. The Sections were busy finding agents in Antwerp, Bruges, and Ghent, seeing the concrete results of their work and feeling themselves part of the Divisions that were doing the fighting. I could only move around, visiting, watching, making a suggestion; it didn't require a Protestant conscience to feel guilty and unnecessary.

The sense of being almost a bystander came home sharply late one afternoon. I had been out on the isthmus of South Beveland all day visiting a Section at Goes and watching the troops working their way forward to the causeway, preparing for an attack that would coincide with an assault from across the Scheldt to take Walcheren Island and clear the estuary. The terrain on both sides of the road was low-lying, wet, and dangerously exposed. I was tired and hungry and edgy on the return trip, being crowded well over by oncoming convoys, when there, coming toward me in truck after truck, was the Toronto Scottish Regiment. I hadn't seen them as a whole since Normandy, where I had sat in a field with John Ellis (later to be the battalion's colonel) while he described with ironic detachment their first battle. Now, weeks and many battles later, they were moving up. One or two waved and gave me a tight smile. Most were asleep, sprawled on their equipment. Many I had never known; but some that I had known well were not readily recognizable behind the grey masks of exhaustion and shock which I had seen first on our landing in Normandy; seen on the faces of men from 3rd Canadian Division who had been in bitter fighting for a month; and seen later on the faces of thousands of German prisoners as they stared sightlessly out of passing trucks or stood in clumps behind wire, like cattle facing a storm, beside the roads to Falaise. My own fatigue and hunger were trivial; I was moving away from the battle area to comparative comfort, and the already tired Toronto Scots were moving into it.

It was consistent with the bizarre contradictions of the times that a Belgian civilian who had attached himself to 2 Division Section in Antwerp suggested that a few of them, and I, should have our pictures taken at the Gevaert film plant. I wasn't enthusiastic but he pressed it. The photography would be superb; "Ça sera pour vous le plus beau souvenir de la guerre." But why, why should Gevaerts do this? He answered that they had for four years taken pictures of Germans because they had to; now they would like to take pictures of some Canadians because they wanted to. It didn't appear so extraordinary in a town where life went on with considerable gaiety, while day and night the sound of gunfire could be heard as the Germans clung to Merksem on the north-eastern edge of the city. And it almost seemed churlish to refuse so handsome an offer — besides Christmas was coming — so three or four of us went along. The pictures were taken, and they were indeed excellent, truly *un beau souvenir*. When a few days later a Belgian Intelligence group took in some of the Gevaert people for questioning about collaboration with the Germans we were bound to wonder whether the motives of our genial photographers had been quite as pure and generous as they had been represented to us. But we were not asked by anyone whether they were fine photographers or fine fellows.

Set against all the background of war oddly juxtaposed with peace, of soldiers hurrying past to fight as civilians went to work or play, it was refreshing to find that several of the men from Corps Headquarters during a static period had been helping some of the farmers on neighbouring lands to get the harvest in. My batman told me he had a fine day, with his shirt off and handling a scythe in the sun. I asked him whether he spoke any French or Dutch. "Oh no," he said, "but we understand each other pretty good. When you are used to working on a farm you all sort of talk the same language."

·13·

WITH THE BATTLES to free the Port of Antwerp finished, advance elements of 2 Canadian Corps moved up to the Nijmegen area and I went with them. We were taking over from 30 British Corps, which in September had driven a long wedge north into the German defences in Holland only to fall short of a junction with the airborne forces at Arnhem. It had been a daring, and perhaps mistaken, gamble that might have ended the war by Christmas and might have changed in an important way the subsequent course of European history. But these were all might-have-beens. By late October it looked as though any hope for a quick end to the war had gone, and we would spend the winter guarding what had been won and staring across rivers at what we had not.

The Counter-Intelligence role of defending against covert enemy activity had to be closely tied to the operations of the fighting units. Between us we had to cover a long line, strung out in a great bow for almost 150 miles from the North Sea on our left to near Venlo, south and east of Nijmegen. And paradoxically it was a line that had to be shut tight against our enemies and yet kept open for our friends. Though the battle for Arnhem was over, an unknown number of survivors of the British airborne force dropped around Arnhem was still within the German lines in hiding. What remained of the main body had been brought out in assault boats by daring rescue operations long after the main operation had closed down, but a little trickle of escapees and Dutch Resistance men kept seeping out during the hours of darkness from the marshy areas bordering the misty rivers. A part of the escape machinery that made me very nervous was an open telephone line from a powerhouse near Nijmegen to a terminal in German-occupied territory. It seemed incredible that in the years of occupation the Germans had remained unaware of it; if it hadn't been cut, was it not because it was tapped? But experts were certain it was not tapped and the people using it at each end used and guarded it carefully; those at the German end of the line were told only what they had to know for the escape operations they were conducting.

Gradually the machinery of controls of the forward areas was fitted into position, with close liaison between the Counter-Intelligence Sections and the forward units. Back of them was a loose screen of Dutch police cycling along remote roads at all hours, challenging any civilians they didn't know. Our control problems were compounded by patriotic Dutch rivermen who knew the mysterious waterways as no one else could, and who would not be persuaded that control of movement on them must be ours. One notorious and stubborn patriot, King Tom, who had been warned by Captain Ernest Sirluck, Intelligence Officer of 4th Division, persisted in playing his games until a frightening stream of red tracer bullets across his bow turned him back — in a rage, but for the moment tamed.

Some weeks later our control program produced an interesting side-effect. I had moved to Army Headquarters and one morning a young British officer, whom I had seen at planning meetings in England before the invasion, came in to ask for a pass to the forward area to assist in escape operations from the Arnhem side. His credentials were those of people working in IS9, the escaping organization whose course I had attended. Making out the pass I asked his name — Captain Maurice Macmillan. "Are you any relation to the publishing family?" I asked casually. Very stiff and correct, he said, "Harold Macmillan is my father, sir." I told him then that I had been with Macmillans before the war and hoped to return to them after it was over. Moreover, I had met his father when a Macmillan group had lunched with him in Toronto in 1938. Parting, I said, "Let's have dinner some night; we can talk about books and forget the war." He said he would like that very much, but we weren't to have our talk for another two years.

The most precious prize salvaged out of the battle for Arnhem was the great bridge at Nijmegen; its huge span on massive stone piers soared across the Waal River and with its approaches extended almost half a mile. Defence against conventional attack, by aircraft, artillery, or ground troops, was not our responsibility; but defence against covert attack — especially underwater attack against the stone piers — was a Counter-Intelligence task. Once, soon after its capture, German frogmen had been sent downstream with explosives and had damaged one pier. Thereafter midget submarines, manned torpedoes, and floating mines disguised as logs were launched against the bridge. Against all this we had only vigilant riflemen to shoot or throw grenades at any menacing shadow in the water. One explosive charge did get between the piers to blow a hole in a pontoon bridge downstream. That was easily fixed. Damage to the great bridge was limited to torn-up flooring and twisted bits of metal in the superstructure as the Germans shelled and mortared it — noisy and occasionally frightening but not serious.

It was soon apparent that all hope of a quick end to the war had not been given up. Planning began for a break-out from the Nijmegen area and a clearing to the Rhine. There came a sudden demand from General Simonds, commanding 2 Canadian Corps, for Counter-Intelligence to assure him that no information was reaching the Germans from within or behind our lines. Wasn't it the kind of assurance that no one could give? The long perimeter along the dark and mist-filled rivers seemed beyond closing, though with armed troops on both shores a crossing was obviously a dangerous enterprise. More than once German patrols had come into our forward areas led by an English-speaker calling out, "Don't shoot, don't shoot, we're friends," until the patrol itself was close enough to fire. But at least a watch could be maintained on the outer edges where few travelled. The teeming towns of Nijmegen, Breda, Tilburg, and 's-Hertogenbosch were all within easy wireless contact of the Germans. It was perhaps natural for us to assume that Nijmegen, close neighbour to Germany, was full of German sympathizers, many of them not enjoying our occupation and only too ready to send messages to our enemy. Along the margins of the Reichwald Forest to the east all units were warned to be doubly alert for people trying to pass through to the Germans. Perhaps the warning was not needed. The units were alert on their own account and the ground between the armies was mined. Only a mad or desperate person would try to cross the lines alone after dark.

There was still the wireless as a method of vaulting safely over troops and mines and gun-lines. With the help of special secret units we set up a wireless watch, strategically placed so that illicit traffic could not only be detected, but in due course its place of origin identified. It must have been boring work for the operators but they stayed with it faithfully, and dropping in at the vans at any hour of the day or night I would find the intercept boys sitting alert in their head-sets listening patiently, week after week. And most boring, and best of all, nothing happened — no excitement of suspicion to relieve the monotony. Against all probability I was able to report with confidence that we had good reason to believe no information was passing from our area to the Germans; they were effectively blinded as to what was happening behind our lines, so short a distance from theirs.

And what was happening would have interested them. The roads at night were crowded as elements of 30 British Corps moved in back of Nijmegen and supplies and munitions from the now open port of Antwerp began pouring up all the roads.

Then, in early December we had reason to wonder whether we were going to attack or be attacked. In the fields north of the rivers, facing our spread-out left flank, aerial photography began to show more and more haystacks and barns that hadn't been there before, and imperfectly hidden vehicle tracks — these looked like gun emplacements or supply dumps. It was difficult to believe that the Germans were in a position to launch a major attack, but almost impossible to doubt that a large build-up for some purpose was going forward. With the fierce and active patrolling now taking place along our front — swift raids across the river that made the dike roads as dangerous at night as gunfire did by day — we expected at least a spoiling operation. The site of Corps Headquarters in a village outside Nijmegen and close to the Waal River was probably known to the Germans, and certainly vulnerable to a bold raid. We were ordered to carry arms at all times and I marched around peaceful streets carrying a German semi-automatic rifle. I was uncertain of how dangerous I might be with it and to whom, having on one occasion smashed a pencil stuck up in the snow and on another missed a pigeon on a low bough just over my head — the pigeon had looked down at me with incredulity bordering on contempt and had then flown away.

In fact, with the evidence of build-up growing daily and the beginning of the German attack from the Ardennes, our own tensions grew. The purpose of the build-up opposite us seemed clear now. If the dramatic break-out — the battle of the Bulge — succeeded in taking Antwerp or Brussels, an attack from across the river, through our thin perimeter and on to Antwerp, could put First Canadian, Second British, and Ninth U.S. armies all in a bag that might make the Falaise Pocket and Stalingrad look like minor engagements. The menu at our mess Christmas dinner in an old monastery had a picture of Santa Claus in a German helmet swinging down in a parachute and carrying a German Schmeisser sub-machine-gun under his arm. As a caption we borrowed a brave sentiment from Henry v: "And gentlemen in England now abed shall think themselves accursed they were not here".

The German Intelligence effort seemed to be stepped up at this point, but we could see no evidence of its being more effective; it appeared to be as cynical or desperate as before. One night many of us were conscious of a low-flying plane. Later we learned it had missed its target area and dropped a clutch of agents in northern France. Three men had been strapped into a contraption that looked like a huge badminton bird. When the bird parachuted down, the cage was opened on impact and they were bounced rudely out. The wretched men — themselves Dutch policemen — had thought they were in Holland or just over the Belgian border. Their shaky morale was not braced by a meeting with French policemen on a lonely road in the early morning. In this state they were arrested and taken to a nearby police station where they were given the French police treatment known as *passez le tabac*. Passing the tobacco meant simply knocking a man back and forth across the room from one French policeman to another, and as the unhappy Dutchmen didn't enjoy the game, they made a partial confession at once. They were sent up to us, where they readily explained their mission: to blow up Intelligence Headquarters with explosives buried near by. The big cache of explosive materials and arms to which they led us was largely British material parachuted in for use by Dutch agents and Resistance groups but captured by the Germans. What they had been told was Intelligence Headquarters was in fact our Interrogation Centre.

A few days after Christmas I learned that I was to be GSO2 1b at Army Headquarters, and was to move at once; Tex Noble would replace me at Corps. I suppose I was glad to be a major and certainly I enjoyed the prospect of working more closely with my seniors, Lieutenant-Colonel Graham Macdougall and Colonel Peter Wright, but to leave my friends in 2 Corps was a wrench. With the German break-out from the Ardennes now contained and thrown back by the Americans, 30 British Corps, which had moved south and taken up a blocking position, now began to move back to our area. The threat of attack from north of the rivers appeared to have gone away as mysteriously as it arrived, and it was now our turn to threaten — without appearing to do so.

One morning in January we had a message from the American 9th Army area. A Dutchman from Goch had just brought in a colonel of the U.S. Air Corps who had been in German hands and had escaped. He had brought him across the Meuse at night, delivered him safely, and left. He was now on his way to see friends in our area. Would we give him the help he had so richly earned? An hour or two later came another message — a second thought — saying to hold the colonel's guide until we had a detailed report now being sent by dispatch rider. It didn't take us long to get patrols out on the road. They made at best a loose sieve and yet within a few hours they had scooped him up and brought him to my office. For the time being he was sent to the Interrogation Camp, though he was not to be questioned.

Almost at once we had visits from three dignitaries from the area including, I think, two burgomasters. Was it true that we had arrested so good a man, such a brave patriot, as Mynheer Denhaff of Goch? I answered that we had detained him for questioning; arrest was too strong a word. I had never been sure of the meaning of having someone talk to one like a Dutch uncle; now this gap in my knowledge was filled in. More in sorrow than in anger, they all scolded and pressed their argument; to arrest this man who had risked so much for so long — the lecture or plea went on and on. I tried to remain patient and courteous while matching their stubbornness. Their view of Denhaff was that throughout the war he had been assisting escapees, hiding people from labour round-ups, and generally acting as a bulwark; now for a final and brave act of direct assistance to the allies he was arrested. I could only repeat that he was not being, and would not be, harshly treated at our hands, but we were not yet prepared to let him go.

Up to this point we had not questioned Denhaff while we waited for the detailed report from 9th U.S. Army. The report when it came explained the second message, that he should be held, though it didn't make clear why he had been turned loose in the first place. The colonel when shot down had evaded capture, and had appealed to some civilians in an isolated area for help. He had eventually come into Denhaff's care and been hidden in a ruined cellar for some days. To this point it was a conventional escape story. The night before, he and Denhaff had come down close to the River Meuse on bicycles. They had hidden the bicycles and Denhaff went forward to a German bunker while the American colonel stayed out of sight but watching. A German soldier had come up out of the bunker and after some talk had led them both down to the water where he inflated a rubber boat and rowed them across to our shore. In the early morning the colonel had been delivered free and safe into the hands of his friends.

We had already heard from the Interrogation Centre that Denhaff was protesting strongly against being held, as a penalty for his good deed, and I now had him brought up with an interpreter for questioning. He was a small, unsmiling man, full of formal courtesy — bows and crisp, correct answers. He had a small head and a brown face like a russet apple with rather hard blue eyes. He demanded at once to know when he would be allowed to return home — many people depended on him. Playing for time I asked how he proposed to cross the river. He took me to a large-scale wall map and studied it carefully. Then with a little grin of triumph he pointed to a precise spot and said that if we would guide him to that point on the river bank after dark he could cross. But how? He would flash a short signal and the Germans would come over in a rubber boat and pick him up. It was a fantastic proposal and I began to press him. Didn't he understand that we couldn't let people move back and forth? And neither could the Germans, so how was it that the Germans had helped him out and would help him to get back?

He gave a crafty little smile. He had had to make friends with the Germans, had got things for them in the black market, had played up to them as a cover for his activities in helping escapees and sending out information to the Resistance. Had they sent him over, and what would he tell them when he went back? No, they had not sent him. He had given them a story about why he must cross. As to what they would ask him and what he would say, he hoped we would give him some information that he could pass on — either innocuous information or even misleading information. I said that he must have known that we might not let him return; if his presence on the other side of the river was so important, why had he crossed? Because he thought a colonel so vital to us that he must take the risk.

What to make of this man and his legion of influential friends! He had apparently covered himself with both sides; both thought him a supporter. So who was he really for? What was probable at least was that he now knew too much of our affairs, had seen too much as he made his way up the back roads from 9th Army. Having heard him out, I said firmly that I was sorry if his family would be worried but we couldn't allow him to go back. He began to scold, then to storm, and finally to plead. The hard face became first fierce and excited, then close to breaking. He had to go back — he must — or some sixty people and a whole escape line would be endangered. Sorry, no. Sixty people? Sixty people who had risked everything for escaping allied airmen and soldiers. Were they nothing, would we not think of them and save them? How were they to be endangered by his failure to return? If he didn't go back his house would be searched and his papers would compromise these people. They would be rounded up and shot. I returned him to the Interrogation Centre.

Though I couldn't entirely believe his story, its possibilities were hard to live with. A report from the Interrogation Centre said that Denhaff was behaving wildly, pacing his cell without rest, round and round, up and down, and muttering incoherently — they thought he was on the point of a breakdown. I was doing some walking myself and late in the evening took my problem to Colonel Wright, as Graham Macdougall was in England on leave. He was not unsympathetic but quite clear and firm: we could allow no one to cross; the balance of risk was on our side. I had known the answer but was glad of the reassurance of his opinion and ruling.

When some weeks later 30 Corps fought its way into Goch we made inquiries. Had there been a round-up and people shot? No, there hadn't been. What about Denhaff? A strange man, they said. What to make of him? You never knew. Was he a good man or a bad man? A shrug. And it wasn't until the war was over that we found among our prisoners the German Abwehr officer who had been in or near Goch at the time. Did he remember Denhaff? Oh yes, he remembered him. Had he sent Denhaff over on a mission to our side? Yes, of course, to find out all he could. It was a good deal short of proof, and I never learned what the Dutch authorities to whom we handed him over made of it all in the end.

At all levels the whole world of espionage had these murky margins, like the Dutch rivers in the dark of winter nights. Whatever people involved in that trade — willingly or by coercion — might say or do, their motives must remain in doubt. Their ultimate intention, their true loyalty — if any — was to what? lay where? The question was to surface again and again. And at the war's end, when many missing pieces in the puzzle fell into our hands, there remained great areas of uncertainty. Almost certainly injustices were done and just as certainly men who had been weak or treacherous went unpunished. And across the world thirty years later men are still hunting and old men still hiding, to satisfy old hatreds or to escape the consequences of old treacheries.

Most of the cases we had to deal with hadn't this kind of magnitude; many were petty, some bizarre. As triumphant armies swept across Western Europe they acquired a retinue of local hangers-on; genuine Resistance fighters who had been longing for this moment to attach themselves to us, as well as interpreters and scroungers. Inevitably some of these were seizing a chance to correct their record, to acquire a piece of paper testifying to their valuable service on the side of the winners. Some undoubtedly had hidden similar pieces of paper bearing a German stamp, which they just might need again.

The Queen's Own Cameron Highlanders of Winnipeg, fighting out of Antwerp, had picked up a clever and bold young man who spoke good English — and of course French, German, and Flemish — so they carried him along when they moved up to the Nijmegen area. He was an asset in many ways, an honorary member of the officers' mess, and an amusing companion; he had even gone out on patrols with them and done well. He must have felt that he had cleverly changed his spots and it didn't occur to the Camerons that he had any to change. When, weeks later, a Counter-Intelligence Section arrived at the regiment to arrest him everyone was dumbfounded, but the evidence from Antwerp was unanswerable. He had worked for the Germans and taken training as an agent. After a period of being held under interrogation the young man, trying to expiate his sins, offered himself in the role of double agent. Why not put him in the forward area in Canadian battle-dress where he could let himself be captured? It was a dangerous game for him (and obviously his motives could be suspect), but as the battle swept up into north-eastern Holland and neared the German border it seemed unlikely that he could carry information that would do us harm, and if he was now genuinely on our side he might learn a good deal that would be useful.

He disappeared from view one night in the forward area, perhaps never to be seen again. In about two weeks he was back with a pocketful of snapshots of himself in Canadian uniform carousing with a group of German officers and their girl friends. Once through the lines he had been taken at once to his spymaster in the Sicherheitsdienst and there greeted like the prodigal son. He thought some had doubts about his reliability but since no other agents had been heard from, they had to make the most of this one and claim his return as a brilliant success. But the love feast didn't last and, becoming uneasy, he stole a bicycle and set out at night on his return journey, cycling through groups of retreating Germans. Nearing the battle he hid in a barn under some hay until twenty-four hours later he heard Canadian voices and crawled out into the arms of his old friends the Cameron Highlanders, who greeted him with equal incredulity and distaste. As for the Intelligence staff, the Camerons had thought them incompetent after Dieppe; now they were prepared to certify them. Was it guys like these who were running the war? It explained a lot — but improved nothing.

As the final break-out from Nijmegen began — the battle for the Rhine — I paid a visit to 9th U.S. Army on our right. They were already over the German border and had fought their way into München-Gladbach. I found some excitement at the Counter-Intelligence Section because a German girl had just come in to confess to training as an agent and to take them to where her wireless set was hidden. Under questioning she had given them the name of another girl who had trained with her, and she in turn indicated still others. By evening they had rounded up five or six girls in all, young and frightened and now immensely relieved. The excitement of finding they apparently weren't going to be shot or even tortured set them all to giggling and chattering, so the kitchen of the Counter-Intelligence Section's house sounded like the lunch-room at a girls' school. Not a bit daunted by their inexperience, the Americans, who had just arrived, were carrying on interrogation as a group, everyone asking whatever questions occurred to them interspersed with periodic civilities such as "Have some more cawfee, Gretchen. No, you're Hilda, care for some cawfee?" The girls couldn't believe it — and neither could I. It was all contrary to our way of doing things, but it worked, up to a point. The girls said that they made up the whole class of one agent-training course, except for a man who had been sent down from Cleve on our front. They couldn't give me his right name or any distinctive description, but he had been wounded in the leg on the Russian front and walked with a limp — and, oh yes, he had a gold tooth. Soon everyone tired of the interrogation game. I was staying overnight and sharing a room with the Section commander, an eager, intense little Irish-American. For a while we sat up talking but with difficulty, for in the next room were the girl agents who between giggles seemed to be having a pillow fight. The sinister, deadly German Secret Service had slipped to a depressing extent.

When, soon after, the battle for Cleve — or what was left of it — was over, a man with a limp and a gold tooth was found rooting among the ruins in his garden looking for a wireless set that he had buried, and that our bombardment had further buried past finding. He was herded into a camp with the German prisoners of war and there eventually the description I had circulated caught up with him. The whole of Agents' School Number So-and-so was satisfactorily accounted for, having accomplished none of the tasks for which they had been trained. Did it matter? The war was not being lost or won by such as them — or us.

But it was being won, and quickly now. First Canadian Corps, having fought in Sicily and Italy for a year before the Normandy landings, had moved up to join us and for a few short weeks the whole of First Canadian Army fought together for the only time in the war. As we drove north, 2 Corps wheeled east toward Germany and 1 Corps west into Fortress Holland. Army Headquarters, trying to direct these diverging and swift-moving battles, was in danger of doing the splits, like a circus rider with a foot on each of two spirited horses. First Corps, having been part of the great Eighth Army, left us in no doubt they thought Eighth Army Headquarters much better than we were. Understandably they were making us pay for the bitterness they felt at having fought first and hard and successfully for what had turned into a sideshow, while the spectacular triumphs had been won by those who came later into Northwest Europe.

Peace was only days away, and yet to the last minute we heard of friends being killed on both fronts. Plans were being hastily put together for defining occupational responsibilities, though not until the end was it clear what the situation might be. There were rumours — inevitably — about a formidable resistance movement, the Werewolves, forming in Germany; that the ss in Fortress Holland would not recognize the cease-fire. Planning for war is continuous and detailed and it is not easy to change gears. Planning for peace is arranging for proper administration within a framework of law. About Fortress Holland at least there was little need to worry. We had already seen in freed areas how eagerly and efficiently the Dutch picked up the pieces and put them together; how they had never really let go what the Germans had snatched at and the

307

war seemed to have broken irreparably. Would the great cities of the north — Amsterdam, Rotterdam, the Hague — be different? We didn't really know how much they had suffered, but we would soon find out.

One night early in May a casual conversation in the back of a truck parked and serving as sleeping quarters outside Hengelo on the German border was interrupted by a yell in the darkness. The war was over. There had been a signal from General Montgomery's headquarters. The war was over — or would be tomorrow. There were more yells and excited talk round about. People were repeating the news in a kind of wonderment; trying to understand it, to feel it. Peace meant that the shooting stopped; then what? How soon could it mean going home? And what would it be like, back on civvy street? No one, it seemed, wanted to take up his pre-war life just where he had left it. War had given people new perspectives and increased confidence. Like everyone else I had been over these questions, and was resolved to do things differently — to carve out more time for writing. I would be happy enough to go back to publishing, but the future at Macmillans didn't look attractive. Harvey had been made president a year before and though it sounded as though the Company was prospering, I couldn't believe I would be returning to a head man who had suddenly become bold and stimulating and knowledgeable. The only prospect I could see ahead with unclouded joy was a return to Tony and to young John. Given that, other questions could wait. Meanwhile we would see what peace felt like.

We had twenty-four hours to savour peace and then began the moves to allotted stations and the beginnings of a dismantling of the German Army. Within that the Counter-Intelligence role was the rounding up of German Intelligence personnel; those in the arrest category were not to be treated as prisoners of war but were to be locked up like criminals. For the SS Intelligence Services, the Sicherheitsdienst, and its most hated section, the Gestapo, the arrest category laid down by 21 Army Group included virtually everyone above the rank of corporal. It wasn't going to be pleasant work, though I didn't know how unpleasant. Wallowing in triumph did not seem attractive to me, though clearly some were getting ready to make the most of it. The roads on which Canadian Army moved into Germany — Maple Leaf Up — bore the legend "You are entering enemy territory, behave like conquerors". I never knew who thought that up, or just what he meant by it; perhaps he didn't either.

Since my own posting was to be Holland I didn't have to understand that particular direction. I was to be Area Security Officer, South Holland, with Sections based on Leyden, the Hague, Rotterdam, and Dordrecht. My headquarters would be in Rotterdam. Our responsibilities would clarify once we were on the ground. Apart from these general plans I had a specific order to find and arrest the Chief of the ss and Police, Brigadeführer Schoengarth, assumed to be in the Hague or its suburb, Scheveningen. This man had only recently taken up his appointment on the assassination of his predecessor — Rauter — by the Dutch Resistance. For that assassination the Germans had imposed brutal reprisals. Whether this was Schoengarth's work or not, he was believed to have directed some of the most savage actions against civilians in Poland in 1939. He sounded like a monster and I looked forward to our meeting with mixed feelings. When I arrested the monster — if I arrested the monster — what would I do with him? Having gone into war as amateurs, and become pros, we had now to learn the arts of peace-keeping with its hardly foreseeable problems, at which we were once again amateurs.

But the early part of the day was joyful, the kind of moment for which, consciously or not, we had all been waiting. My little party was carried in two jeeps and included my friend Antz, the French liaison officer, and Captain John Stonburgh, a Cambridge University graduate of distinguished Hungarian background, who had somehow landed in the Canadian Army. My driver was a small, silent Pole, Jan Mischa, who had arrived from no one knew quite where, but had been in Dachau; he spoke almost no English and only a little French but he made it clear he was enjoying this day. Someone had supplied us with bully-beef sandwiches and hunks of apple pie, and I think we had some of the Alsatian wine with which Antz had returned laden from a quick trip to Colmar after it was liberated. We were to travel the width of Holland at almost its widest point, from Hengelo to Rotterdam.

The early part of our journey was through country that had been liberated for some weeks, and then we began reaching areas that had been fought over only a few days before. It was a brave sunny day, a day for calling out and waving flags, and there were people out to wave and sing on the edges of the villages and towns we skirted. We were travelling on the main autobahn and began overtaking long convoys of trucks filled with troops wearing the famous Red Patch of First Canadian Division. They had only just stopped fighting a few days before but they were trim and smart and looked like the first-rate soldiers they were; we were overtaking in our little scuttling jeeps some of the most famous regiments in the Canadian Army: the Royal Canadian Regiment, the Royal 22nd, the Hastings and Prince Edward, the 48th Highlanders, the Loyal Edmonton Regiment, and many more. Up ahead somewhere, in their gleaming armoured cars, rolled the Divisional Recce Regiment, the Princess Louise Dragoon Guards — a regiment I had last seen in a splendid cavalry charge across Barriefield Common outside Kingston almost twenty years before.

The war might have been all futile madness but this seemed to me a splendid moment, if only for the excitement and the joy and the tears of the people beside the road. And then, incredibly, as we passed a big house the windows and the yard outside were full of German soldiers waving and yelling excitedly, as joyously as the liberated Dutch. This we weren't quite in a mood for yet, and we hurried by with only a perfunctory acknowledgment of this forgive-and-forget gesture. It wasn't just a rough hockey game we had all been playing, and even if these men had not committed the mindless bestialities of the Nazis — of which we had still to learn the full story — they could not expect us to stop thinking them loathsome just because pieces of paper had been signed saying the shooting would stop. We could acknowledge them as brave men and superb soldiers, not as friends.

Somewhere on the margin of the great road, high above the flat fields, we picnicked and hurried on. We had bypassed most of the large towns and cities in our path, and though we had seen lots of joy and celebration on our way we were not prepared for the great crescendo of pent-up emotion that burst over us as we drove into Rotterdam. Having left the long, disciplined convoys behind, it looked as though we were the first Canadians to arrive, but elements of the Recce Regiment were ahead of us. It was not for a couple of unimpressive jeeps that the people had crowded the streets all morning, but we were at least a further confirmation that the Canadians were coming, trailing visions of sugarplums; the Germans were going and the war was over. Even on the outskirts of the city the police were hard-pressed to keep the narrowest of lanes open for traffic. The crowds were all the direction we needed into the city centre; there was only one way to go, and all that way we moved in a great rolling wave of cheers, and calls, and waving flags. From strong people this outburst would have been wonderful, but what we didn't fully understand until later was that this great welling up came from people who were weak from months of cruel undernourishment, who had been standing for hours and now were drawing on the very essence of the life force within them to have this great day for which they had waited five years.

Somehow with a minimum of asking we found our way to the Stadthuis — the City Hall — fronting acres of weed-covered open spaces that the German bombers had burned out in 1940; now they were filled with people. My jeep was allowed in through a great iron gate which was with difficulty closed against the crowd. John Stonburgh, left outside and fearful that he and his jeep were going to be loved to death in the surging mass, climbed cheerfully onto the bonnet to a roar of applause and led the crowd in singing — the only song he could think of: "It ain't gonna rain no more, no more". No doubt it should have been something more splendid but as a safety valve it was just right, and the Dutch people sang it as though it was for this, too, they had been waiting for five years. My business inside was soon done; there was friendly confusion but someone was able to tell me that the headquarters of the Resistance was at Heineken's Brewery and guides were not lacking. As I came out of the Stadthuis a dozen or fifteen young men were standing around my jeep, longing to do something — to sing, to shout, to shake hands. As I was about to climb in I saw the cardboard box with the remains of our lunch — sandwiches and pie. If these men were hungry — would it be resented? I asked a man who seemed to be a leader was this of any use to them? He looked into the box and stared at me incredulously — any use? He climbed onto the bonnet of the jeep and began to break the sandwiches into little bits and to give each man a small handful. They crowded forward then, reaching up so that he had to kick at them to restore some order, then went on doling out the little shares. They ate slowly, relishing every crumb, licking at their hands to get the last taste. Some got sandwich, some pie, but all had something, relishing it, smacking their lips and raising a little chorus of "dat is heerlyk", "dat is lekker" — delicious, lovely. Many soldiers had a similar experience that first day and in the days that followed; and to many Dutch people the very taste of liberty remained for a long time a mouthful of good bread or pastry such as they had almost forgotten.

Heineken's Brewery was less crowded but no less joyously confused. This was the Resistance's night of the long knives. Cars and motor-bikes raced in and out of the great courtyard designed for teams of mighty horses pulling great drays loaded with beer. Petrol was scarce, so cars went out packed to the running boards, while the bikes had pillion riders all dressed in blue denim and flourishing Sten guns. Greetings were cordial but as yet no one knew much. Were the Sicherheitsdienst and the Gestapo going to fight on as we had been told? No one knew. Were any of them still in Rotterdam? It was thought they were all in or near the Hague in a fortified area. A couple of officers from First Canadian Division overheard, and the younger one, wearing a Military Cross, rubbed his hands together and said to his companion with relish, "Let's have them for breakfast." I couldn't help wondering whether at his age, if I had survived, I would have loved war, as once when roused I had loved fighting and bruising games. All I knew was that if it had ever been possible it wasn't possible now; whatever had to be done I would have tried, but I would no longer have gone hunting it, lusting to play at Guns.

So it was up the great road again to the Hague, seeing the towers of Delft, past the windmills and across the beautifully cultivated flat fields to our left as we drove by. It was a Dutch painting. The Hague, smaller and more sedate than teeming Rotterdam, was almost as excited. It was to be days before one could see properly the classic beauty of the city and its centrepiece, the Binnenhof.

Again willing hands led us to Resistance Headquarters where a meeting was in progress. We were admitted at once and made welcome. They didn't know whether the ss and sd were going to recognize the cease-fire, but it was easy to ask the German Kommandant whose office was just across the street. In a few minutes the plump and nervous little Kommandant appeared and clicked his heels. He wasn't certain about the surrender but he took it for granted the wanted people were going to observe it. Would he guide us to them? Reluctantly he agreed. First, if we would accompany him he would try to telephone ahead from his office. As he led the way into the office a clerk sprang up and in the same motion flung out his arm in a Nazi salute; then, seeing me, he quickly tucked it away and tried to look as though he hoped I would forgive his nervous tic. Apart from newsreels I had only seen the Nazi salute once before, and that was when a German hiding in Abbeville, in France, had been brought in to the Polish Armoured Division's Counter-Intelligence Section. He had had the audacity to greet the Sergeant-Major with a "Heil Hitler". It was a cardinal mistake with the Poles, who of all the allies probably hated the Germans most, and with good reason. Before anyone could intervene — even had they wished to do so — the posturing young Nazi had been slapped silly by the Sergeant-Major. In contrast now the wretched clerk got off with a cold glare.

The military phone appeared to be dead and we prepared to go. Antz took me aside. Very gravely and arguing from his hard realism he urged me not to go. I was the senior officer and if Schoengarth, surrounded by his supporters, refused arrest I could only withdraw in humiliation or undertake a wildly rash and doomed gesture. If a junior officer were refused he could withdraw to seek further instruction. I knew this was sensible advice, but I could not accept it. This might be a tough assignment. Yet Schoengarth might surrender to me when he would not to a junior; anyway, the assignment was mine. Antz waggled his head and gave me a wry grin. He thought it silly but understandable.

I ordered the German Kommandant to sit in the front with my Polish driver, Jan. I sat in the back with, I think, Captain Basil Torry of British Intelligence — our star interrogator. Our plump guide sat stiffly in front, directing the driver. It was no distance to Scheveningen, but the last stretch was over open ground to an area of fine trees. In front of the trees the road was closed by a barbed-wire hurdle flanked at each end by a German sentry with rifle and fixed bayonet. As we drove up they moved together and crossed their rifles in a smart drill movement to indicate the road was barred. On a sharp order from the Kommandant they swung the hurdle away and we drove in. Down the first avenue we found ourselves driving toward a medium machine-gun sighted along our road. As we drove by, the gunner stood up in his slit trench looking frustrated and bewildered; to be offered such a target and to have a German officer sitting in the middle of the bull's eye! We drove on down a series of leafy avenues, past fine houses, all looking empty, or occupied by German soldiers. A pleasant and privileged life had gone on here — and no doubt would again. We began to think the Kommandant had lost his way when after some hesitation he indicated a right fork and we rounded a corner into a small, trim courtyard in front of a handsome house. But it was not the house that interested me. In the courtyard facing the doorway was a smart-looking sergeant wearing the red patch of First Canadian Division and beside him an armoured car, with its gun trained on the house. I stopped holding my breath.

After a cheerful exchange with the sergeant (beginning "My God, am I glad to see you") I went into the house. Off the handsome hall in a big living room twenty or thirty officers, in their best uniforms and wearing their medals, stood chatting together. Hard faces, some of them distinguished; they might have been about to pose for a painting of The Congress of Vienna. In my rumpled battle-dress tucked into dusty flight boots I must have cut a poor figure — except that the battle-dress, the army patch, the balmoral with the badge of the Toronto Scottish, belonged to the Canadian Army.

There was one other Canadian uniform in the room. To one side I saw a Canadian colonel talking with a tall, thick-set German officer with a strong, rather brutal face complete with duelling scars. The colonel, Charlie Petch of the Princess Louise Dragoon Guards, I had not seen since we took our commissions together at St. Johns, Quebec, in 1930, when he was a provisional lieutenant in the Black Watch and I in the Glengarrys. When he turned toward me our exchange was cordial, but in front of the watching Germans correct, brief, and business-like. His regiment too had been ordered to find and arrest Brigadeführer Schoengarth, and this they had now done. His whole group would remain under arrest within this area, which was surrounded, and would be kept under guard. Schoengarth would provide nominal rolls in triplicate of all the people in the camp within forty-eight hours.

Back on the streets of the Hague we were again in the world of peace and laughter. People were pouring out of the houses and down every side street, hurrying and jostling good-naturedly, and all heading for the great main boulevard. We wondered why, and then we saw the answer. Driving slowly through the crowd in a rain of orange streamers and a great welling up of song — Oranje Boven — up the House of Orange — came the Princess Irene Brigade, Holland's soldiers come home. Some had fled to England after the capitulation in 1940;

others had escaped and crossed the North Sea in small fishing boats; still others had slipped across the lines. A pretty girl with tears in her eyes came up to me, full of the wonder of a moment she would never forget. "Oh, I saw them," she said, as though her eyes had seen the glory of the coming of the Lord, "I saw the Princess Irene Brigade." It is at moments like this, on a note of joy like this, that wars should end. So it seemed on that short and splendid day. But to those for whom wars end gloriously will not wars seem glorious? Most of the survivors forget most of those who do not survive.

It was early evening when we returned to Rotterdam and the exhausted crowds were dragging their way homeward through the streets. The cars loaded with excited Resistance men were still dashing about dangerously; no doubt some of the activity was legitimate and necessary, some of it merely aggressive and vengeful. From the rooms in our commandeered hotel came giggles and bursts of laughter and song; in the dark streets there was yelling and singing and frequent gunshots. But it had all been too exciting to go on much longer. Sitting on the sill of my open window thinking about the day — a great day? Well, at any rate never to be forgotten. Movement had almost stopped in the great city. The war in Europe really was over.

⁓14⁓

OW TO RECALL the kaleidoscope of moods and events
of that wonderful summer the war ended: wonderful
alone in the fact of the war being over, so that I
seemed to waken to happiness every morning,
happiness in myself and in those around me; wonderful in the
soft early-summer days that flooded the morning streets with
golden light; wonderful to feel the returning pulse of normal
life and energy to the great cities of Holland. That aspect is
personified in my memory of a man whose name I never knew
and to whom I never spoke; my early-morning visitor.

I had been billeted along with Bill Tenhaaf, a young Canadian officer of Dutch background, and Antz in the house of Mr.
Nygh, owner and publisher of the *Rotterdamsche Courant* newspaper. It was a fine house and perhaps it was the ample comfort
or the excitement of a bed and a room of my own that wakened
me early the first morning. There was a little balcony outside
my room overlooking the sidewalk, a roadway, and beyond it a
canal — the Westersingel. I stood in pyjamas, smoking and
looking at it all, the rising sun through the trees and the still-
sleeping houses, and then I heard someone approaching with
slow, clumping steps. A man came into view, a young man
dressed like a workman and wearing Dutch clogs. His slow
walk came to a stop at our gate and without seeing me he stood
still, looking at the two jeeps parked in the little courtyard in
front of the house. Cautiously he came in a little and stood staring with intense interest at the jeeps, walked around them

317

without touching anything, and then he looked up. I lifted a hand and smiled, and all his tiredness was thrown off as he flung up an arm in a happy salute. We stood there smiling up and down at each other and then his hand came up to his mouth in the international gesture, almost like blowing a kiss but meaning only one thing: smoke? I dropped him half a package of cigarettes. He caught and stared at it as if he had found a gold nugget, then he carefully took one out, lighted it, and drew down the smoke deep into his lungs. He stood there for a moment or two longer and then went on his way, turning at the gate to smile and wave his thanks. For the next two or three mornings he was back, for cigarettes and a smile, walking more briskly each day. I looked forward to this cheerful start for the day, but inevitably the morning came when he did not appear and I didn't see him again.

The first few days were filled with little happinesses and ceremonies that the excitement in the air turned into events. At first it was natural, if startling, to encounter a squad of German soldiers marching smartly through the echoing streets on the way to their concentration areas. One morning outside the city, driving alone in my jeep on a lonely dike road high above the surrounding polders, I found myself overtaking a long marching column of grey uniforms, a ripple of shoulders, a German regiment. The one or two men in the rear looked round, and the look was not friendly. What to do? Half a dozen of them, in the rage they might well be nursing, could tip me and my jeep off the narrow road without anyone seeing, and I would probably not survive to testify — it would just be an accident; there were no Canadian troops for miles, and no Dutchmen in sight. I could have slowed down to a walk; I could have stopped and waited; both alternatives seemed feeble and demeaning. I felt bound to go on as boldly as I could. With honks, as unaggressive as possible, I overtook the rear files. They crowded over, but there was little enough room for us both as I crept up the column. I was too busy driving to look much at the men I was brushing by. To many my arrival seemed startling as I came abreast of them. Just a few glared; whether it was as enemy soldiers or merely irritated pedestrians I didn't inquire, and eventually I passed the head of the column and sped away. Peace still seemed as brittle as an egg-shell.

As the days went by there were no more marching Germans to be seen, and after a church parade and a fine march-past of First Division the first Sunday in Rotterdam, there were few Canadians. In great camps near the sea the unarmed Germans waited to be shipped home while round them, at ease but watchful, the regiments of First Canadian Division played shepherd. Very shortly, having left Canada almost six years before, they too would go home.

With offices in a small apartment building near what remained of the centre of Rotterdam, the Area Security Organization, its motor-bikes and jeeps parked outside the building, remained one of the most visible signs of Canadian Army; the catchment area for a blizzard of inquiries, complaints, and revelations. We fielded and handled or redirected as best we could, trying meanwhile to get on with our major task.

The whole of the group at Scheveningen, put under guard on VE Day, had to be sorted out, put in prison, interrogated, and held for future disposal. The nominal rolls promised, and delivered, by Brigadeführer Schoengarth read like a list of the most-wanted men in Holland. Virtually all the people whose names we had come to know from the interrogation of agents, virtually all the perpetrators of the most vicious exploits in the reports of the Dutch Resistance, almost all were here. Looking at the list I felt both astonishment and a kind of grudging respect. These men, who must have known they faced trial, imprisonment, and perhaps execution, had stayed, when many of them might have slipped away; they had stayed and now stood up to be counted. (The decision may, of course, have been Schoengarth's, not theirs.) There was one man missing — Hauptsturmführer Frank, one of the heads of the Gestapo in the Hague and a man with a reputation for brutality. He was on the list, but at the bottom, and after his name the single word "Deserter".

Within the list were a number of names that were well

319

known to us but not as members of the SS. They belonged to the Abwehr, the old German Secret Service; an organization that was loyal to the German state and the armed services, but was believed to contain many anti-Nazis. They were not gentle men, but their record was not generally of war by atrocity. They were tough, highly professional Intelligence men who had been recruited within the armed services, unlike the branches of the Sicherheitsdienst recruited from the police and the original para-military forces of the Nazi party — the Brown Shirts (the storm-troopers) and Hitler's black-shirted bodyguard that grew into the SS. The Abwehr, like most professional soldiers, had by report stayed clear of politics and in the early part of the war had maintained an aloofness from and often a destructive competitiveness with the Sicherheitsdienst, and especially with the Gestapo arm of the SD. But after the attempt on Hitler's life at Rastenburg in June 1944, its leader, Admiral Canaris, had been executed and the whole organization, though kept separate, had been placed under command of the SD. Now they were lumped in with bullies and criminals and found it the ultimate humiliation, as we were to learn.

Meanwhile, we had to deal with all of them. Looking at the lists I could see very few who by rank or association were not in the arrest category laid down by governments or High Command. It was a rough-and-ready classification, but it was all we had. We were faced with sorting and imprisoning, for immediate interrogation and perhaps later for trial, some 1200 to 1500 men. Since this covered only a small part of the German Army, and since the little machines of Justice were going to be required to work over much of Central Europe, it seemed to me that the mills of God were going to be grinding slowly for years. Yet though many of the men on our list had real crimes to answer for, few of them could be counted among the names that had brought a shame on Germany the world would be a long time in forgetting.

Our plans for preliminary sorting and imprisonment were quickly made. My own little establishment included Captain Eddie Corbeil's Corps Counter-Intelligence Section, several clerical workers, including some civilians recommended to us by the Resistance, Major Basil Torry of British Intelligence, Major Antzemberger, and Captain Bill Tenhaaf. It also included Lieutenant Jim Tassie, a German-speaker, and a lively little blonde Dutch Resistance girl (ultimately to become Professor and Mrs. James Tassie at Carleton University in Ottawa). We had two or three able Dutch sergeants who spoke English, German, and Dutch, and I had a Dutch liaison man from the Resistance who insisted on being known only as Chris.

The large Nordsingel prison in Rotterdam had been almost emptied for us, the 48th Highlanders from Toronto provided the needed troops to guard the sorting operation, and the first three or four hundred men on our list, starting from the bottom, were ordered to parade with all their gear to an empty house in Scheveningen. It was to be a long, miserable afternoon as the line of prisoners, watched by smart and tough-looking Highlanders, filed in one door and on through a series of rooms. All papers were taken away and placed in big envelopes, which formed a mountainous pile as the day went on. All the prisoners were stripped and their bodies and gear searched for weapons or articles useful for escape or suicide. Extra blankets and all food and drink, of which there were quantities, were confiscated and piled in an extra room from which late in the day the Dutch Red Cross took away a small truckload. At the other end of the dis-assembly line the men were packed tightly into trucks like bunches of asparagus. The trucks then took them to Nordsingel Prison, where they were clapped into the cells to which they had been committing people with gusto for five years.

No doubt there was a grim satisfaction to be taken from the work, but it was at best rough justice; a necessary cleaning up of a battlefield, but unpleasant. There were harsh little reminders of what was back of this when some of our Resistance helpers, who were there for a kind of identification watch, spotted someone at whose hands they or their friends had suffered; they fired harsh questions, shouted abuse, and once or twice came close to attacking a prisoner. To the Resistance, who had fought half-blind against a constantly shifting opponent, most of these prisoners — police and security or intelligence personnel — were Gestapo, a generic term spat out with hatred.

Though the operation was effective, the amount of activity as the lines moved through and sometimes blocked up — the searching, the questioning, the stripping — produced an impression of confusion. At one point a sergeant from the 48th came over to me with a cash-box. He said one of the prisoners had given it to him and the key "seemed to be lost" — what would he do with it? I told him to chuck it into the room with the pile of envelopes, and was to wish afterwards that I hadn't been quite so offhand, quite so busy supervising and holding chaos at arm's length.

At last it was over. The final two truckloads of prisoners stood ready to take off and a staff car was being loaded with the brown envelopes as the sun set across the space in front of the house. Hurrying to his car went a little British officer attached to us, I think, from the Lowland Division. He looked like a junior clerk from an office fussily going home to his fussy wife, except that while in one hand he carried his briefcase, in the other he had a pair of German officer's jackboots. One or two of the stern German faces twitched into a near smile of bitter cynicism. Whatever image of stiff but proper behaviour I had hoped to establish, it must appear that we were simply playing at ins and outs; winner take all.

Undoubtedly many men in the Canadian Army felt that that was the game — and ought to be. I thought trophies from the enemy were only an entitlement of fighting soldiers. Once near Caen I had passed one of our men in tin hat and shirt-sleeves stepping along in high excitement, his rifle with bayonet carried at the high port; around his waist was a Luger pistol and on his wrists two or three handsome German watches. I said something about his fine souvenirs and in his mood of nervous excitement he pointed to a burnt-out patch in the field below; "Jerry machine-gun nest," he said; "they got this," he patted his bayonet, "and I got these." Those were legitimate spoils of war, but the clever boys from various auxiliary units or

322

staff jobs — too often officers — sometimes gave the impression that loot was what they were there for, the object of their war.

Some of the pillaging was imaginative, some amusing, while the soldiers who had won whatever it was we had won got on with parades and polishing their boots, kissing Dutch girls and waiting to go home. One officer, I think in Military Government, pushed ahead into Germany charged with securing the postal services; what he secured from the postmasters he ordered around was jeep-loads of Hitler stamps in mint condition which he later sold in Paris for a large sum. Another, when the Dutch currency was about to be revalued, took advantage of the extra negotiable time allowed Canadian forces to gather large quantites of old paper money which was to be had for a song and mailed it to a brother who was a banker in London; it went in brown paper parcels marked "laundry", in time for the brother to convert the money at par. Such stories were to grow as active men without enough to do thought up schemes and lost the high sense of purpose we had seemed to share.

Meanwhile in the north of Holland at Den Helder the German regiments were marching in and boarding transports for return to Germany and demobilization. Here again we had Resistance people watching the gang-planks, peering into faces, grabbing at this last chance of finding wanted men before they slipped into anonymity among the shifting crowds of refugees and transported labourers in Germany making blindly for homes that might or might not exist; a world in which people could easily be lost, especially if they wanted to be.

Our work was closing in, though it was clear it would never be finished. The examining of papers, the interrogations, and the following of clues went on — and would go on for years, but in other hands. Meanwhile I was trying to clear lesser matters that had been set aside. One morning on opening a drawer in my desk I came for the third or fourth time on the cash-box that had been given me weeks before. We must do something with it, not just keep shutting the drawer on it. I asked Bill Tenhaaf to find a locksmith and have it opened. He was back in an hour breathless and a little white, saying I would never guess what was in the box: 50,000 guilders. This was before the money was revalued, so it was worth about $25,000, which had been lying in a locked small box, but in an unlocked drawer, for weeks. I looked at the packets of crisp new bills. It seemed we had arrested a paymaster or the custodian of the Gestapo's slush fund. We had had it too long and now I wanted to get rid of it — quickly. Away went Bill Tenhaaf again, this time to Corps Headquarters at Utrecht with orders to get a receipt. In a few hours he was back again and this time he was white. "Do you know what they did?" he said. "You're not going to believe this. They put it in the furnace, shovelled it in. I saw them." The wonders of the post-war world were beyond me. I took the receipt, "Received 50,000 guilders", and filed it away. It seemed that we might just as well have sent the money to England, marked "laundry".

We were constantly required to interrupt our tunnelling into the research mountain growing out of interrogations to deal with visits and inquiries from a variety of nuts, vague enthusiasts, along with nervous and genuinely unhappy people in need of help. Characteristically Dutch was a man from Dordrecht who applied for a pass to allow him to go to Hamburg to find a Hauptmann Schmidt at a very precise address there. He added that Schmidt had been in Dordrecht in 1940, Alkmaar in 1942, Groningen in 1943, and now was in Hamburg. I was impressed and asked how he knew all this. "I haaf take my informatio̱ns," he said rather smugly. "But why, what do you want him for?" His answer didn't seem surprising to him, but it grounded me. "He stole my bicycle," he said. I had a vision of an aroused Dutch people, looking more or less like the fierce lady on the Dutch Cleanser can, swarming over the German border looking for all the things the Germans had stolen, and with their stubborn determination finding and retrieving them. I thought his persistence splendid, but in the present confused state of Germany, frivolous.

This relentless, unsmiling determination was not always attractive, but it was admirable. It had made a small people into a great and rich nation; it had kept one of the most densely populated countries spacious in appearance, handsome, tidy, and giving the impression of superb management.

So it shouldn't have been a surprise when one morning a Dutch officer was announced. It was my friendly German agent, Volendam, last seen at the Interrogation Centre, then at St. Omer, prior to his departure for England almost a year before. He was now in uniform, fully cleared and reinstated, a captain, and on his way to Germany to look for and reclaim rolling stock stolen from the Dutch railways. Even as I congratulated him, I understood the reason for his visit. Did I still have his pistol? I said light-heartedly that I had promised to return it when we sent him back into Calais, but we hadn't done so and now it was one of my pet souvenirs. He pulled a long, sad face, an "aw c'mon" expression, and I gave him back his pistol.

Too often I was reminded that all our cleverness and all our industry would leave some problems unsolved, some ghosts not laid to rest, some wounds we could not heal. One morning the British Town-Major of Rotterdam came to my office with a pretty woman to ask our help for her. She proceeded to tell her story. As she spoke I realized that Chris, my Resistance Liaison Officer, who normally sat at a desk opposite me, had turned away on her arrival, and then slipped out of sight.

Her story was that her fiancé, a Dutchman who she thought had worked for the Resistance — and, he had said, for British Intelligence too — had late in the war been ordered to cross the lines to go to Prince Bernhard's Headquarters in Eindhoven. He had not returned and she now had reason to believe he was dead. Moreover, it had been suggested that he had not been what he seemed, that he was a traitor. How could she find the truth?

She spread her hands in a gesture of despair. "I'm over the worst of this," she said, "but I would like to know the truth, if only to be able to tell his parents. I know now that he lied sometimes but among his things there was a Czech cross for bravery. All I can tell you is that he was called 'Mac', he said his code name was Elst, and he worked for a man who was known as Breda. Also he wore a little blue button as a lapel badge." She stared at me searchingly to see whether I reacted to Breda, or the blue lapel button. They meant nothing to me, but sounded like someone playing at spy games. "I just can't leave it like this," she said, and then locking her hands she leaned forward and said in a low, intense voice, "This is pretty bad." I believed her, but I could only promise to make inquiries. "British Intelligence" was a vague term that covered a variety of groups, but — we would do our best.

After they had gone Chris reappeared. "What did she want?" he asked in a harsh, defensive voice. I said that she was looking for her fiancé, and he said brutally, "He's dead." When I asked how he knew, he launched into a confused story that reflected the kind of half-light in which the Resistance had worked, and the ruthlessness they found essential to their survival. Chris said the man the Resistance called Mac was one of the most recklessly brave men he had ever met. He was also one of the greatest liars, and wildly indiscreet. In the end the Resistance had come to distrust him. Out on a job he didn't keep position but wandered around to see what other people were doing, and he always asked far too many questions. They decided that whether foolish or treacherous he endangered their whole group, their work and their lives. So he had been lured to the Biesbosch — the area of marsh and small streams northeast of the junction of the Waal and Maas rivers — and there he had been ambushed and killed.

Afterward the Resistance had gone to his bank manager and demanded the contents of his safety-deposit box. The manager refused. They threatened to blow up the bank, because they believed the safety-deposit box contained lists of names which if known to the Germans would destroy the organization. Reluctantly he undertook to burn the contents of the box, without looking at it or showing it to them; and this strange ritual was carried out in the middle of a field in open country while Resistance men, discreetly concealed, looked on.

As far as Chris was concerned that was the end of the story, though it was evident that it would be there to trouble him for a long time. The girl's story I took to a very mysterious British organization that was set up near the Hague. Some days later they reported that they knew nothing and could find out nothing about Mac, or Elst, or Breda, or blue buttons. Of course there was a variety of organizations doing special jobs, so they couldn't swear that he hadn't been working for us in some capacity, but it all looked unlikely, a bit fanciful.

When I told my inquirer this much she looked despairing. Could he after all have worked for the Germans? "If he did, then I worked for the Germans, because I worked for him: carried messages, and did whatever he told me to do." In the circumstances it was easy to ask the Germans. Most of the people he might have worked for were in our hands and seemed quite willing to answer our questions. But none of them knew, or knew of, any such man. Had it all been acting on his part; had he just been playing exciting and dangerous games? It seemed unlikely that we would ever know; but whatever the explanation, it had cost him his life. I could only make a sad, negative report; she had asked an unanswerable question.

The winding down of a war was going steadily on, though not fast enough for me. Canadian forces were being returned home on a point system, those who had served longest going first. It was a fair and sensible arrangement and I couldn't expect to go among the first, but it was hard to be patient. Having been moved back to Utrecht I was content enough for several weeks trying to put together a coherent account of German Intelligence activities in Holland since 1940 out of the great volume of Interrogation Reports we had amassed. It was no longer easy to dig further because most of the Germans held in the prisons of Rotterdam and the Hague had been sent back to camps in Germany. I was at once glad and ashamed to see them go. The administration of the prisons had been in Dutch hands and there was good reason to think, seeing the gaunt men come out of their cells and climb into the trucks bound for Germany, that many of the rations supplied for the prisoners by the Canadian Army had found their way into Dutch homes or onto the black market. It was easy to understand Dutch resentment and vengeance, and certainly these men didn't look like their counterparts in German concentration camps, but once again we seemed to have lost some of the moral authority that should have added lustre and meaning to our triumph. I reported my suspicions to the Dutch authorities and things improved.

It was time to go. We had grown slack and we were wearing out our welcome. The smart, well-disciplined troops that had waved and smiled their way into Dutch hearts and homes in the delirious weeks following VE Day had become just another Occupation Army, not hated yet, but standing in the way of a return to normal life in Holland. The race-tracks, the theatres, the playing fields, the dance halls were for Canadian troops, where Dutch girls might be entertained, but not Dutch men. A Nijmegen paper finally said in a resounding editorial what many had been muttering; the gist of it was, "Let them go home. We are grateful to them, but let them go home. We won't forget these nice smiling boys, and they will always have our good wishes and our gratitude, but let them go home. They are not happy here and we are no longer happy to have them; so let them go home."

It was a plea in which we joined, most of us fervently. What we were doing to the Dutch was perhaps less regrettable than what we were doing to ourselves. On a short leave in Paris I talked in the Canadian Officers' Club with a colonel who was returning to British Columbia in a mood of sad bitterness. He had been so proud — bursting with pride — to be part of the Canadian Army. Now he was not; he wanted out. We had not stood success well, but perhaps we were expecting too much. Good soldiers are not necessarily good citizens, and some who had risen to senior rank had neither the taste nor the character to keep them steady and sensible in the role of the glorious conqueror. A less glorious day lay ahead, and many seemed to be snatching at pleasure and treasure against a mundane future when they would be turned back into pumpkins. We projected an image of the greedy boy, and it was hardly an accident that a senior Canadian officer in Amsterdam, the diamond capital of Europe, came to be known in the army as "Diamond Jim".

Perhaps I was too busy to think much about publishing; possibly I was just putting away an aspect of peace that didn't appeal, the returning to work at Macmillans under Harvey. But in the Officers' Club in Paris I met two war correspondents who were going home to write books: Ross Munro, who, though I didn't know it, would publish his account of the Canadian Army in battle, *Gauntlet to Overlord*, with Macmillans and win great and deserved success, and Lionel Shapiro, who was to write two best-selling novels for Doubleday. Shapiro talked to me a lot about runaway book sales that were taking place, and the eager and affluent public. I couldn't believe him, but the idea that this could happen was wonderful; the idea that reading had suddenly become general and important to people. Time was to show that it wasn't a Renaissance, merely too much money chasing too few things; books were available while luxury goods were not. Like many others, I thought briefly and mistakenly that we had broken into a new day.

But the new-day idea was reinforced and enlarged by someone telling me about a book called *Two Solitudes* by Hugh MacLennan; he said, "You'll like it; it's the real stuff, has the feeling of Canada." To my surprise I found it in an army library in Utrecht and read it through in a single late-night's reading, consumed with excitement and exhausted as daylight appeared over the city's spires. What wouldn't I give to be able to write such a book — or even to publish such a book. Excitement at the idea of being once again in publishing stirred in me in spite of my misgivings.

But the book had done much more. It had evoked almost unbearably the sights and sounds and smells of Canada, had recalled sharply my time in Quebec — a time I had loved, and loved to remember; it had reminded me of people I knew and of my beloved St. Lawrence River. Apart from the importance of its insight into French-English relations, the book had made me homesick.

My report and my time in Utrecht came to an end. I was moved back to Apeldoorn at Headquarters Canadian Forces in the Netherlands. Graham Macdougall had gone home and Colonel Peter Wright was just going. I was left for a few bleak weeks as the senior Intelligence Corps Officer in Holland to wind up the affairs of the Corps, assisted by Captains Claude Tetrault and John Prefontaine. There was much we didn't know, and no one who could tell us.

On all sides there was similar confusion. Intelligence Corps records showed, among other things, that we were missing about 250 jeeps, staff cars, and trucks, and the people who might have had at least some explanations had all gone home. In my dilemma I went to a senior staff officer: what could I do? "Oh, forget it," he said. "There are about 5,000 vehicles missing in the army and someone is just going to have to assemble a Court of Inquiry and write them all off." So I filled in a form saying the vehicles were lost by enemy action, or some equally likely story, and breathed a sigh of relief. Up and down the halls there was a cynical light-heartedness. (One morning in the hall someone called out, "Would you like a Dutch decoration? We have some left over." I said not that way.)

If the books wouldn't balance — well, get the bottom line right. No one was going to care. I heard of one regiment that had had a very enterprising Quartermaster — a great scrounger — and now found itself embarrassed by far too many uniforms, boots, blankets, and sundry stores. It was, of course, a crime to sell surplus stores and almost as great a crime to give them away (since no one would believe they hadn't been sold anyway). They couldn't be returned to senior headquarters stores without awkward explanations. The problem was really quite simple: balance the bottom line. So while Dutch people in need of boots and blankets and warm clothing against the approaching winter stood around and shivered and watched in disbelief, a giant bonfire — made more gigantic with surplus petrol — brought the bottom line into balance.

At last in late November I was warned for repatriation — at least to England. Shipping was tight and unpredictable and there might still be weeks of waiting. But I packed with joyful excitement; it couldn't be long now. I paid a last round of fare-well visits to friends in Rotterdam and the Hague; left Chris richer by a pair of flight boots, a German Schmeisser, and my semi-automatic rifle, for shooting pigeons. I was happy, wildly happy, to be going, but I was closing what had been an impor-tant and often heart-warming chapter in my life.

In the Hague I called on one of the Resistance men, Chief Inspector Van der Speck of the police, a man for whom I had a great respect, and at the Joint Intelligence Headquarters now being shared by British and Dutch. There we talked a little about my report, which had been well received by both British and Dutch, and about going home. And then just as I was leav-ing, either Andy Noest (the British Officer) or Peter Gerbrant (whose name I probably mis-spell) said, "You might be able to solve a problem for us. An ss paymaster who has been returned to Germany claims that 50,415 guilders were taken away from him here in the Hague by the Canadians. Would you know anything about that?" Laughing, I told them my story of the 50,000 guilders put in the furnace. And where was the receipt? I shrugged: wherever the records from the Rotterdam office had gone — perhaps to Canada, perhaps into another furnace. As for the 415 guilders, I could only guess that the wily sergeant who reported the key conveniently lost had scooped up the change first. "Well," said Major Noest, a little doubtfully, "it's lucky we know you." I was amused rather than embarrassed, and not unhappy to be leaving someone else with a little teas-ing puzzle of which some of the pieces were irretrievably lost.

I don't even remember the name of the Transit Camp in Surrey to which I was posted — comfortable enough, but fea-tureless and dull — where it seemed I might stay forever. At one moment of wild frustration in Holland I had sworn I would be sent home for Christmas or I would desert, and half believed I meant it. Graham Macdougall had talked me around to a more reasonable frame of mind, but now it looked as though, infinitely more dreary, I would spend Christmas in a transit camp. Then overnight it was changed. I had gone up to Lon-don for the day and had visited old friends at Canadian Military Headquarters in Cockspur Street. They were in a relaxed and happy state. Someone asked when I was due to sail. I didn't know — at His Majesty's pleasure. Would I like to sail on the *Queen Elizabeth* in three days' time? I couldn't believe they were serious. The *Queen* was said to be filled to overflowing. In happy wonder I sat and listened while a couple of phone calls were put through. And when Colonel Bob Raymont said, "All fixed, you're on the *Queen*," I sat, unbelieving and hardly able to breathe, let alone express my thanks. I had just witnessed what felt remarkably like a miracle.

In all the times I had been in and out of London in my two years in England I had only once gone to Macmillans, and that was to get some money, after banking hours. Now on impulse I went there again; presumably it was the fact of sailing that suddenly swung me back to a realization that soon I would — or would not — be back at Macmillan Canada. The London office was in St. Martin's Street, just back of Canadian Military Headquarters, and in the euphoria of being homeward bound I marched in to the handsome, rather formidable building and sent up my name to Rache Lovat Dickson, the Director in charge of Canadian Company affairs in London. He had been a friend of Hugh Eayrs and we had met once briefly in Toronto. The wonders of the day were prolonged with a lunch at the Garrick Club and talk about publishing, in fine rooms echoing with memories of Samuel Johnson, Sir Joshua Reynolds, David Garrick, and their nest of singing birds.

We talked a little about Macmillan Canada, who, Rache reported comfortably, were doing very well. I wasn't to know for months that though the balance sheets looked rather impressive, the London Directors had been less than reassured by some accounts of the management in Canada. Meanwhile, I faced the prospect of going back to work under a man who I was certain still knew nothing about books and little about publishing, or Canada; a man I didn't dislike but couldn't warm to or respect, from whom I could draw none of the stimulus, and the fun, I had known with Hugh Eayrs. I said that I was hoping to make an arrangement under which I might work part-time, and have, say, three or four months in the year in which to write. Mr. Dickson countered at once that I should be careful lest people think I wasn't interested in the business. Just then I came close to spilling out my gloomy views on the future at Macmillan Canada, and expressing something like indifference, but I held back. It would have been quite improper and possibly inaccurate, though I didn't think so. I wasn't concerned whether anyone thought I was serious or interested; if things didn't work out at Macmillan Canada, they would work out somewhere else.

I wasn't home for Christmas but I was at sea. Standing with thousands of others on cold, wet decks, staring at the heaving grey Atlantic and trying to look beyond the horizon to the west. The mighty *Queen* ploughed on while we chatted or lay in our bunks and tried to read or merely to understand what was happening. We were going home. Though Cunard or the Army did its best, Christmas was much like any other day. There were church services and singing and a Christmas dinner, but it was a dry ship and if we were inwardly happy, we were not merry; just waiting, as soldiers learn to do.

A day or two later came the morning with New York dead ahead, rising suddenly out of the sea; the Battery, the emerging profile of tall buildings, and the Statue of Liberty. We hung over the rails and watched breathlessly. The continent seemed to be rushing to meet us, to welcome us back. Little boats and ships passed or circled round the *Queen*, whistling salutes, and as we entered the Hudson River and moved up past office and apartment buildings, people cheered and waved and threw paper streamers from a thousand windows. And from the *Queen Elizabeth* 12,000 of us gave back the generous cheers until we were dry-throated and hoarse. Below us, a pigmy beside the towering *Queen*, a scow with about twenty American soldiers was putting out into the river on some fatigue job. A few thousand from our crowded rails gave them a cheer, then into a moment of silence one of the American boys threw a question-mark, a reminder, a warning: cupping his hands he called, "Yoooool be sorreee." We roared with laughter but the mordant playfulness lit up an alarming truth. Soon now, in a few days, even hours, the Army would stop feeding us and paying us, telling us what to wear and what to do; if not what to think, at least what not to think. Being fortunate enough still to have them, we had now to take back our lives and manage them. After a separation we were about to remarry civilian life; for better or for worse, for richer or for poorer, in sickness and in health. The idea didn't alarm me but it brought a little tingle of apprehension. It had been a long time. What had Colonel Frost said that night in Aldershot long ago? "The years go by." It was unthinkable, unacceptable, at the time, but they had; three and a half of them. I had been in the Army for almost five years.

Meanwhile, the last day was to be the longest. After such a brilliant, swift beginning there were hours of waiting and then we were edged in to the pier. It was said that the Prime Minister of Canada, Mackenzie King, was coming on board to make a speech; 12,000 hoarse throats groaned. In the end it was the voice of an old friend from Cornwall, Lionel Chevrier, now a Cabinet Minister, that came on the loudspeaker: "Men and women on board the *Queen Elizabeth*, welcome home." It was less than a moment of splendour, but because we had played hockey and football together — and bridge on the train journeys back to university for me and to Osgoode Hall for Lionel — I suppressed my groan, though no one else did. From down the corridor a voice thick with rage yelled, "Oh, for Christ's sake."

But disembarkation started at last. Endless lines of soldiers, grunting and sweating, began to struggle up narrow companionways, carrying heavy packs and dragging kit-bags, then poured down gangways along the side of the great ship and flowed onto the pier, formed up, and marched away. It was dark by the time I came down the gangway to be greeted by kindly women serving milk such as I had almost forgotten and chocolate-covered doughnuts; food for the gods. In between our lines a band of middle-aged Canadians living in New York, looking half-frozen, paraded up and down playing the bag-

334

pipes with a kind of desperation; beneath the kilts their bony knees looked blue. I was torn between gratitude for their intentions and wishing they would go home.

Late at night our train pulled away from the Jersey side and started an interminable crawl towards home; for the next twenty-four hours it stopped more readily, if not more often, than it started. We shook down as best we could, fully dressed, to wait it out; an interminable night and day, while other trains crawled away across the wintry countryside towards Montreal and Winnipeg. And at last in the late evening Toronto became a possibility, and then a probability. Men were dropping off as we stopped at their home stations, Niagara, Brantford, Hamilton. We scraped away at the frosted windows to peer out and watch as they were greeted by friends and families. Tension was mounting now. Who would be there? Would it be all right? Could Tony and I meet almost as though three and a half years had not intervened, or would we be strangers at least for a time? In the long past one of our playful courting songs had been Noel Coward's

> *Someday I'll find you,*
> *. . . true to the dream I am dreaming.*
> *As I draw near you*
> *You'll smile a little smile.*
> *For a little while*
> *We shall stand*
> *Hand in hand . . .*

Would it be like that? Tense, making small talk, I sat with Peter Osler, with whom I had served at RMC, and drank out of a flask of his whisky which had somehow survived the voyage in a dry ship. We were at Sunnyside; we were running alongside the Coliseum and the train was slowing down. Long since we had put on greatcoats and gathered up haversacks. Now we had only to stand up and move with all our questions to the door.

Awkwardly in the wet darkness we lined up. I found myself

335

in command of a squad, and though we were exhausted and rumpled with travel I sensed that everyone wanted this last parade to be a smart one. And then we were through the doors and marching into the bright lights of the Horse Palace, where many of us had signed up and drilled all those years ago. As we came into the light there was a burst of cheering and clapping from the crowded seats. We came smartly to a halt, bracing ourselves for the horrors of more speeches, more official welcomes. But someone had been compassionate and sensible, and there were none. Immediately, and for the last time, it was "Dis-miss". Even as we broke ranks the crowd poured over the barrier and flung itself at us like a wave breaking on a beach.

It was to be, and to remain, a breathless, joyful memory beyond description. The frantic hunting around, the finding of each other, the wordless clinging together. Hoisting up the boy who had perched on my arm in that terrible moment at Kingston, and now was a chunky small man almost nine. Words that were meaningless whirled around, handshakes, hugs, kisses, tears — a joyful confusion. Then, somehow the three of us were alone in the dark, walking toward the car, going home. True to the dreams I'd been dreaming? I don't know. But it wasn't important.

The joy persisted in the weeks that followed, but it had to accommodate uncomfortable realities. My gear and I were oversize for the small flat that had suited Tony and John. Though I was happy and wanted to make them happy, I was as embarrassing as a large dog crowded into a small car and unable to sit still; I was noisy, excited, and talked too much. I found the little flat hot and opened the windows until Tony complained that she was turning blue. Worst of all, without action or responsibilities — though I couldn't quite define my problem — I was bored.

I went to the office and met a welcome that was guarded from some, kindly and enthusiastic from others. Harvey, stiffly cordial, was quick to suggest I take a good long rest — glad to have me back, of course, but why not have a good holiday, take

336

a month or more, "you deserve it," he said. It sounded a bit hollow. When I was ready I could come back at my old salary. I don't know what I had expected. I hadn't any fixed idea of what was appropriate, but that was a shock. So, nothing had changed. I objected rather mildly, reminding him that I had been earning more than that in the Army and had had five years' more experience in dealing with people and problems. He stared at his desk, playing with the pencils, then, having braced himself, increased his offer from $4,000 to $4,800. Not impressed, but reluctant to start with a row, I accepted, and he was all smiles again. Have a good long holiday, a good rest, he said heartily.

I went upstairs to see Frank Upjohn, who had been back for a couple of months, and found him depressed. He was brief and firm; he hated the atmosphere at the office, thought the Company had been prospering because in wartime it couldn't do otherwise — selling everything it could find paper to publish, but he thought their editorial work and judgement and book production deplorable. If there were not basic changes, and soon, he wouldn't stay. I had seen a lot of Frank in England where during service with the RCAF his Kensington flat had been a rallying-point for former members of the Beer and Literature Club; such a popular place that there was not always a spare couch, and one night with the buzz bombs snoring overhead I had had a comfortable sleep in his bathtub. His war experience had given him strength and confidence, and it seemed to me he would be a great loss to the Company if he left — I couldn't imagine being happy there without him. I begged him to stay on a bit until I had tried the water and until we found if together we could help to get things moving in a better direction. He gave no blank cheque but undertook to try to be patient.

The suggestion of a nice long rest had sounded fine, but quickly I had had enough. Tony and I paid a visit to my parents in Cornwall where my still young and pretty kid sister, Joan, was also visiting with her second husband, her first, a very young flier, having been killed in a flying accident two or

337

three years before. We went on for a few days of celebration in Montreal. I was still in uniform because I had nothing else to wear, but except for seeing a few old army friends I was eager to put the war behind me. My father's war effort had been a continuous shopping prowl around Cornwall with his dog in search of articles for food parcels to send to Bob and me and to various remote connections in England; my mother said that his bedroom had looked like a small grocery warehouse and in between shopping expeditions he listened to the news, wrote long letters to us, sorted his groceries, and wrapped parcels with meticulous care. Now, though he had largely lost his occupation the old soldier was quietly content. He had his two sons home, which he had not counted on, having told me in a kind of agony early in the war that he had dreamt of seeing me lying in the mud, shot between the eyes.

A month or so of "holiday" turned me into an uncomfortable problem. I was sleeping badly, reading at all hours, grouchy when I wanted to be pleasant. After watching and enduring this Tony suggested gently I should go back to work. Wouldn't I be happier? I fought the idea a little because the prospect at the office was a part of my tension, but I knew she was right.

Finding my way back into the work at first only transferred my scratchiness. I knew that even my friends and supporters in the office, though they might welcome me back in theory, found the business of moving over and making room for me uncomfortable. Probably the person most affected was Gladys Neale, who had been quite a junior girl when I left, though showing enough promise for me to single her out in my recommendations to Harvey as someone I thought capable of handling much more responsibility. She had proved that and more, having risen to become acting manager of the department. Attractive, hard-working, and forceful, she was already well known and much respected by educators across the country. Though she didn't in any way challenge my right to take back my job and some of the important travelling, it was clearly not going to be pleasant giving up much of what she had won.

Not only was I turning a fresh eye on the work, but I had a

briskness and often an impatience that was upsetting. There were little flare-ups, and people could at once wish me well and wish me elsewhere. It was typical of these tensions that on one occasion as we discussed a problem, and I asked rather casually for some papers bearing on it, people started to run around in excited circles, searching, fussing. I roared, "Oh, for God's sake, we're not building a battleship." It came out more brutally than I had intended, and it hurt. One of the senior girls in the group, a conscientious and able if nervous worker, and an old friend, suddenly, on the edge of tears, said, "I imagine a lot of the things we've been doing here don't seem very important to you." The words sketched our problem exactly. Knowing I had sounded harsh and unreasonable I could only apologize and promise to try and do better.

I took up my travels again, and meeting old friends in Western Canada made me wonder how I had been able to shut it all out, forget it, for five years. Though the Company seemed to have lost some ground, the warm welcome, the wrestling with publishing problems, and the realization that I hadn't forgotten all I knew, or been forgotten, helped steady my nerves. In some ways this was where I came in; in others it was different enough to be stimulating. The war's end was also ending restrictions. Canada was feeling a new confidence, and educational authorities were bending to new excitements and pressures, preparing to change courses and books. I had always travelled without a fixed itinerary, staying in a city as long as it seemed useful to do so, then moving on. Now with hotels and trains full, I had to move in a world of reservations and closely plotted time-tables. Before I finally accepted this aspect of postwar Canada, I had repeatedly to doss down like an old soldier in any corner the hotel could find — and that it only found because they remembered the days when I had been one of their few customers. One night, lacking a stateroom, I rolled up in my overcoat and slept comfortably on the floor of a corridor on the ship from Vancouver to Victoria. Some senior educators found my casualness a bit rough, even shocking.

Many of my old friends in education had moved up the ladder and by the same kind of osmosis I had been converted from a relatively junior man to one who was treated like a senior, almost like a man of some consequence. If the process was mystifying it was also pleasant, and best of all there was a warmth of friendship in many of the associations that the interval had only strengthened. One of my old friends, Bill Noble, who ran the Provincial Textbook Bureau in Edmonton, had hung a picture of me in uniform on the wall of his office, and there it was — a young soldier I couldn't believe had existed — when I walked into the office five years later. The new Director of Curriculum in Saskatchewan was Alan Macallum, a man I had admired as a teacher at RMC, and later had come to value as a close friend. It was all like a second homecoming.

Because we were still working with the Ryerson Press, now on a revision of the reading series developed fifteen years before, I made part of the trip with Lorne Pierce, Editor of the Ryerson Press and a national figure. It was very different from the travels with Hugh Eayrs, and yet it had some pleasant similarities. We had the same long talks in the evenings, after the last dinner-guest had gone; the publishing shop-talk that made me forget the war and the uncertainties. Conversation wasn't easy because Lorne was deaf, but it was worth the effort.

On one of these occasions Lorne startled and flattered me by suggesting that I join the Ryerson Press and train as his successor. He led into it gently by telling me of one of the great moments of his early publishing career. While spending a sleepy, restful Sunday in Winnipeg with his friends the Watson Kirkconnells, he had been rudely intruded on by a gaunt, unsmiling man with a brown paper parcel. The man introduced himself as Frederick Grove — and thrust the brown paper parcel at the reluctant Lorne, who wasn't to have been disturbed. Against all his inclinations he agreed to read the book, bowing to Grove's earnest forcefulness. And against his intentions he had started reading that night when he returned to his hotel. Instead of reading only a few pages he had finished at four o'clock in the morning. At eight o'clock he was wakened by his telephone; it was Grove demanding to be told whether Pierce had read his book. The unyielding man was invited to break-fast and given a promise of publication. The book was, I think, *Settlers of the Marsh.*

Today it would shock no one, but in the early nineteen-twenties many people found Grove's book raw and objection-able; publication produced an unpleasant controversy. In par-ticular many authorities of the United Church, owner of the Ryerson Press, were scandalized. Dr. Pierce had grave talks with the Book Steward — I think Dr. Fallis — and his future with the Ryerson Press seemed precarious. But one day changed it all. The morning mail had brought a letter to the Book Steward expressing thanks to the Ryerson Press for hav-ing the taste and the courage to publish so fine and important a book. The letter was from Arthur Meighen, leader of the Con-servative Party in Canada and a man of intellectual capacity and integrity. To Dr. Fallis, a great admirer of Meighen, this was proof that Dr. Pierce was right and everyone else wrong. He had marched into Pierce's office and flung the letter on his desk saying, "I have the finest editor in Canada." With Dr. Fallis on his side, Pierce had no need to worry about lesser figures in the Church's publishing hierarchy, and from that time on he had a free hand to publish what he wished to.

He finished the story with a characteristic little quirky smile and sat still, remembering a great moment. Then in the rather high-pitched, hard voice that came from his deafness he said, "I have the finest job in publishing in Canada. I plan my own list, do the things I think are needed, ask no one's permission." I knew this appeared to be true and that his list was the most ambitious and idealistic in Canada — or anywhere — if a bit dull and probably not very successful in business terms. And then he put the question to which this had led without my rec-ognizing it. "How would you like my job?"

It was only at the last minute that I somehow guessed where this was tending and couldn't prepare myself for it. Perched on a radiator with a drink in my hand, I sat transfixed. It was a fine, prestigious job, and a compliment I had not earned, but it was no place for me. Lorne was watching me closely. Slowly, and smiling my appreciation, I shook my head. I said he did me great honour, but it wouldn't work. Cupping his hand around his ear he leaned forward, "What's that?" "I'm not the type," I roared. "Why not?" again sharply. Thinking of the stiff rectitude of the United Church legend — easy to respect but for me hard to love — I could only hold up my glass and my cigarette. "I drink," I said, "I smoke." Lorne himself had a drink in his hand, but it was a very small Scotch and a rare indulgence, when he was tired, or to keep me company. "Do you have to do these things?" I answered, "No, but I intend to." He left it there and said good-night. He watched me during the rest of the trip, on our visits to Deputy-Ministers of Education, to authors and school inspectors, and returned again and again to the proposal (including Frank Upjohn in the plan), which I fended off laughingly — "I would let you down, Lorne. We might be a horrible embarrassment."

Soon after my return from the West, full of concern over ground we seemed to have lost and change we had not prepared for, there was word of a visit from London; Rache Lovat Dickson was coming out. No doubt it could be regarded as an evidence of merely normal interest, but visits from London had not been normal in the past — Daniel Macmillan I knew had visited us for a few days in 1922, and Harold Macmillan for a day in 1938; otherwise Hugh Eayrs had reported on our affairs by correspondence and by trips to London every year or two. London had not seemed to know much or care greatly about us, so news of the Lovat Dickson visit sent a little current of excitement through the Company; through those who hoped for change and presumably those who did not. The outwardly calm Frank Upjohn said fiercely to me that Rache Dickson must not be allowed to leave Toronto thinking all was well.

Whatever its outcome, it seemed inevitable that the visit was going to be some kind of milestone; whether things were to be better or merely different, they would never be quite the same again. And yet through a series of meetings and social events I couldn't feel the earth moving under my feet. Harvey was a hearty host and an enigmatic chairman, winding us all up and

342

letting us talk, his contribution being a sage nod or a non-committal word from time to time. Rache Dickson asked questions and made notes and at times looked a little baffled. Watching it all I was both fascinated and frustrated; Frank looked as though he was merely frustrated. Rache, handsome, sophisticated, and experienced, seemed to be playing the role of an amiable, occasionally heavy-handed, but fairly relaxed London partner. He hadn't had — and wasn't going to have — time to dig deeply into our affairs; and without that could he report adversely on management?

The little publishing world of Toronto was watching events, as far as it could, apparently with some interest. At a cocktail party at the Granite Club to publicize the visit Mac Seccombe, Editor of *Quill and Quire*, the magazine of the Canadian book trade, insisted on getting a picture of Tony and me along with Frank Upjohn and E. J. Pratt. With a mischievous grin, and without bothering to lower his voice very much, he said that he would like to have this, it might be quite an historic picture. Hope spurted up. If people outside the Company felt that our situation must change, wouldn't Rache catch some hint of this? But if he had, he gave no sign of it. He seemed judicial, calm, and a bit remote.

And then with the visit almost over, everything opened up. By what seemed sheer chance, but wasn't quite, Frank and Rache and I had dinner together at the King Edward Hotel, where Rache Dickson was staying. Through dinner I think we talked mostly about London and the war and, inevitably, its effect on publishing. It was like a gavotte as we moved closer to our subject and backed away. And then after dinner we settled down to talk over a drink and began to discuss the object of Rache's trip. He didn't ask any leading questions, nor were we quite ready to break the subject open. I found I shrank from saying the things that needed to be said — the personal attack on poor Harvey. Six years before, we had told Billy McLaughlin that if he was allowed to get out on the end of the limb he now straddled, he would be able neither to hang on there nor to get back.

343

But suddenly, after all the preliminary footwork, the subject came wide open and we were all talking at once. Frank, usually less aggressive, had probably suffered more and certainly longer than I; he was now blunt and decisive; give us a publisher, someone who understands and cares about the business or I, for one, won't stay. The easing of the tension that had begun to make us edgy released a nervous excitement in all of us that made our talk more frank than I would have believed possible an hour before. Metaphorically Rache rubbed his hands together as he said again and again, "This is exactly the kind of thing I came to find out." He added an account of an evening's talk that week with Ellen Elliott, formerly Hugh Eayrs' secretary but for the last six years the effective head of the publishing side of the business. She had talked frankly and emotionally to Rache about her plans and aspirations for a publishing program — among her dearest hopes was a uniform edition of the books of Frederick Philip Grove — and in doing so had horrified him; he thought she lived in cloudland. I liked, though I distrusted, her enthusiasm, but what had often since my return filled me with dismay was her airy way of saying, "Oh, I don't know anything about figures, you'll have to talk to Mr. Harvey about that," and yet she pushed her pet schemes. For his part, Harvey wouldn't say, "I don't know anything about publishing," but then he didn't need to. What was all too clear was that we were travelling on a ship without an effective captain and with a first mate who didn't know anything, or care much, about navigation; and the weather forecast was stormy.

Something of this was conveyed to Rache and finally we were talked out — exhausted and elated. Driving home, Frank and I were in a mood to pinch ourselves or punch each other and dance around like schoolboys. It was sheer relief; things were going to change. We did not assume that either of us would replace Harvey, but someone would; and if it was someone who knew publishing and was a reasonable person, we could work with him and between us do great things. So ran our simple melody. No doubt it was naïve, for there were people in publishing, more knowledgeable than Harvey, who could have been even less congenial to work with. But over a final drink and talk in Frank's apartment — while at home poor Tony bit her fingernails and wondered what had happened — we continued to talk and point, like people who have glimpsed the Promised Land.

And then came weeks of waiting. Hateful weeks because people seemed happy that the visit had gone well — and why shouldn't it, after all; Mr. Dickson must have seen that things were in good shape. One of the painful realizations was that the staff included many gifted people who had worked very hard in the war years and done it gladly; who except in the matter of spending had had a rather free hand. To some at least change would be a shock and unwelcome. For many who knew only their corner of the business this had seemed on the way to being the best of all possible worlds. Meanwhile Frank and I waited, and it began to appear that talk of change had been an illusion; had it really happened — and was it going to come to nothing?

It was in that moment of impatience turning to a dumb despair that Harvey walked by my office one morning. It was one of those clear-glass cubicles in which my periodic sillinesses could never be hidden — leaning too far back in my chair and finishing "arse over tin cup", or setting fire to my wastepaper basket with a carelessly thrown match. I had said good morning and Harvey had answered, almost reluctantly. Then on his way back he said in a tight voice, "Jack, will you come to my office in a few minutes, please."

If it hadn't been that his manner was strange the request would have carried no special significance. But as I put on my jacket and straightened my tie I was jumping with questions: Was this it? Could this mean that I . . . ? My mind backed away from completing the question. But something was up; must be. I walked into his ground-floor office on the edge of excitement and sat down. This was where I had sat when I first talked with Hugh Eayrs in 1930 and where I had said good-bye to Harvey in 1941. With its mullioned windows and handsome fireplace it was the original office of the President, abandoned years before by Hugh Eayrs, who had fled upstairs to more space and more privacy. Harvey had never taken over Hugh Eayrs' upstairs office; the girls said it was so no one would see how little work he did.

I sat looking a question at Harvey and he sat looking at me in silence for a moment, fiddling with pencils as he had the day I left. And then in a voice he had trouble controlling he said, "I guess you know all about the changes that are coming here." I said I didn't. Then, roused as I had never seen him, heaving himself up like a wounded buffalo, in a voice cracking with anger he said, "Oh, I think you do."

I faced him straight on then and said, "I don't know what changes are coming. But if you ask me whether I thought there was going to be a change, yes I did think so, and I thought there should be. I thought it was a mistake for you to take this position, and I tried to prevent it. But I don't know what the change is to be."

Obviously he didn't know whether to believe me or not, perhaps couldn't quite take it all in. Then he dropped his bombshell: "Well, I'm retirin' and you're takin' over. You're to be Manager, and Frank Upjohn your second in command." I suppose it is legend and apocrypha that produce the splendid statements with which some men are said to have met great moments. All I could manage with a kind of strangled earnestness was, "I certainly didn't know that."

He looked at me in silence, then made the kind of stupid remark that was characteristic and smothered some of the sympathy I couldn't help feeling for him. "I never did you any harm," he said. Thinking back to his attempt to withhold the differential in pay, to his attempt to hire Cecil Eustace of Dents to take my job when I was away at the war, I said, "No," and just barely stopped the imp inside me from saying, "but it wasn't for lack of trying."

And then it was as though he was suddenly relieved — as though for six years he had been waiting, knowing that this moment would come; that the enormous bluff he had consciously or not been running would be called. He said London

346

had treated him very decently, given him a pension for life (quite a modest pension I discovered later). I would have to get a figures man, and pretty quick, because I didn't know anything about figures (this uncomfortable reminder gave him evident satisfaction). But on the whole the rest of our little talk was easy, agreeing on a time for the announcement and change of command and some other details. I had trouble paying attention. Within me excitement, apprehension, delight, a sense of my inadequacy, and a confidence that I could make it, all fought to be heard.

A few days later the announcement was made to the whole staff in the Company library and the response was what might have been expected: a good deal of sadness and sympathy for Harvey, a barely concealed delight from a few old friends, some excitement, and over all a sense of uneasy waiting to see what this would mean. One of the gifted, sophisticated girls on the staff said to me that Mr. Harvey would have been all right if only he had read the books. Irene Welsh, the mighty atom I had hired just before going into the Army, sent me a little quote (as she was to do on occasions for many years): "The things that are for you gravitate to you — Emerson".

Just as welcome was a letter from Professor B. C. Diltz, the distinguished head of English at the Ontario College of Education, which recalled an almost-forgotten accomplishment: "When the author of 'The Silver Whale' becomes head of Macmillans in Canada that is news." No doubt it was as extravagant as it was graceful — but it was also bracing and welcome at a moment of excitement heightened and corroded by doubt and apprehension.

Isabel Syme, who had been my secretary and then been taken away for Hugh Eayrs' staff, came to ask what office I would use. I hadn't thought about that, as I hadn't thought about much else. I said at once I would take Mr. Eayrs' old office, which for six years Harvey had left vacant. I might fail, but I intended to leave no one in doubt, I was going to be manager; I was going for broke.

347